D0619162

NEWS, PUBLIC RELATIONS
AND POWER

The *Media in Focus* series provides students and lecturers with an authoritative, that is, balanced and informed account of the media communication field and its many sub-fields of contemporary research. The editor of each volume, an expert in the media sub-field in focus, contributes an introductory 'mapping essay' charting the perspectives, debates and findings of major studies before introducing the reader to a carefully commissioned and structured range of chapters authored by international researchers. In this way, readers gain a relatively compact and structured overview of the media sub-field in question as well as exposure to a judicious range of writings selected to illuminate theoretical and methodological frameworks, key research findings, and defining debates. The *Media in Focus* series, then, is informed by strong pedagogical and scholarly emphases throughout and provides media communication lecturers and students with an accessible and authoritative resource for teaching and learning.

Simon Cottle, Series Editor

Simon Cottle

NEWS, PUBLIC RELATIONS
AND POWER

PERTH COLLEGE
Learning Resource Centre

ACCN No:	SUPPLIER:
007 05435 Ⓢ	Dawsons
CLASSMARK: 070-43	COST: 19.09
LOCATION: Loan.	DATE RECEIVED: 04-03

SAGE Publications
London • Thousand Oaks • New Delhi

© Simon Cottle, 2003

First published 2003

Apart from any fair dealing for the purposes of research or private study, or criticism or review, as permitted under the Copyright, Designs and Patents Act, 1988, this publication may be reproduced, stored or transmitted in any form, or by any means, only with the prior permission in writing of the publishers, or in the case of reprographic reproduction, in accordance with the terms of licences issued by the Copyright Licensing Agency. Enquiries concerning reproduction outside those terms should be sent to the publishers.

SAGE Publications Ltd
6 Bonhill Street
London EC2A 4PU

SAGE Publications Inc
2455 Teller Road
Thousand Oaks, California 91320

SAGE Publications India Pvt Ltd
B-42, Panchsheel Enclave
Post Box 4109
New Delhi – 100 017

British Library Cataloguing in Publication data

A catalogue record for this book is available from the British Library

ISBN 0 7619 7495 4
ISBN 0 7619 7496 2 (pbk)

Library of Congress Control Number available

Typeset by Mayhew Typesetting, Rhayader, Powys
Printed and bound in Great Britain by The Cromwell Press Ltd, Trowbridge, Wiltshire

Contents

Acknowledgements

The chapters in this book, in line with the pedagogical and cutting-edge aims of the *Media in Focus* series, present and summarize current arguments and research findings within the field of journalism studies. These have sometimes been published at greater length elsewhere, and where this is so this is acknowledged by the various authors in their respective chapters. All chapters in this volume, however, have been carefully prepared specially for this volume. A special thanks is here made to Roger Dickinson, Course Director of the MA Mass Communication Distance Learning Program at the Centre for Mass Communication Research, University of Leicester. A number of chapters in this book first began life as teaching units in Module 10 (option 5) 'Journalism: News Access and Source Power' commissioned by Roger Dickinson and the editor. The authors of Chapters 1, 4, 6, 7 and 8 would like to thank Roger Dickinson for granting permission to refashion these teaching materials for publication in *News, Public Relations and Power*. The editor also thanks Mugdha Rai for her detailed eye and diligent help in preparing the manuscript for publication.

List of Contributors

Alison Anderson is Senior Lecturer in Sociology, University of Plymouth, UK. She is author of *Media, Culture and the Environment* (UCL, 1997). She is co-author of *The Changing Consumer: Markets and Meanings* (Routledge, 2002). Forthcoming publications include: *Tourism, Consumption and Representation: Narratives of Place and Self* (Cab International, 2003) and 'In Search of the Holy Grail: Media Discourse and the New Human Genetics', *New Genetics and Society* (in press) 21 (3). She is currently conducting an international study of journalistic practices and the reporting of environmental issues.

Simon Cottle is Professor and Director of the Media and Communications Program at the University of Melbourne, Australia. His books include: *TV News, Urban Conflict and the Inner City* (1993), *Television and Ethnic Minorities: Producers' Perspectives* (1997), as co-author *Mass Communication Research Methods* (1998) and as editor *Ethnic Minorities and the Media: Changing Cultural Boundaries* (2000), and *Media Organization and Production* (2003). He is the Series Editor of the Sage *Media in Focus* series. He is also currently writing *Media Performance and Public Transformation: The Case of Stephen Lawrence* (Praeger, 2003) and conducting a major international comparative study of TV news and current affairs entitled 'TV News, Current Affairs and Deliberative Democracy'.

Aeron Davis is a lecturer in Sociology at City University, London. He is the author of *Public Relations Democracy* (Manchester University Press, 2002) and several articles on the impact of public relations on the news media and political process. He is currently working on an edited book on political communications and researching the influence of promotional culture on markets.

David Deacon is Senior Lecturer in Communication and Media Studies, Department of Social Sciences, Loughborough University, England. His publications include *Researching Communications* (with Mike Pickering, Peter Golding and Graham Murdock), *Taxation and Representation: The Media, Political Communication and the Poll Tax* (with Peter Golding) and *Mediating Social Science* (with Natalie Fenton and Alan Bryman). He has written widely on political communication and media issues and has just started collaborating on a major research project on textual and content analysis methods, funded under the Economic and Social Research Council's 'Research Methods' Programme.

Bob Franklin is Professor of Media Communications in the Department of Journalism Studies at the University of Sheffield, UK. He is editor of *Journalism Studies* and has published widely on political communications. His publications include *British Television Policy: A Reader* (Routledge, 2001); *Social Policy, The*

Media and Misrepresentation (Routledge, 1999): *Making the Local News: Local Journalism in Context* (edited with David Murphy, Routledge, 1998); *Newszak and News Media* (Arnold, 1997); *Packaging Politics: Political Communications in Britain's Media Democracy* (Arnold, 1994); *Televising Democracies* (Routledge, 1992); *What News? The Market, Politics and the Local Press* (with David Murphy, Routledge, 1991); *Social Work, the Media and Public Relations* (with Nigel Parton, Routlege, 1991); *Public Relations Activities in Local Government* (Charles Knight, 1988). He is currently researching New Labour's news management and advertising activities, while writing a second edition of *Packaging Politics* and editing the MacTaggart Lectures for Edinburgh University Press.

John Langer is located in the Department of Communication, Language and Cultural Studies at Victoria University, Melbourne, Australia where he teaches media and film studies, and radio production for community broadcasting. He has written on popular forms of television, the phenomenon of celebrity and has published the book *Tabloid Television: Popular Journalism and the 'Other News'* (Routledge, 1998). Currently his research interests include multicultural community radio, the institutional and social movement contexts of media democratization, and media literacies and internet usage in South East Asia.

Philip M. Taylor is Professor of International Communications at the University of Leeds, UK. His publications include *War and the Media: Propaganda and Persuasion in the Gulf War* (1992, 1997), *Munitions of the Mind: A History of War Propaganda from the Ancient World to the Present Era* (1990, 1995), *Global Communications, International Affairs and the Media Since 1945* (1997) and *British Propaganda in the 20th Century: Selling Democracy* (1999).

Gadi Wolfsfeld is Professor and holds a joint appointment in the departments of political science and communication at the Hebrew University in Jerusalem. He has served as chair of the department of communication and as director of the Smart Family Communication Institute. His books include *Media and the Path to Peace* (in press), *Media and Political Conflict: News from the Middle East* (1997), and *The Politics of Provocation: Participation and Protest in Israel*. He has also been co-editor for two additional volumes: *Political Communication in a New Era: A Cross-National Perspective* (with Philippe Maarek, in press) and *Framing the Intifada: People and Media* (with Akiba Cohen, 1993).

PART I
INTRODUCTION

CHAPTER 1

News, Public Relations and Power: Mapping the Field

Simon Cottle

We are living in increasingly 'promotional times'. Today states, corporate organisations as well as diverse pressure groups and new social movements all seek to put their message across via the media in pursuit of disparate organisational interests, collective aims and public legitimacy. The study of media sources and public relations, therefore, takes us to the heart of key concerns and debates about the media's relation to wider structures and systems of power. It invites us to reconsider the relative power of the media in relation to other organised interests, as well as the nature of the mechanisms that link them and through which they interact. Small wonder, perhaps, that the study of media sources and public relations is fast becoming a key area for empirical research and theorisation within the broader field of media communications study.

The field of journalism, by definition, occupies a pivotal site in the communication of conflicts and in relation to the surrounding voices that vie and contend for media influence, representation and participation. Who secures media access, and why and how, inevitably raises fundamental questions about the nature of media participation, processes and forms of mediated citizenship, issues of media performance and the play of power enacted between the news media and their sources. Public relations (PR) also occupies a central position in today's wider promotional culture. Defined here as 'the deliberate management of public image and information in pursuit of organisational interests', the practice and institutions of public relations have grown across the twentieth century into a major industry. Indeed, in recent years this growth has assumed exponential proportions. The rise of the public relations industry, and its associated army of public relations consultants and so-called 'spin doctors' employed by governments and corporations, pressure groups and celebrities, mirrors the rise of an increasingly media aware, and 'mediatised' society – a society where both commercial interests and cultural identities seemingly compete for media space and strategically mobilise forms of communicative power.

News, Public Relations and Power aims to introduce some of the most important theoretical ideas and empirical findings delivered by researchers working in this field and so help us to better understand the complex relations of power enacted between media sources and journalism. The chapters that follow are written by leading international researchers in the field, and their contributions address diverse source fields and media public relations strategies, as well as the characteristic forms and opportunities that attend news access and participation. Specific areas covered include:

- the recent rapid growth of public relations and its impact on news production;

- state information management strategies in times of internal political dissent;

- political parties and mediated 'spin' conducted at national and local levels;

- the historically changing nature of journalist and source strategies in times of war and international crises;

- comparative analysis of non-governmental organisations – quasi-autonomous non-governmental organisations (quangos), trades unions, voluntary groups and charities – and their efforts to secure media access;

- the communication strategies of environmental pressure groups and ecological and cyber-activists;

- tabloid television and forms of cultural representation; and

- the 'deliberative' architecture of television's news and current affairs programmes and how this variously enables and disables the public engagement of contending views and voices.

In these ways this book examines media source involvement and public relations strategies across different fields of organisational activity, in relation to different collective interests, and across time. It thereby provides a comparative base from which to appraise competing theoretical and explanatory frameworks and different levels of analytical approach. The collection throws its net much wider (and critically deeper) than narrowly conceived ideas of public relations as the technical organisational accomplishment of 'effective' communications, and encompasses a wider range of theoretical approaches to the study of sources than is usually the case. This is designed to encourage a more conceptually nuanced and theoretically sophisticated appreciation of the multidimensional nature, dynamics and complexities of media–source interactions and forms of public relations. Together, then, the nine chapters that comprise this book serve to provide the reader with an entrée into the latest thinking and research findings concerning this historically changing, organisationally complex, and often politically contingent field.

This first chapter now sets the scene for the chapters that follow by mapping the broad contours of theoretical approach, empirical study and defining debates that have informed the study of media sources and mediatised public relations.[1] On this basis we can better understand the continuing relevance of past media communication research and appreciate the productive departures of more recent researchers in this key area of communication enquiry.

Media Communications: Research Traditions

Questions of media source involvement raise fundamental concerns about who is delegated to speak or pronounce on social affairs and wider conflicts, of how exactly this communicative entitlement is conducted, and by whom it has been authorised. Profound questions of 'representation', 'social and cultural power' and 'citizenship' are all thereby raised. Putting the matter succinctly, whose voices and viewpoints structure and inform news discourse goes to the heart of democratic views of, and radical concerns about, the news media. Traditionally, liberal democratic theory contains an implicit concern with questions of news representation and access. Here the liberty of the press (and wider news media) must be protected so that dissenting views can be aired, opinion formation facilitated and 'representative' democratic process sustained (Mill, J. 1997; Mill, J.S. 1997). Variants of critical theory, for their part, have generally been more explicit and observe how the news media in fact routinely access and privilege elite 'definitions of reality'. These, it is said, serve ruling hegemonic interests, legitimise social inequality and/or thwart moves to participatory democracy (e.g. Golding and Murdock 1979; Gitlin 1980; Hall 1982; Herman and Chomsky 1988).

Both liberal and critical theorists, in their different ways, point to the fundamental, pivotal even, concerns of media source involvement and media representation. Whose voices predominate, whose vie and contend, and whose are marginalised or rendered silent on the news stage are questions of shared interest. How social groups and interests are defined and symbolically visualised is also part and parcel of media source access. Whether social groups are representationally legitimated or symbolically positioned as 'Other', labelled deviant or literally rendered speechless can, of course, have far-reaching consequences as shown, for example, in studies of media representation of youth subcultures (Cohen 1972), ethnic minorities (Van Dijk 1991), political dissidents and 'terrorists' (Gerbner 1992) or the victims of 'risk society' (Cottle 2000a).

Much depends, therefore, on how we conceptualise and theorise the relationship between the news media, their sources and wider society, and how we understand the mechanisms and meanings that surround and inform processes and patterns of news representation and entry. Liberal democratic theory and variants of critical theory have traditionally staked out, in broad terms, an area of common concern and debate – the role of media in giving voice to surrounding political interests (or elite views) and the articulation (or ideological manufacture) of public opinion. These views have also informed more recent debates centred on the media approached as 'public sphere' (Habermas 1989) – a space constituted by the media, available to all, and in which public debate and reason prevail for the benefit of public opinion and political will formation (Elliott 1986; Garnham 1986; Curran 1991; Frazer 1992; Hallin 1994; Dahlgren 1995; Murdock 1999; Husband 2000). Here theorists debate as fiercely as ever the operations of power – economic, political, social, cultural – and how these variously condition and shape, or erode, the contribution of today's media to forms of 'citizenship', 'rational' opinion formation and 'consensus', while nonetheless acknowledging the less than ideologically closed and less than individually open nature of public communications. This turn to a more historically nuanced, empirically differentiated and politically contested view of 'the media' as a site of struggle, in which contingencies as well as determinisms are thought to inform the operations of material and discursive power and representational outcomes, provides a foundation for much current work in the media communications field, including the study of media–sources interactions. Developments in both society and social theory have added new levels of inflection as well as urgency to this concern with media approached as 'public sphere'.

New(s) Times: Contested Fields

Contemporary social theorists maintain that we live in globalising, post-traditional and uncertain times. Each of these characteristic features of late-modern societies point to the increased centrality of the media in expressing the profusion of competing interests and associated discourses that now clamour for public representation. Processes of globalisation assisted by new forms of communication technology and delivery have accelerated the collapse of space and time, stretched and intensified social relations conducted at a distance (Giddens 1994), and given rise to a global 'network society' (Castells 1996). Globalisation has also prompted increased flows of finance, peoples and cultures around the globe (Lash and Urry 1994) and contributed to the undermining of nation states and their ability to control and manage economic and political processes – both within and without territorial borders (Held et al. 1999). In such ways, the contemporary world generates new economic and political conflicts, exacerbates problems of state legitimation, and has prompted the rise of the 'public relations state' (Deacon and Golding 1994).

Globalisation also consolidates modernising impulses, including the disenchantment of the world where faith and tradition become subject to Max Weber's 'iron-cage' of instrumental reason. Pronounced individualism, consumerism and technical rationality undermine traditions and belief systems once taken for granted. In 'post-traditional times', however, traditions do not necessarily disappear but, paradoxically, can assume a more assertive and combative stance in response to modernising/globalising forces. The point is that they are now expected to defend themselves in reasoned and self-reflective terms and cannot assume unquestioning adherence on the basis of tradition alone (Giddens 1994). Traditional solidarities of class and political allegiance rooted in the social relations of mass production have also been weakened in respect of new flexible arrangements of social production and cultural patterns of consumption; this has given rise to new forms of identity politics, new social movements and other extra-parliamentary 'subpolitics'. Together these constitute an expanded field of 'the political' within civil society (Hall and Jacques 1989; Mouffe 1996; Beck 1997; Castells 1997). Such social transformations have also produced a cacophony of discourses as different state, corporate and group interests and cultural identities

compete, contend and promote a diversity of values and aims via communicative action in the media 'public sphere' (Habermas 1996).

   This profusion of contending discourses is also encouraged by today's
increased 'social reflexivity' which questions knowledge claims and expertise,
including the 'certainties' of science and the technocratic administration of 'risks'
– those potentially catastrophic 'manufactured uncertainties' of late modernity
now circumnavigating the globe and possibly affecting generations yet unborn
(Beck 1992; Beck et al. 1994). Anthony Giddens maintains that such powerful
forces of social change have given rise to feelings of 'ontological insecurity'
(Giddens 1990), fuelling the rise of environmental consciousness and grassroots
protests conducted at local and global levels – protests that are invariably
played out in the mass media spotlight. All this contributes to the growth of
'subpolitics' – a politics from below – questioning 'normative' goals of economic
growth and state-sanctioned environmental exploitation. Powerful states as well
as individuals inhabit uncertain times of course, as the events of September 11,
2001 bear witness (Zelizer and Allan 2002). This has prompted renewed efforts
at an international 'suprapolitics' – a politics from above – and this too is no less
dependent upon the legitimating arenas of the mass media and its public
relations capabilities.

   The foregoing points to some of the profound processes of social transformation that today are thought to underlie the profusion of discourses that
clamour for media access and public representation. The mass media constitute
a prime arena in which the contending interests, values and viewpoints that
comprise this 'radical pluralism' seek to engage in communicative action in
pursuit of public recognition, legitimacy and strategic aims – whether by strategies of 'disclosure' or 'enclosure' (Ericson et al. 1989). But how have theorists
researched, theorised and explained the involvement of media sources in
processes of news representation? What are the principal complexities involved
and what are the key questions that we need to pursue today?

   The following maps in more theoretically proximate terms the different
paradigms and range of approaches that have helped to define the current field
and stake out its fundamental concerns with media–source interaction and
participation. The first, broadly sociological, paradigm is generally concerned
with how sources strategically pursue their organisational interests via media
access and aim to secure 'definitional advantage'. The second, broadly culturalist,
paradigm pursues the representational nature of media portrayal and access and
examines questions of 'symbolic power'. And the third, emergent 'communicative', paradigm develops on and departs from the previous two by focusing
more explicitly on how forms of 'communicative power' are performed and
enacted in the media with a heightened awareness of the contingencies involved –
whether in relation to the potentially transformative aspects of 'ritual processes',
or the less than certain outcomes associated with live mediated encounters and
'risks' of public performances. While there is certainly overlap between these
three paradigmatic orientations, each nonetheless pursues different questions and
emphasises different aspects of news media–source interaction. Importantly, each
also serves to illuminate different dimensions of power informing media–source
relations, whether strategic, symbolic or communicative. These paradigms will be

reviewed in turn, but first it is useful to revisit briefly the tradition of symbolic interactionism. This earlier sociological approach has proved to be seminal, bequeathing influential ideas to later sociological studies of sources strategies, culturalist approaches to the study of the symbolic nature of media representations, as well as studies of communicative action and the dynamic nature of mediatised encounters.

Seminal Beginnings: Symbolic Interactionism

The sociological tradition of symbolic interactionism (Blumer 1969, 1971) sought to explore how labels, symbols and meanings inform human interactions and understanding. Influential studies of how 'outsiders' were labelled as deviant (Becker 1963), how 'others' were stigmatised (Goffman 1963), and how 'moral entrepreneurs', 'control agents' and 'folk devils' featured within moral panics (Cohen 1972) have informed countless studies of media representation to this day. In extreme cases of deviant labelling, social groups have become dehumanised, demonised and their aims depoliticised and delegitimated (Cohen and Young 1981). This early sociological approach with its concern with processes of labelling and symbolisation influenced the early development of cultural studies (Hall 1974), but it also prompted a more strategic view of social power. Howard Becker's (1967) notion of a 'hierarchy of credibility' helps us to map the evident patterns of elite access within the news media (and documented across countless empirical studies) and he explains this with reference to the social structure and cultural mores of the wider society.

> In any system of ranked groups, participants take it as given that members of the highest group have the right to define the way things really are. And since . . . matters of rank and status are contained in the mores, this belief has a moral quality. . . . Thus, credibility and the right to be heard are differently distributed through the ranks of the system. (Becker 1967: 241)

Becker's formulation, though suggestive, nonetheless remained theoretically underdeveloped. It offers a far too static and ahistorical view of 'social hierarchy' and cultural 'mores' and thus begs questions concerning the role of the media in mediating change, conflicts and contending interests. However, when aligned to Herbert Blumer's views on processes of 'collective definition' and the so-called 'career' of 'social problems', a more processual and strategic view on news access is opened up (Blumer 1971: 301). As 'social problems' proceed through Blumer's discerned stages of 'emergence', 'legitimation', 'mobilisation', 'formation' and 'transformation', so the strategic activities of key players become crucial, as do the news media – one of the 'key arenas of public discussion' (Blumer 1971: 303). In a statement remarkably redolent of more recent theoretical positions on news source interventions (see below), Blumer usefully draws attention to the dynamics and political contingencies involved in mobilising social problems.

How the problem comes to be defined, how it is bent in response to awakened sentiment, how it is depicted to protect vested interests, and how it reflects the play of strategic position and power – all are appropriate questions that suggest the importance of the process of mobilization for action. (*Blumer 1971: 304*)

Symbolic interactionism, then, with its seminal ideas of 'labelling', 'hierarchy of credibility', the 'play of strategic position and power' and 'the mobilization of action' contributes valuable analytical tools for the interrogation of media sources strategies, the symbolic nature of media representations, as well as the investigation of interactional forms of communicative action. Nonetheless, for the reasons mentioned, these remain theoretically underdeveloped in respect of the exact mechanism(s) linking the strategic promotion of particular 'social problems' with the news media.

Moral panic theory, as elaborated by Stanley Cohen in *Folk Devils and Moral Panics* (1972), promised to bridge this gap. Moral panic theory explores how public anxieties are generated by the media through processes of media amplification involving sensationalising, exaggerating, distorting and symbolising 'problematic' events and social actors which, in turn, leads to processes of societal reaction (typically a tough law-and-order crackdown) and the resurrection of a 'societal control' culture. Cohen's theory of moral panics thus served as a bridge between symbolic interactionist ideas of labelling and neo-Marxist ideas of ideological legitimation. But again we can note how the exact mechanisms linking the news media to a discerned wider 'societal control culture' remained empirically under-explored, as did the possible motivations informing the so-called 'control agents' and 'moral entrepreneurs' manning, courtesy of the news media, the moral barricades. Moreover, in today's promotional times, we can no longer assume that dominant social interests have it all their own way; yester-year's 'folk devils' have increasingly learnt to 'fight back' on today's media stage (McRobbie 1994).

Media Sources and Strategic Power

Sociological studies of media sources and news–source interactions encompass a range of influential theoretical approaches: neo-Marxism, the sociology of news production and the sociology of source fields. Each contributes important insights and conceptualisation for improved understanding of the strategic nature of media source power and source interventions into the world of news discourse.

Neo-Marxism and Legitimation

The early works of the Glasgow University Media Group (GUMG) (1976, 1980) and Stuart Hall and his colleagues (1975a, 1978) are in many respects similar. Each builds upon the ideas of symbolic interactionism, each is informed by neo-Marxist views of society structured in dominance, and each seeks to move beyond interactionist ideas of 'labelling' to those of ideological 'legitimation'. Importantly, each also identifies the role of a dominant 'world-view' or 'dominant culture' and structured hierarchical access as the key mechanisms accounting for the privileging of dominant ideas by the news media. Thus, according to the GUMG,

> television news is a cultural artefact; it is a sequence of socially manufactured messages, which carry many of the culturally dominant assumptions of our society. From the accents of the newscasters to the vocabulary of camera angles; from who gets on and what questions get asked, via selection of stories to presentation of bulletins, the news is a highly mediated product. (GUMG 1976: 1)

These 'culturally dominant assumptions' are said to inform journalist's views and, in turn, to inform the systematic and preferential patterns of news access: 'Access is structured and hierarchical to the extent that powerful groups and individuals have privileged and routine entry into the news itself and to the manner and means of its production' (GUMG 1980: 114). A slightly less static account of the news media and their sources is provided by Stuart Hall, who maintained: 'broadcasters and their institutions mediate – hold the pass, command the communicative channels – between the elites of power (social, economic, political, cultural) and the mass audience' (Hall 1975a: 124). Hall and his colleagues also provide a twin-pronged approach to news access and the reproduction of the voices of the powerful.

> These two aspects of news production – the practical pressures of constantly working against the clock and the professional demands of impartiality and objectivity – combine to produce a systematically structured over-accessing to the media of those in powerful and privileged institutional positions. (Hall et al. 1978: 58)

In these ways, Hall et al. maintain that the news media reproduce the voices of the powerful who become the 'primary definers' of events. Though subject to some limited opportunities for challenge in the news media, the 'primary definers', via routine access and news legitimation, command the discursive field and set the terms of debate there. The voices of the powerful are translated into the 'public idioms' of different newspapers, which thereby serve to invest them with 'popular force and resonance' (Hall et al. 1978: 61). For both the GUMG and Hall, questions of news 'mediation' ultimately boil down to the reproduction of the 'culturally dominant assumptions of society' (GUMG 1976: 1) and how different news outlets become 'inflected with dominant and consensual connotations' (Hall et al. 1978: 62). In both cases, ideas of news mediation are effectively reduced to a view of ideological translation and transmission that leaves little room for consideration of the characteristic forms, differentiated appeals and discursive possibilities inhering within different journalist genres and in relation to differently organised source fields. We need to know more about the interactions within and between news sources and news producers before we can simply position the news producers as 'unwittingly, unconsciously' serving 'as a support for the reproduction of a dominant ideological discursive field' (Hall 1982: 88) – a point that has also been recognised by more recent work by members of the GUMG (Eldridge 1993; Miller et al. 1998a).

Perhaps too, ideas of 'dominant culture', like those of its correlate 'dominant ideology', were always too generalising, too nebulous to substitute for an analysis of the complex of forces at play (Abercrombie et al. 1980). But the most serious limitation of these studies is that neither examines the complexities and interactions informing the professional and organisational worlds of news production and news sources. This is so notwithstanding the GUMG's partial (but aborted) production study, self-described as a 'reconnaissance into alien territory' (GUMG 1976: 58) and Hall's theoretical acknowledgement of the role of bureaucratic routines and the professional ideology of objectivity in accessing primary definers (Hall et al. 1978: 53–77). For a more grounded appreciation of the role of 'strategic position and play of power' in respect of these, we have to look elsewhere.

Sociology of News Production: Behind the Scenes

Studies in the sociology of news production, many based on considerable time in the field and drawing upon different news outlets, have revealed something of the normally concealed internal workings of the 'black box' of news production and the routine professional practices and organisational and cultural norms informing its operation (Epstein 1973; Altheide 1976; Tuchman 1978; Schlesinger 1978; Golding and Elliott 1979; Gans 1979; Fishman 1980; Ericson et al. 1987; Cottle 1993a). Their findings help to throw light on source–news interactions.

According to Gaye Tuchman's observations, for example, news is a bureaucratic accomplishment organisationally geared up to 'routinizing the unexpected' and 'taming the news environment' (Tuchman 1973, 1978). Here processes of news manufacture must ensure that sufficient amounts of news, comprising a certain mix of news subjects, are produced and packaged on time and to a predetermined and professionally understood organisational form (Rock 1981). This bureaucratic goal necessitates a newsroom division of labour, organisation of journalists into 'news beats' and the setting up of news bureaux (Rock 1981; Tuchman 1973; Fishman 1980), as well as the development of a 'vocabulary of precedents' that helps journalists to 'recognise', 'produce', 'source' and 'justify' their news stories (Ericson et al. 1987: 348).

It is these practical responses to news work, it is said, that lead to the systematic accessing of powerful, resource-rich institutions and their definitions of events – and to the marginalisation of resource-poor social groups and interests (Goldenberg 1975; Gitlin 1980). Society's major institutions – government, the courts, and police and so on – are thereby positioned to pronounce on social affairs and command both the physical resources and the authoritativeness to define and pontificate on newsworthy events. They also have the organisational capacity to manage professionally the flow of news material or even produce their own 'pseudo-events' (Boorstein 1964; Sigal 1973), encouraging favourable coverage through the provision of bureaucratically useful (and commercially beneficial) 'information subsidies' (Gandy 1982). In the terms of Harvey Molotch and Marilyn Lester, such 'event promoters' enjoy 'habitual access' to the news media, in contrast to those who must resort to 'disruptive access'. The latter can only '"make news", by somehow crashing through the ongoing arrangements of news making, generating surprise, shock, or some more violent form of "trouble"' (Molotch and Lester 1981: 128).

Clearly, the organisation of news is not geared up to the needs of the socially powerless. Specialist news reporters and correspondents daily enter the professional worlds of key institutional sources and negotiate a long-term exchange relationship based upon trust and mutual benefit (Tunstall 1970), a relationship that all too often is thought to result in news compromise and newsroom dependency (Chibnall 1977). Subtle socialisation processes generating intra-group norms established in interaction with 'competitor-colleagues' (Tunstall 1971; Dunwoody 1978; Fishman 1981; Pedelty 1995) as well as incremental inter-source socialisation where the journalist steadily becomes immersed into the professional world-view of his/her principal source – whether, for example, the police (Chibnall 1977) or the military (Morrison and Tumber 1988; Morrison 1994; Pedelty 1995) – combine to narrow differences of news perspective from those of their sources.

Moreover, in an increasingly competitive (Ehrlich 1995) and commercially driven news environment (Altschull 1997), the 'market model of news discovery' is likely to prevail over the increasingly mythical 'journalist model of discovery' or in-depth and independent investigative journalism (McManus 1997: 287), adding a commercial impetus to the organisational dependence upon official sources. In short, according to Michael Schudson, 'it matters not whether the study is at the national, state or local level – the story of journalism, on a day-to-day basis, is the story of the interaction of reporters and officials' (Schudson 1991: 148).

The professional ideology of objectivity also contributes to the profession's subservience to elite views. As John Soloski argues, 'objectivity is the most important professional norm, and from it flows more specific aspects of news professionalism such as news judgment, the selection of sources and the structure of news beats' (Soloski 1989: 213). Journalists socialised into the professional pursuit of (philosophically elusive) 'objectivity' settle pragmatically for balance, fairness and impartiality. To achieve this end and, importantly, to be seen to be so doing by their sources, audience/readers and colleagues, journalists engage in the 'strategic ritual' (Tuchman 1972) of seeking out authoritative voices whom they deem to be knowledgeable and socially accredited to pronounce on newsworthy events.

While these broad findings remain insightful, they tend to exaggerate the uniformity of news output across the differentiated ecology of news forms as well as the invariant cast of news sources found on the news stage (Eliasoph 1988; Cottle 1993b, 2000b). Closer attention to the different cultural forms of news, their associated professional practices and how these influence patterns and processes of news access, suggests that issues of media access cannot be reduced wholesale to bureaucratic routines and/or a presumed subscription to a generalised professional ideology of 'objectivity' – other cultural factors are also (literally) at work.

Sociology of News Sources: Behind the Producers

If studies of news organisation and professional practices point to the bureau-cratic, professional and, to some extent, cultural dimensions involved in the accessing of voices on to the news stage, so others have sought to investigate the interventions of sources into the news theatre from the source point of view. Herbert Gans (1979: 117), after analysing the commentary of news producers, concludes that the success of source interventions in their 'tug of war' with the news media, will depend on (a) their incentives, (b) power, (c) ability to supply suitable information, and (d) geographic and social proximity to the journalists.

Philip Schlesinger (1990), developing on earlier source studies, has argued for a more 'externalist', less media-centred, approach to sources and their 'strategic activities' that are seen as organised within 'competitive fields'. Though recognising the material and symbolic advantages enjoyed by the state and powerful institutions, he also acknowledges the importance of non-official source activities.

> [I]t is necessary that sources be conceived as occupying fields in which competition for access to the media takes place, but in which material and symbolic advantages are unequally distributed. But the most advantaged do not secure a primary definition in virtue of their position alone. Rather, if they do so, it is because of successful strategic action in an imperfectly competitive field. *(Schlesinger 1990: 77)*

When conceived of in this way, static views of definitional advantage secured by social dominance alone are found theoretically and empirically wanting. Schlesinger (1990: 66–7) takes the 'primary definer' thesis to task for not taking account of:

1 the contention between official sources;

2 the behind-the-scenes manoeuvrings of sources, rendered methodologically invisible by culturalist readings of texts;

3 the competitive and shifting nature of key sources *within* privileged elites;

4 the longer-term shifts in the structure of access; and

5 for assuming a *uni-directional* flow of definitions from power centres to media.

These more complex views on source power and strategic activity have subse-quently informed growing numbers of empirical studies of different 'competitive fields', including studies of environmental pressure groups (Anderson 1993, Hansen 1993a), health professionals working in the field of HIV/AIDS (Miller and Williams 1993), competing pressure groups and professional interests in the criminal justice field (Ericson et al. 1989; Schlesinger and Tumber 1994), non-official sources working in the voluntary sector (Deacon 1996), political party and pressure group contestation of a controversial government policy (Deacon and Golding 1994), trades unions (Davis 2000a; Manning 2001) and the complex (and historically changing) interactions of state and other sources in the 'Troubles' in Northern Ireland (Miller 1993, 1994).

If these predominantly British studies implicitly question earlier positions for assuming guaranteed elite access without attending to relevant contexts and strategic activities, predominantly US-based studies have highlighted the changing nature of elite political consensus and how this too shapes processes and patterns of news access. Lance Bennett (1990: 106) explicitly formulates the 'index' model of news access as follows: 'Mass media news professionals, from the boardroom to the beat, tend to "index" the range of voices and viewpoints in both news and editorials according to the range of views expressed in main-stream government debate about a given topic.' The model maintains, in other words, that in times of elite political consensus, the news media will tend to support government policy and access voices that give vent to this support; in times of elite dissensus, however, the news media will also take their cue from this and be prepared to access a wider range of voices than normal and may even be emboldened to adopt a more engaged and challenging stance. In-depth, longitudinal studies of media reporting of wars in Vietnam (Hallin 1986), El Salvador (Bennett 1990; Hallin 1994; Pedelty 1995), the Gulf War (Bennett and Paletz 1994; Wolfsfeld 1997) and the changing state 'aperture of consensus' informing media reporting of Northern Ireland (Butler 1995) all lend empirical support to this thesis. In sympathy with this model, Deacon and Golding (1994) draw attention to the distinction within elite sources between professional experts or 'arbiters' and 'advocates'. The former are accessed by the news media to help 'legislate', that is, to make informed evaluations of statements and opinions advanced by 'advocates' on a particular debate or issues and can prove extremely influential (Deacon and Golding 1994: 15–17).

In their different ways, then, all the studies referenced above have helped shift attention away from media-centred views to examine the complex of vying interests and temporal processes informing news access and representation. In short, source strategies and political contingencies are found where once social dominance alone was assumed sufficient to guarantee successful news entry. To be clear, none of the authors above would theoretically seek to discount the unequal weighting of resources, social credibility or legitimacy distributed across source fields, nor their continuing influence on processes of news access. Nonetheless, together they point to the multiple factors and contingencies that unfold through time and that cannot, therefore, be easily predicted in advance nor better understood without recourse to empirical examination. Persuasive, insightful and necessary as these sociological approaches to media sources undoubtedly are, when approached from the perspective of the culturalist paradigm, they nonetheless remain insufficient in so far as they appear to underestimate the shaping impact of news as a cultural medium and form of symbolic expressions. Here we need to turn to studies conducted within the broad orientation of the culturalist paradigm.

Media Sources and Symbolic Power

The sociological paradigm, as we have seen, pursues questions of media sources and news access principally in terms of the activities of news producers and strategic interventions of sources. What this lacks, from a culturalist perspective, is a sense of the culturally mediating nature of news approached not just as a cipher of social interests and political power, but in terms of its very constitution as a cultural medium of communication and purveyor of symbols. Drawing upon the more textually sensitive approach of cultural studies to the structures and forms of story and narrative, some researchers have pursued the cultural nature of news further, and in so doing have opened up further insights into the nature of news media–source involvement.

Story, Myth and Narrativity

As all journalists know, the 'news story' is at the core of their professional activity. Ronald Jacobs, for example, has argued that '"Narrativity" is the central factor structuring newswork' (Jacobs 1996: 73) and, as such, it continues the tradition of storytelling. This tradition has long provided the means by which society can tell and re-tell its basic myths to itself, and in so doing reaffirm itself as collectivity or 'imagined community' (Smith 1979; Barkin and Gurevitch 1987; Campbell 1987; Bird and Dardenne 1988; Bird 1990). Approached this way, news becomes a symbolic system in which the informational content of particular 'stories' becomes less important than the rehearsal of mythic 'truths' embodied within the story form itself: as Elizabeth Bird and Robert Dardenne have argued, 'News stories, like myths, do not "tell it like it is", but rather, "tell it like it means"' (Bird and Dardenne 1988: 337).

This clearly has relevance for understanding of media sources and news involvement. According to Dan Berkowitz (1992: 83), 'newsworkers develop a mental catalogue of news story themes, including how the "plot" will actually unravel and who the key actors are likely to be'. Bird and Dardenne also point to the implications of news 'story' for concerns of access, and the mythical role performed by news more generally.

> In newsmaking, journalists do not merely use culturally determined definitions, they also have to fit new situations into old definitions. It is in their power to place people and events into the existing categories of hero, villain, good and bad, and thus to invest their stories with the authority of mythological truth. (*Bird and Dardenne 1988: 345; see also Lule 1997*)

John Langer, in his study of tabloid television, also points to the deep-seated influence of cultural forms when he argues that, 'What journalists like to refer to as news sense has as much to do with the priorities of "form" as it does with institutionalized sanctioned content' (Langer 1998: 133). His study details how a limited repertoire of news narratives position 'celebrities', 'ordinary people' and 'victims' symbolically in standardised roles within the mythic structures of tabloid news stories. These symbolic roles are not confined to popular and populist forms of journalism however.

Media Events: Scripts and Roles

Daniel Dayan and Elihu Katz, in their study *Media Events – the Live Broadcasting of History* (1992), examine those pre-planned, live, and generally state co-ordinated interruptions to the routines of broadcasting such as ceremonies of state and other major events (the so-called 'high holidays' of mass communications). They make the case that the broadcasting of such historical events is made to conform to genre types; moreover, that these genres determine roles and condition forms of access accordingly. Dayan and Katz identify three genres within their category of 'Media events': *Contests* or epic contests of politics and sports (for example, the Senate Watergate hearings, the World Cup, the Olympics); *Conquests* or so-called charismatic missions (for example, the moon landing, President Anwar el-Sadat's visit to Israel); and *Coronations* or the rites of passage of the great (for example, the coronation of Elizabeth II, the wedding of Prince Charles or the funeral of Princess Diana).

> [T]he corpus of events can be subdivided into Contests, Conquests and Coronations. These are story forms, or 'scripts' which constitute the main narrative possibilities within the genre. They determine the distribution of roles within each type of event and the ways in which they will be enacted. *(Dayan and Katz 1992: 25)*

Collectively, then, these authors recognise the structuring power of narrative and storytelling and how these apparently position news actors symbolically to serve wider cultural myths. From a sociological perspective, however, they risk reifying news structures and cultural myths as seemingly immutable and determining forms outside of the historical play of power and the strategic interventions and struggles of contending social interests.

'Postjournalism': beyond Access?

Some theorists go even further in their theorisation of the power of form and suggest that the conventionalised formats of news now effectively make concerns with media sources and news access redundant. David Altheide, for example, discerns a generalising 'media logic' which produces standardised news formats or templates that condition how stories are scripted and how sources behave (Altheide 1995; Altheide and Snow 1979, 1991). The all-pervasive influence of such media formats, it is argued, conditions other arenas of society, whether politics or sport, producing both a 'postmodern' age and a new form of 'postjournalism' – a situation effectively 'beyond access'. In the 'postjournalism era', then, politicians and others are said to have succumbed to the logic and formats of the media and therefore deliver to the entertainment and commercially driven media exactly what they require – the death knell of independent and investigative journalism thus rings.

Is Altheide too pessimistic, too generalising in his claims? In so far as today's news ecology continues to demonstrate at least some important differences of format and political outlook, and in so far as vying social interests feel the need to enter the news domain and discursively engage the definitions, accounts and prescriptions of others and strategically win some opportunity to do so, the claims that we are entering the doomsday scenario of a 'postjournalism era' may be premature.

Media Sources and Communicative Power

Finally we come to a range of studies that both build on and in some respects depart from the sociological and culturalist approaches reviewed above. These studies exhibit a heightened awareness of the contingencies of 'communicative power' at the moment of its enactment. Here the broadly sociological emphasis upon the play of power of social interests organised within competitive source fields and strategically pursuing definitional advantage within the media, is extended to an examination of how this is actually played out in communicative practice. The culturalist sensitivity to textual forms and conventions and how these 'mediate' source participation is also brought into view, but now in a far less closed and deterministic way. Studying forms of communicative action at the moment of enactment, the accent shifts to a more politically contingent and communicatively less settled or predictable outcome. Mediatised communicative action is based on the performances, institutional opportunities and interactional encounters of engaged participants rather than a reading of static cultural forms and myths or the closed textual determinations of fixed story-types, scripts and allocated roles and so on. Again, the differences between this approach to 'communicative power' and sociological approaches to 'strategic' power and culturalist approaches to 'symbolic' power should not be taken as mutually exclusive, but rather as serving to capture important differences of emphasis and insight.

Mediated Ritual, Scandals and Public Performance

Studies of mediated news 'ritual' and associated performances have helped to highlight how these often involve dynamic processes and social tensions that unfold through time. Far from serving in Durkheimian terms to 'integrate' the social order by re-establishing social consensus and maintaining the status quo, mediated 'rituals' can also, according to theorists, serve conflicted interests and potentially be transformative (Elliott 1980; Chaney 1986; Wagner-Pacifici 1986; Alexander 1988; Alexander and Jacobs 1998; Ettema 1990; Jacobs 1996; Hunt 1999; Cottle forthcoming). Here, then, a *processual* view of 'ritual' is opened up, one in which the script is not thought to be exclusively owned by any one party whether news producers or particular sources, and where 'ritual' is often mobilised and contested in an unfolding 'social drama'. The idea of 'social drama' has been developed by the anthropologist Victor Turner (1969, 1974) and helps to map how social conflicts often move through time, involve different political opportunities and risks, and embroil diverse social actors and powerful institutions in public performances in their struggle to maintain or win public legitimacy and support.

> I have used the notion of a social drama as a device for describing and analyzing episodes that manifest social conflict. At its simplest, the drama consists of a four-stage model, proceeding from breach of some social relationship regarded as crucial in the relevant social group, which provides not only its setting but many of its goals, through a phase of rapidly mounting crisis in the direction of the group's major dichotomous cleavage, to the application of legal or ritual means of redress or reconciliation between the conflicting parties which compose the action set. The final stage is either the public and symbolic expression of reconciliation or else of irremediable schism. *(Turner 1974: 78–9)*

Turner's ideas of 'social drama' have been put to work in a number of applied studies of mediated conflicts and public crises often involving highly ritualistic elements. These include a study of the mediated coverage of the US 'Watergate' scandal (Alexander 1988), Italian terrorism and the killing of Aldo Moro (Wagner-Pacifici 1986), British press performance and the reporting of IRA acts of terrorism (Elliott 1980), the reporting of a conflictual race relations story in the US (Ettema 1990) and media reporting of the racist killing of the British black teenager Stephen Lawrence, murdered in London in April 1993, and the institutional and cultural responses that this subsequently unleashed (Cottle, forthcoming).

As these case studies of mediated rituals indicate, questions of news access and source power are rendered more complex and politically contingent when approached through this more *processual* view. Political contingencies and 'risks' also attend mediatised scandals where the 'transformation of visibility' brought about by modern forms of media communication can unseat the powerful and prompt public performances designed to hold on to the reins of power (Thompson 1995, 2000).

> [p]olitical scandals are not only personal tragedies: they are also social struggles which are fought out in the symbolic realm, in the to and fro of claims and counter-claims, of revelations, allegations and denials. They are struggles which have their own protagonists, each pursuing their own strategies in an unfolding sequence of events which often outpace the individuals involved and which, thanks to the media, are made available on a public stage for countless others to watch or listen to or read about. *(Thompson, 2000: 7)*

In circumstances of mediatised scandal, the balance of media and source power can easily shift, once again underscoring the reality of the contingencies and political 'risks' of performance involved.

Forms of Talk: Interactive, Communicative, Deliberative

The influence of earlier ideas of symbolic interactionism, as we have seen, influenced both later developments in the sociology of 'strategic power', and cultural studies of 'symbolic power'. Erving Goffman had also defined human interactions or 'encounters' as one of the 'primal scenes of sociology' (Goffman 1963), for it is in and through encounters that human relationships and meanings are daily recreated and roles and statuses are reproduced. This focus on 'encounters' has subsequently informed theoretical developments in ethno-methodology and conversation analysis and a number of studies of 'talk-in-interaction' in media settings. Collectively these contribute to our third 'emergent' paradigm of approaches to 'communicative action' which are pro-ducing new insights into forms of mediated talk and the institutionalised nature of broadcast encounters. Attending to forms of talk conducted in news interviews, for example, has revealed how these institutionalise, that is regulate and normalise, certain procedures of turn-taking, agenda-setting and agenda-shifting between interviewers and interviewees; moreover they reveal how these, and other powered features of the conduct of talk, are differentially available to those involved (Greatbatch 1986; Heritage and Greatbatch 1993; Clayman 2002).

Paddy Scannell has helped to historicise and institutionally contextualise this attention to forms of broadcast talk, and recovers the 'communicative inten-tionality' of different programme forms in radio and television and how this has broadly shifted earlier distant and authoritative relationships between broad-casters and audiences to more equal, open and accessible relationships (Scannell 1992, 1996, 2003). This shift in communicative ethos across the years is recovered in part by attending in close-grained and sympathetic ways to the programmes themselves.

> In attending to the institutional features of broadcast occasions we can specify how power works in them, by the study of 1) the distribution of communicative entitlements,
> 2) participatory statuses and performative roles and 3) the organization and control of talk.
> (Scannell 1996: 18–19)

One of the fascinating features of this historical recovery of broadcast forms of talk is the way in which 'liveness' and the often unscripted and spontaneous nature of the talks themselves produces enhanced opportunities for debate and engaged discussion.

The different forms of television news and current affairs programmes rou-tinely structure the presentation, hierarchies of access and discursive possibilities for engaged talk and deliberation for the 'benefit' of an overhearing, overseeing audience – vital resources for processes of 'democratic deepening' (Giddens 1994) and the development of a more deliberative democracy (Dryzek 2000). Attending to the presentational architecture of television journalism can help reveal how these structures regulate, constrain and facilitate the public elaboration and dialogical interactions of divergent views and interests for an overhearing, overseeing audience as well as the public display and performative features of engaged participation (Cottle 2001, 2002).

Considerations of 'communicative power' thus invite us to examine empiri-cally how mediated encounters and the interactions of accessed participants are variously enacted and performed, and how these are both constrained and facilitated by the institutionalised arrangements and systems of delegation in which they take place. Contrary to theoretical determinisms, which all too readily presume forms of ideological or textual closure, attending to mediated forms of talk can often reveal the contingencies and opportunities that attend engaged public encounters, and not just their containment.

Media–Source Paradigms: Summary

As we have seen, researchers working within the *sociological* paradigm have tended to forefront and investigate media–source interactions in terms of strategic and definitional power, examining patterns of news access, routines of news production and processes of source intervention, and how each conditions the production of public knowledge. Researchers working within a *culturalist* paradigm, on the other hand, have tended to theorise news access in terms of cultural representation, and are sensitised to the symbolic role of news actors and how these are positioned according to the conventions of news – story, narrative, form – and thereby help contribute to and sustain wider cultural myths that resonate within popular culture.

These broad paradigmatic differences, rooted in the academic divisions of the social sciences and the humanities – a division that continues to structure much of the work undertaken in our multidisciplinary field of media communication – provide powerful optics through which to view media sources and news access. While the sociological paradigm encourages us to look at the role of strategic power in the public representation of politics (broadly conceived), the culturalist paradigm invites us to see how cultural forms and symbols are implicated within the politics of representation (more textually conceived).

A third emergent paradigm, that of *communicative action*, both incorporates and in part departs from the previous two, and examines communicative power at the moment of its enactment. Attending to the dynamics and contingencies of ritual processes, live performances and engaged encounters within the institutionalised forms of media representation, these studies open up a more processual and less deterministic view of media participation – returning the study of media participation and performance to the world of engaged strategic interests, the enactment of communicative action and contingencies of political struggle as well as the complexities of mediating forms.

With these three broad theoretical orientations to the study of media sources and their interactions with the journalist field in place, we are now equipped to consider some of the recent contributions to this area of study and how each deepens our understanding of its specialist focus of enquiry.

Plan of the Book

News, Public Relations and Power is structured into five main sections, each of which contributes to the overall thematic approach informing this volume. The next section, **Promotional Times: the Growth of Public Relations**, alerts the reader to the wider field of public relations and how this has grown exponentially in recent years. Chapter 2, 'Public Relations and News Sources' by Aeron Davis, charts this rise of public relations in Britain and then explores and theorises its impact on media–source interactions and news production practices. Davis observes how a wide range of organisations have adopted public relations as a means of achieving particular goals through media coverage. At the same time, media institutions have experienced tighter editorial budgets and have therefore become more dependent on information supplied by external sources. These two trends have resulted in the sudden growth of the professional public relations sector and changes to patterns of source access. Davis thus examines whether public relations is simply another means by which institutional and corporate organisations are managing to secure access advantages, or whether in fact the changes described represent a new means whereby non-official sources can also gain media access.

This is followed by the first of two major sections on source fields. The first, **Source Fields: Dominant Interests**, examines how dominant institutions and interests – state, political parties, military – seek to manage and manipulate news agendas in the furtherance of their own goals. This, of course, has long been of concern to critical media communication scholars and informs influential ideas of 'hierarchies of credibility', privileged 'elite access' and 'primary definition'. Here three authoritative chapters attend to the complexities involved. Chapter 3, '"A Good Day to Bury Bad News": Journalists, Sources and the Packaging of Politics' by Bob Franklin, examines the important arena of political communications focusing upon British party political communication strategies and attempts at news management conducted at both national and local levels. The discussion is based on the recognition that the media have today become an integral, indispensable even, part of political communications. Politics, according to Franklin, has become 'packaged'. Political parties and politicians increasingly seek to exert some degree of control over their media representation whilst also acknowledging that the media operate according to a different set of priorities and logics. Based on his recent research, Franklin confirms his general thesis of 'packaged' politics while nonetheless teasing out important differences and complexities that characterise national and local media–political party interactions. Nationally, an analysis of the Labour government's relationship with journalists reveals the dominance of sources, while an analysis of the relationship between journalists and parties at the local level reveals the dominance of local news media and journalists.

Chapter 4, 'Journalism under Fire: the Reporting of War and International Crises' by Philip Taylor, examines historically the competing interests that characterise journalism, military and government interactions in times of war and acute international crises. Public knowledge about foreign events, including wars and international crises, relies heavily upon the mass media. Yet, asks Taylor, how much public understanding is there of the ways in which the media interact with, and report on, such events? Taylor expertly charts the changing, sometimes difficult, relationship between journalists, governments and the military with respect to the reporting of wars and crisis situations from the Crimean War to the Gulf War and, most recently, the wars in Bosnia and Kosovo and the 'war against terrorism' following the events of September 11, 2001. Here the competing logics of media and state, and the strategies of information management that inform these, are explored historically, revealing both continuities and change across time and in relation to different wars and international crises.

Chapter 5, 'The Political Contest Model' by Gadi Wolfsfeld, outlines his influential model for analysing political conflicts and the media and sets out to identify the key factors and political contingencies that determine the nature of media representations of conflict. Media conflict reporting, he observes, is far from linear or constant, notwithstanding material advantages of dominant groups. Sometimes, he says, it is as if the media arena is used for lavish spectacles in which the officials show off their most colourful costumes and weapons; at other times it is a place for fierce contests in which challengers and authorities square off in brutal combat; and at other times it becomes a theatre for putting on tragic morality plays about the plight of the oppressed and the need for social change. The aim of Wolfsfeld's chapter is to explain how and why the media perform these different roles in political conflicts, based on an understanding of the political, social and situational factors involved. The chapter thereby helps to open up for consideration a politically nuanced and historically contingent view of elite, and challenger, news access. This takes us into the second of our two sections on source fields.

The next section, **Source Fields: Challengers**, focuses on a range of different groups and interests that occupy varying positions in the social structure but all formally outside of dominant state and government organisations. Chapter 6, 'Non-governmental Organisations and the Media' by David Deacon, therefore shifts the empirical focus of the preceding three chapters and attends to a range of organisations and interests that are often overlooked in the media communications literature and debates about media–source power. Studying comparatively and in detail trades unions, voluntary/charitable organisations and quasi-autonomous non-governmental organisations ('quangos'), Deacon provides a more empirically nuanced and theoretically discriminating analysis of how sources interact with the media and what affects the outcomes. David Deacon's chapter provides a welcome and authoritative discussion of this important and, until recently, relatively under-researched area of news–source interaction.

Chapter 7, 'Environmental Activism and News Media' by Alison Anderson, also examines non-official sources in the context of her discussion of environmental pressure groups and ecological activism – possibly some of the most successful 'challenger' groups in contemporary society. Based on detailed empirical research and study, Anderson addresses: different source strategies deployed by these pressure groups and activists; their hostility to mainstream media; and the use of alternative channels of communication including the Internet by cyber-activists. With the help of empirical examples drawn from the UK and elsewhere, the discussion analyses the complexities that inform the way in which different environmental groups and activists seek to secure media representation, and the reasons for their eventual news representation.

Together these two chapters and their empirical case studies help to document how, despite inequalities of capital, organisational capability and, possibly, social prestige, the voices and views of challenger groups in society occasionally manage to gain a foothold on the slippery slopes of news access and representation, and they provide grounds for understanding why and under what circumstances this can come about.

Finally, a section on **Mediating Representation and Participation** provides two chapters that explore how the cultural forms of television tabloid news, and the 'deliberative architecture' of television journalism, condition and mediate access, representation and participation. Chapter 8, 'Tabloid Television and News Culture: Access and Representation' by John Langer, also examines non-elite news access and news representation. Here, however, he invites us to contextualise and interpret how 'ordinary people' feature in tabloid television news in terms of its characteristic appeals and use of formulaic news stories – whether those of tragedy, disaster or exceptional happenings. These types of news stories, too readily dismissed as 'unworthy' from the point of view of democratic models of news conceived purely in terms of information and public opinion formation provide, Langer argues, important insights into the nature and appeals of tabloid news and its relation to everyday culture. This discussion, then, examines concerns of access and representation through a cultural reading of tabloid TV news and helps to explain the conventions of this popular news form and how it shapes and symbolically positions news entry.

To end, Chapter 9, 'TV Journalism and Deliberative Democracy: Mediating Communicative Action' by Simon Cottle, examines how the conventionalised architecture of television journalism shapes and conditions the public performances and 'encounters' of accessed voices. Through examples of news portrayal of major issues of 'risk society' and anti-World Trade Organization demonstrations, and current affairs programmes about September 11, 2001 and its political aftermath, the author demonstrates how the presentational forms of television journalism can both discursively constrain and facilitate the public elaboration and dialogic engagement of contending political views and cultural outlooks. Cottle argues that forms of news and current affairs programmes potentially contribute invaluable resources for an overhearing, overseeing audience and can thereby be viewed as a key means for the extension of processes of 'democratic deepening' and 'deliberative democracy' – processes that today deserve increased recognition by media scholars.

Together these sections provide a multifaceted understanding of the complexities of media–source interactions, public relations strategies, and forms of media representation and participation. The study of media sources, as we have heard, constitutes a rich field of study and encompasses broad concerns to do with: the rise of 'promotional society' and the role of media in public relations within this; of how and why organisations' PR strategies are aimed at today's news media, from different source fields, and with what discursive effects; as well as the patterns of news access, forms of cultural representation, and the contingencies of public performance and encounter enacted within and through the news media. Attending to each of these, we are able to build a sense of the relative power of media and media sources and their contribution to the clash and clamour of contending interests and identities that today seek public recognition, legitimacy and support via the news media.

CHAPTER SUMMARY

- The study of media–source interactions, public relations strategies and forms of media access and participation goes to the heart of current debates about the relative power of the media and sources in today's society.

- Both traditional liberal democratic theory with its injunction that liberty of the press be protected so that dissenting views can be aired, opinion formation facilitated and 'representative' democratic process sustained, and critical theories which challenge the news media for privileging elite views, legitimising social inequality and/or thwarting moves to participatory democracy, share a fundamental concern with media source involvement and representation.

- Three broad paradigms currently organise the field of media communication research into media–source interactions, representation and participation. The sociological paradigm is generally concerned with how sources strategically pursue media influence and aim to secure 'definitional advantage'. The culturalist paradigm pursues the representational nature of media portrayal and access and examines questions of 'symbolic power'. And an emergent 'communicative' paradigm focuses on forms of 'communicative power' and how these are enacted within the contingencies of media forms and encounters.

- In today's promotional and 'public relations' society, in which contending organised interests and cultural identities clash and clamour for public recognition, support and legitimacy in pursuit of their claims and aims, the media have become a central arena for the conduct of communicative action.

- Today the study of media–sources interactions and relations necessarily involves attending to: (a) the complexities of different source fields and how strategic interests are mobilised in relation to the news media; (b) the political contingencies of struggle and temporal processes involved; (c) the mediating cultural forms and logics of the media; and (d) the enactment of communicative action within the media.

Note

1 This introductory essay, in parts, updates and reformulates ideas first published in Cottle (2000c). See also the excellent discussion by Paul Manning (2001) *News and News Sources: A Critical Introduction*. London: Sage.

PART II

PROMOTIONAL TIMES
The Growth of Public Relations

CHAPTER 2
Public Relations and News Sources

Aeron Davis

This chapter looks at the recent rise of professional public relations in Britain and attempts to gauge its impact on news production and media–source relations. Its basic premise is that the PR (public relations) industry has, in recent decades, come to play an increasingly important part in the reporting process. Behind the media interest in a few key 'spin doctors', there has developed an extensive and well-resourced profession that services a wide range of source organisations. In contrast, the news-gathering resources of journalists have declined. As news organisations have been forced to make cuts while simultaneously increasing output, so their dependency on PR 'information subsidies' has grown. On the one hand, this suggests that public relations is having a stronger influence on the profession of journalism. On the other, it might also be concluded that traditional hierarchies of media–source relations are being altered significantly in the new PR-saturated media environment.

How is the use of public relations altering the media–source relations of various types of organisation? According to critical researchers, there is a strong case to be made for arguing that it has simply helped resource-rich sources, namely governments and corporations, to further extend their control and influence over news producers. Conversely, for liberal pluralists, the evidence suggests that it has enabled resource-poor sources, such as pressure groups and trade unions, to gain a level of media access that was previously denied them. Much of this chapter explores these somewhat contradictory accounts. In so doing it attempts to identify the various means by which public relations can help different types of source to improve their news access and media–source relations. This, in turn, leads towards more definitive conclusions about which types of organisational source have benefited most from public relations in Britain and for what reasons.

Throughout, the study focuses solely on research on British public relations, journalism and news sources. The thinking here is to maintain a comparative focus on a number of competing industries and sectors. Its conclusions, therefore, relate most accurately to the 'British experience' but also contribute to a better understanding of 'promotional' societies more generally.

The Rise of Professional Public Relations and the Rise of Media Dependency

Professional public relations has been a developing profession for most of the twentieth century. However, over the last two decades, the growth and dispersion of the industry in the UK has been considerable. Most documentation of this expansion has been concerned with the rise of government, political party and election communications (e.g. Franklin 1994; Jones 1995, 1999; Scammell 1995; Rosenbaum 1997; Schlesinger et al. 2001). In terms of political parties, the impressive increase in election campaign expenditure is a significant indicator of the expansion of communications in this sector (see Figure 2.1). Government communications expenditure has also risen strongly during the period. In 1979, the Central Office of Information (COI) budget was £27 million and government advertising expenditure was £44 million. By 1988 these figures had risen to £150 million and £85 million respectively (Scammell 1995: 204–6). The number of information officers employed by the Central Office of Information increased from 36 in 1979 to 160 in 1996 (COI directories). Employment of information officers (see Table 2.1) has more than doubled in many Whitehall departments, with the number of communications 'special advisers' in government doubling just since New Labour came to power.

However, media fascination with spin doctoring around Westminster has obscured the fact that professional public relations has been widely adopted by a range of institutions, organisations and interest groups. This expansion has been most marked in the business community. According to surveys by Carl Byoir and Associates (PRCA 1986), it became the norm rather than the exception for top companies to use PR. In 1979, 20 per cent of the top 500 companies, as listed in the Times 1000, used PR consultancies. By 1984 it was 69 per cent (90 per cent of the top 100). In spite of the recession of the early 1990s, the consultancy sector in the UK expanded considerably – as evidenced in Figure 2.2, which details the

| **Figure 2.1** | General election expenditure at constant prices, 1983–97 (£m, expenditure at 1997 prices) |

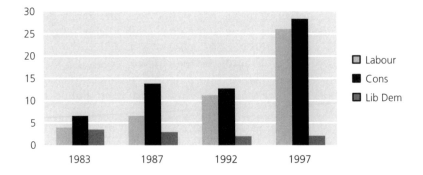

Source: Neill 1998

| Table 2.1 | Changes in numbers of information officers employed in government departments, 1979–2001 |

	MoD	FCO	Home Office	DTI	Cabinet Office	PM's Office	Treasury
1979	58	19	27	38	–	6	12
1983	34	17	25	77	–	6	12
1987	34	13	33	67	11	6	13
1991	36	20	37	62	10	6	9
1995	36	22	43	69	13	10	13
1997	47	30	50	67	14	12	16
2001	87	51	80	77	28	17	30
% change	+50	+168	+196	+103	+155	+183	+150

Source: COI directories, 1979–2001

Note: All figures accumulated from 'The IPO Directory – Information and Press Officers in Government Departments and Public Corporations' (formerly called 'Chief Public Relations, Information and Press Officers in Government Departments, Public Corporations, etc.'). Departments of Trade and Industry were separate until 1985. Figures before 1985 are the sum of the two departments.

| Figure 2.2 | Growth in PRCA members' fee income, 1983–2000 (£ millions) |

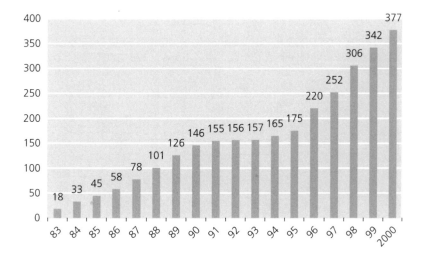

Source: PRCA Year Book, 2001

growth in the fee income of members of the Public Relations Consultancy Association. According to Miller and Dinan (2000) corporate sector PR rose as a whole by a factor of 31 (or eleven-fold in real terms) between 1979 and 1998.

The growth rate for public relations in local councils and other state institutions has appeared to match that in central government. By 1994, according to Franklin (1994: 7, 1997), 90 per cent of metropolitan local authorities had established PR departments, employing 2,000 full-time staff and spending £250 million annually between them. Deacon and Monk's study (2001) of quangos found that 68 per cent had at least one staff member employed to do media/ public relations work, 67 per cent had increased their media/publicity work in the last three years, 88 per cent conducted media monitoring and 84 per cent used news releases. Looking at Table 2.2, it is clear that institutions such as the BBC, the Metropolitan Police and Buckingham Palace have expanded their public relations significantly. Such institutions, along with schools, universities (Wernick 1991) and health authorities (Miller and Williams 1998), have all been encouraged to adopt public relations to pursue specific aims.

Indications are that, during the 1990s, professional PR has also begun to spread into many other sectors of British civil society. Media campaigns have always been a means for pressure groups, charities and trade unions to raise interest and support. What has changed in the last decade is the influx of PRPs (public relations professionals) into these sectors. Deacon's (1996) survey of the voluntary sector found that 31 per cent of organisations had press/publicity officers, 43 per cent used external PR agencies and 56 per cent monitored the media. These figures were increased to 57 per cent, 81 per cent and 78 per cent for organisations with annual budgets over £250,000. A survey of the trade union sector by Davis (1998) found that two-thirds of unions had at least one part-time press officer, 25 per cent used PR consultancies and 57 per cent used agencies to monitor the media and provide other services – significantly more than observed in earlier studies (Philo 1995; Manning 1998). That such

Table 2.2	Changes in numbers of information officers employed in public institutions, 1979–2001					
	Buck. Palace	CBI	Inland Rev.	Met. Police	BBC	CRE
1979	3	8	5	6	5	5
1983	3	10	4	8	9	6
1987	4	19	8	12	12	6
1991	9	16	13	53	12	6
1995	12	18	18	61	35	8
1997	10	18	15	42	34	8
2001	11	19	34	65	20	11
% change	+266	+138	+580	+983	+300	+120

Source: COI directories, 1979–2001

organisations are increasingly using professional PR methods to achieve political and economic objectives is further evidenced in research on campaigning organisations, in work on: environmental issues (Hansen 1993a; Anderson 1997; Allan et al. 2000), the 'criminal justice arena' (Ericson et al. 1989; Schlesinger and Tumber 1994), gay and lesbian pressure groups (Miller and Williams 1993), industrial disputes (Jones 1986; Manning 1998), and paramilitary organisations in Northern Ireland (Miller 1994).

All these organisations have found a need to identify their significant audiences and communicate with them via the media. For governments, public institutions and businesses there is a need to communicate to large groups of consumer-citizens to sell policies and products and compete for resources. For interest groups there is a need to attract funding and members as well as influence corporate and government decision-making. What was once therefore the exclusive domain of government in Britain has moved, first to business, and then into every sector of society that feels a need to compete in the public sphere.

The PR industry may have expanded considerably, but is there any indication that it is becoming more a part of news production? This is a difficult question to assess because of the difficulty in identifying what is PR and what is 'pure' journalism. The only thing that can be definitively concluded is that public relations and news production are highly dependent on each other. Indeed, the influence of public relations practitioners (or sources using PR techniques) was always much greater than scholars recorded, journalists admitted, or news consumers were aware of. This working relationship between PRPs and journalists, although never part of the media fourth estate ideal, was not a serious matter – as long as public relations remained an underdeveloped and under-resourced profession and journalists retained a certain level of day-to-day editorial autonomy. However, that is increasingly not the case with either industry in the UK. In the last couple of decades, just as the public relations industry has expanded, so editorial resources have declined.

News production in Britain has been subjected to intense competition – driven by new media, global media concentration and conglomeration, and deregulation (see Tunstall 1996; Curran and Seaton 1997; Franklin 1997). With far more readers, viewers, sponsors, advertisers and finance attracted to entertainment, the will to resource costly news programmes and a serious broadsheet press has consequently dwindled. National newspapers have consistently struggled as long-term declines have been hastened by rising competition. Sunday papers, since the mid-1970s, and dailies since the mid-1980s, have steadily lost sales. The BBC and independent television channels have all also seen audience figures (and advertising) decline.

In an effort to remain profitable, news organisations have simultaneously increased output and cut back on staff. Newspapers have introduced multiple new sections to widen their appeal – in most cases more than doubling their size between the mid-1980s and mid-1990s (see *Guardian*, 20 June 1994). Traditional broadcasters have also increased their provision to accommodate multiple channels and 24-hour news coverage. At the same time, it appears that journalist numbers per news product have been cut or, in the best cases, increased slightly. Tunstall (1971) estimated that in 1969 there were approximately 3,550 journalists working on national newspapers. Two more recent estimates, by the National Union of Journalists (NUJ) and Delano and Hennington, are 2,666 and 2,462 respectively – indicating a drop of between 25 and 31 per cent over the last 30 years (Franklin 1997: 51–3). Franklin (1994: 70) estimated that 7,000 jobs (25 per cent) were shed from the BBC between 1986 and 1994 and in 1997 it was announced that a further 25 per cent of staff cuts were to be phased in over five years.

While technology has been responsible for many savings, it is also likely that journalist workloads have increased considerably. In fact, a 1996 industry survey revealed that 62 per cent of journalists claimed to work 59 or more hours in the office each week, and that journalism was now the third most stressful occupation – on a par with airline pilots and prison officers (*Press Gazette*, 12 July 1996). As Tunstall recently estimated (1996: 136), 'Between the 1960s and the 1990s the amount of words written and space filled by each national newspaper journalist certainly doubled and perhaps trebled.' The most significant consequence of the drive for improved reporter productivity, according to a mass of anecdotal evidence, is the decline of costly investigative journalism. As Bill Hagerty (*Press Gazette*, 29 January 1999: 14) complains:

> [T]he system is now dictating that journalists stay at their desks. They are overworked – multiskill mania has taken over – and are not allowed the time to investigate and certainly not the time to go abroad and investigate. That kind of thing is actively discouraged because it costs money . . . It's all fast-food journalism these days. (*See also interviews in Davis 2002*)

Clearly, as British journalism is repeatedly cut and squeezed, so standards drop and the need to cut corners becomes crucial. Journalists must do more with less resources and are becoming outnumbered and outresourced by their PR counterparts. Given this state of affairs, reporters are likely to become increasingly dependent on the steady supply of conveniently packaged (and free) public relations 'information subsidies' (Gandy 1980). Although journalists get to pick and choose what they want to use, and they retain their conscious autonomy, they are, in effect, making reactive choices – rather than pursuing proactive investigations.

Critical Assessments

How has the new public relations environment affected media–source relations generally and hierarchies of source access more specifically? Is public relations simply a means by which particular elite sources can further extend their access advantages and management of media agendas? Or does it enable poorer and more excluded groups to gain a level of media coverage that was previously denied them?

There appears to be a strong critical case for arguing that the main beneficiaries of public relations have been corporate and government elite news sources. Looking at the historical development of the profession, many (Tulloch

1993; Ewen 1996; L'Etang 1998; Cutlip et al. 2000) link its rise to the elite need to manage the public at times of difficult social transition. The recent history of public relations and government policy-making in the UK fits well with this interpretation. As several historical accounts of the period record (e.g. Pollard 1992; Hills 1996; Hutton 1996), the Conservative governments of the 1980s decisively broke with the postwar tripartite consensus and initiated a period of free-market policy-making. Continuing attacks on unions, rising levels of inequality and poverty, extensive privatisation and a weakening of the Welfare State, amongst other things, all necessitated a new period of expansion for the public relations industry. Both government and corporate PR did indeed expand impressively during the 1980s. As Davis (2002) and Miller and Dinan (2000) observed (see also, Franklin 1994; Scammell 1995), several of the top public relations companies that grew to dominate the industry in the UK also worked closely with the Conservative Party, gained many lucrative Conservative government contracts, and were employed by many of the UK's top companies.

Looking at the distribution of IPR (Institute of Public Relations) members in Figure 2.3, it becomes clear that government and the corporate sector continue to dominate in terms of PR employment: 16.6 per cent work in government or state institutions and approximately two-thirds work for the corporate sector – either in-house or through consultancies (90 per cent of consultancy work is for businesses). The state is therefore the single largest employer of public relations

Figure 2.3   Distribution of IPR members in employment sectors, 1998

In-house central government (0.7%)

national government (0.5%)
government information services (0.2%)

Other government (15.9%)

local (6.7%)
education (3.3%)
health (3%)
armed forces (0.6%)
other govt dept/agency (2.3%)

External (45.2%)

consultancy (39.1%)
advertising (0.8%)
sole trader (5.3%)

No response (8.8%)

In-house companies – industries and services (20.2%)

manufacturing (6.1%)
services (7.7%)
finance (3.7%)
hq/holding co. (2.1%)
nationalised industries (0.6%)

In-house companies – cultural industries (2.8%)

tourism/leisure (1.6%)
press/broadcasting (1.2%)
arts/culture (0.1%)

In-house non profit/ pressure group (6.4%)

charities (3.2%)
trade/professional bodies (3%)
political organisations (0.1%)
trade unions (0.1%)

Source: IPR membership survey 1998

in the UK and the corporate world is the largest employment sector overall. Those working for charities, unions, professional associations or other political organisations employ only 6.4 per cent of PRPs.

Although the corporate and state duopoly over the use of public relations has recently been broken, traditional critical work in media sociology suggests that little will change. Critical work has tended to be presented as part of two broad perspectives: *political economy* and *cultural structuralism*. Starting with political economy, a principal concern is that corporate and state sources have massive institutional, legal and economic resource advantages which support their PR operations. This gives them the power to restrict/enable media access to information, censor news reporting, and threaten journalists with legal redress and/ or loss of access to important sources (see Miller 1994; Philo 1995; Manning 2001). Linked to legal and political advantages are economic resource advantages. Employing professional PRPs and running large PR departments is something that only 'resource-rich' organisations can contemplate. In 2000, the average fee per client for a small PR consultancy firm in the UK was £18,920. The larger firms averaged £84,506 per client (*PRCA Year Book* 2001). In terms of in-house operations, the PRCA estimated (DTI 1994: 23) that, in 1994 on average, public relations departments cost £42,000 per head to maintain. In effect, the 'costs of market entry' into the professional PR world excludes 'resource-poor' organisations.

For many authors (e.g. Miller 1994; Davis 1998; Manning 2001), PR efficacy can be broadly correlated with economic resources. More PR resources mean more media contacts, greater output of information subsidies, multiple modes of communication and continuous media operations. Extreme differences in economic resources mean wealthy organisations can inundate the media and set the agenda while the attempts of resource-poor organisations quickly become marginalised. Miller (1994: 132–3) recorded that in Northern Ireland in 1989, Sinn Fein, with five voluntary press staff and a budget of £7,000, attempted to compete with official government sources with 145 communications staff and a £20 million budget. Davis (1998, 2002) noted that public service trade unions working to halt government cuts and privatisations were consistently out-resourced by corporations and state departments during the period of Conservative government. For example, ASLEF and the RMT, with three communications officers between them, had to compete with 47 communications staff at British Rail before its privatisation in 1992. The National Union of Teachers (NUT), with one and a half communications officers, were competing with 37 in the Department of Education (statistics from unions and COI Directories) towards the end of the Major government. The differences take on further significance in times of conflict when companies and government departments rapidly employ more PRPs and/or hire consultancies to manage crises.

Cultural structural approaches focus on an alternative set of advantages which are bestowed on government and institutional sources using public relations. For Hall et al. (1978) such sources are situated at the top of a 'hierarchy of credibility'. Journalists, following news values, are drawn to them because such sources are in positions of power, draw legitimate support from the public, and are expected to provide expert knowledge. In continuing to report them with such frequency and authority, journalists reinforce their legitimacy further. So the 'primary definer' status of official sources is 'structurally determined' by the routine practices and values of journalists.

For many studies of journalism a related factor benefiting institutional PRPs is the 'bureaucratic affinity' (Fishman 1980) that exists between institutions and media organisations. According to many North American studies (Sigal 1973; Fishman 1980; Ericson et al. 1989), institutions tend to attract journalists because they are usually physically accessible, well resourced, and provide a regular supply of 'information subsidies'. Thus institutions have tended to become the most common sources for journalists and, consequently, many reporters and media producers have developed a routine dependence on them. That dependence has ultimately influenced the shape of journalism itself. Manning (1999), Anderson (1997) and Miller (1999) have each argued that the level and forms of government interest in industrial and environmental affairs have determined, to a large degree, the level and forms of news reporting of these issues.

The self-perpetuating result of all these inherent biases is that institutional and corporate public relations operates almost invisibly and on a grand scale. Indeed, numerous studies from a wide range of perspectives have found that sources from government and established state and corporate institutions are dominant suppliers of 'information subsidies' to the news media (e.g. Hall et al. 1978; Miller 1994; Schlesinger and Tumber 1994; Philo 1995; Manning 1998; Davis 2000a). In some areas of reporting, such as coverage of Parliament and the City, journalists appear to have become such a part of the 'issue communities' they cover, they have become all but 'captured' by their sources (Negrine 1996; Schlesinger et al. 2001; Davis 2000c, forthcoming). Under such conditions public relations can be seen to have enabled government and corporate sources to extend their dominance of news still further.

Complicating the Picture: Grounds for Pluralist Optimism

Taking account of recent developments in media studies, this critical description of public relations and news sources now appears to exclude too many concerns. Early works that laid the foundations for critical thinking on the subject (e.g. Hall et al. 1978; Herman and Chomsky 1988; Philo 1995) have been criticised on several counts. These include being overly deterministic, ahistorical, oblivious to agency and altogether too narrow in their research frameworks. Such research tended to be too dismissive of the activities of journalists and non-official sources, assumed 'primary definers' acted in unison, and did not allow for historical shifts in status and access (see critiques in Schlesinger 1990; Curran 1996). More recent work on public relations and news sources (see in particular, Schlesinger and Tumber 1994; Deacon and Golding 1994; Manning 2001; Davis 2002), while continuing to support certain critical findings, has also sought to complicate thinking on the subject. As such, these works have attempted to develop perspectives that involve agency (amongst journalists and the public), complex and evolving power structures, and ever-shifting patterns of source legitimacy and media–source relations – but all within a framework of dominance and inequality. This work, in conjunction with research on the use of PR by 'resource-poor' and 'outsider' organisations, has suggested that there exist some grounds for pluralist optimism.

One way of complicating the picture is to look again at dominant sources. Although government and business figures continue to dominate as news sources, that does not mean that they relay the same, mutually reinforcing messages. Studies of lobby reporting in Westminster (Jones 1995, 1999; Negrine 1996; Tunstall 1996), the communications of different government departments (Schlesinger and Tumber 1994; Deacon and Golding 1994; Miller et al. 1998), and of business interest groups (e.g. Grant 1993; Mitchell 1997), all identify regular conflicts between and within powerful organisations. Political parties and businesses have been greatly divided over such issues as the introduction of the 'poll tax', dealing with public health scares, the funding of public schemes, or the adoption of the Euro. Such conflicts have resulted in conflicting messages being relayed to the media, dramatic 'shifts in elite consensus' and/or periodic confusion and bitter division. In such cases, individuals and institutions have come to be regarded as 'unreliable' by journalists and, on occasion, have lost their standing as legitimate sources altogether.

Critical perspectives are further complicated by the reporter's need to adhere to 'news values' and 'fourth estate' ideals. Such imperatives lead reporters to challenge powerful sources and appeal to their non-powerful citizen-consumers – if only to retain sales and advertising (see Gans 1979; Harrison 1985; Schudson 1991; Palmer 2000). Journalists can thus be highly critical of material coming from corporate and government sources – often to the point of setting news agendas and becoming 'primary definers' themselves. Similarly, the ability of a source, powerful or not, to gain media access is connected to how well the reporting of that source fulfils journalist ideals and news values. In effect, if powerful sources do not naturally appeal to news values they, like resource-poor sources, must struggle to get media access.

This second point is very significant when one looks more closely at business source–media relations. Although the corporate sector has been the largest employer of professional public relations, business sources have frequently failed to become dominant sources in mainstream news. Journalists are unlikely to cover business sources positively for several reasons: they are not part of regular news beats; business stories are complex and require specialist knowledge and research; and business news does not interest the majority of news consumers. The only time businesses are likely to be reported in mainstream news is when they are involved in wrongdoing or economic or environmental crises (see Harrison 1985; Tiffen 1989; Ericson et al. 1989; Tumber 1993). In the few existing comparative studies of corporate and other sources, the data show that business representatives are reported less than either state or protest group spokespersons (McQuail 1977; Harrison 1985; Philo 1995).

There are further grounds for liberal pluralist optimism when one looks at recent research on 'outsider' and 'resource-poor' sources and their public relations in the UK. One key finding is that such groups can operate effective PR operations despite their economic resource disadvantages. Unlike advertising, news coverage is free. The main requirements to operate PR operations are work space, basic communications equipment (telephone, fax, computers) and people. In terms of people, alternative interest groups may not be able to hire professional PRPs in large numbers but they often have access to large pools of voluntary labour. Since PR is not a licensed profession and can be practised without specific qualifications or professional association membership, this suggests that such groups can make use of their sometimes extensive membership resources (see Wilson 1984; Davis 2000a).

From another perspective, large communications operations are not always advantageous. Work on union communications (Davis 1998, 2002; Manning 1998, 2001) and environmental campaigning (Anderson 1997; Palmer 2000) has observed several examples of smaller groups outmanoeuvring their larger oppositions. Large institutional and corporate PR operations were and are often slowed down by layers of bureaucracy, cumbersome checks and balances systems, distant links to organisational heads, and the fact that they are not set up for short-term campaigns. Smaller groups, unhindered by such obstacles, can therefore act with considerable speed and flexibility – a vital advantage in a fast-moving media campaign situation.

In terms of the problem of the legitimacy deficit encountered by non-official sources, recent work also indicates that the 'hierarchy of credibility' is not as entrenched as previously assumed. Schlesinger and Tumber (1994) and Miller (1994) have each suggested that institutional legitimacy and authority are likened to a form of media 'cultural capital' (Bourdieu 1979). Their empirical research observed that non-official sources could use professional public relations to accumulate such capital – in the eyes of journalists and the public. By providing a consistent supply of reliable information subsidies (news stories and research) to journalists, non-official sources could become trusted and regular contacts for journalists. More legitimate media exposure could result in a virtuous circle of greater access, a larger public profile, a further accumulation of institutional legitimacy and, eventually, more routine access. Miller and Williams (1993) observed such strategies being applied by the Terrence Higgins Trust. Schlesinger and Tumber (1994) found the same with trade associations/ unions such as the National Association of Probation Officers (NAPO), the Police Officers Association (POA) and the Police Federation, and by pressure groups such as the National Association for the Care and Resettlement of Offenders (NACRO) and the Prison Reform Trust. Similar accounts of the development of media strategies by Friends of the Earth and other environmental groups are offered in Hansen (1993a) and Allan et al. (2000). All of these organisations tended to avoid dramatic publicity stunts, preferring instead to establish positive media profiles over time and, therefore, overcoming their traditional lack of 'credibility'. (Such studies might be contrasted with the confrontational media strategies of many unions and pressure groups up until the early 1980s – strategies that often resulted in the delegitimisation of those groups in the eyes of the media; see Gitlin 1980; Miller 1994; Philo 1995.)

Clearly, 'outsider' and 'resource-poor' groups in the UK are finding ways round their economic and cultural resource deficits. There is a growing list of successful PR-led campaigns by unions and pressure groups against governments and corporations (Wilson 1984; Anderson 1997; Thomson et al. 1998; Palmer 2000; Davis 2000b). Perhaps more significantly, a number of other long-running campaigns, by environmental protesters and union activists, have managed to ignite public interest and, consequently, to change political agendas. 'Fat Cat' pay, carbon dioxide emissions, education, health and transport have all been tirelessly pushed by campaigning groups and all found themselves on the agenda of the current Labour government. Such successes have led several authors (Shoemaker 1989; Scammell 1995; McNair 1999) to argue that PR brings a number of benefits to democratic politics. In addition to making politicians and businesses more responsive to public opinion, public relations offers far greater potential for non-official sources to gain access than before. In Shoemaker's words (1989: 215):

> Journalistic routines (such as news-beats) result in media content that reinforces the status quo and limits media access to new ideas and organisations off the 'beaten' path. As a result, public relations efforts may be the only realistic strategy for a group to get media coverage.

Public Relations and the Question of Source Access

So what types of source have improved their media relations most by using professional public relations? Before answering this question it is worth summarising the findings of the discussion thus far. Much of the debate about improved media–source relations hinges on a source's ability to improve access to news producers and generate favourable coverage. This chapter has identified four important resources which affect a source attempting to fulfil these aims. The first and second of these, already noted in several studies of sources, are the possession of *economic capital* and *media capital*. In this case media capital (an alternative interpretation of cultural capital) comes in the form of 'legitimate authority', to be identified in external journalist and public responses. In many cases, public institutions and figures are bestowed with an automatic level of media capital that is commensurate with their perceived social and political status in society. In other cases media capital can be accumulated. A third resource, one that has drawn less attention, is *human resources*. Human resources are the main expense for any public relations operation but their costs vary considerably. Different types of organisation use any combination of professional PR staff, media-trained representatives, and groups of well-organised volunteers – all of which can be effective with different levels of expenditure.

A highly significant fourth resource is a source's natural affinities with news producers. *Media–source affinity* is affected by both bureaucratic considerations and by what journalists perceive to be newsworthy. Bureaucratic compatibility is influenced by such things as organisational structures, timetables, and the physical proximity of journalists to source organisations. 'Newsworthiness' equates to the belief of journalists that they should report sources because they judge them to be powerful (fourth estate ideals) and/or on account of audience interest (news values). That also means that they will be reluctant to cover resource-rich sources if they are not considered 'newsworthy' or are practically difficult to cover. These four resources are all related but are not inextricably linked. Media (or cultural) capital and human resources are more likely to be boosted by economic resources but they are not completely dependent on them. Media capital can be used to generate economic capital, and human resources can be used to boost media–source affinity.

Professional public relations practitioners bring to sources an additional set of resources. These include appropriate media contacts, a level of knowledge about how journalists operate, and a range of media strategies. Essentially, their main objectives are (a) to locate and exploit the PR resources available to an organisation, and (b) to match the requirements of that organisation to those of relevant news producers. In other words, PRPs develop strategies that uncover the potential affinities that exist between sources and journalists, and utilise the resources at their disposal to match up these affinities accordingly. Consequently, PR strategies themselves can help to accumulate (or lose) other types of resource. This suggests that variously resourced groups can employ PR strategies that rely on alternative combinations of factors – each of which, if conditions are right, can result in a successful supply of information subsidies to journalists.

However, gaining access is only half the story when it comes to using public relations to influence media–source relations. For high-profile public figures and public institutions, access does not have to be acquired. Public relations is all about managing routine access or, perhaps more importantly, restricting media access. In terms of managing access in the political sphere, this may involve timely releases of difficult information, 'kite-flying', 'spinning' story lines, or fostering individual journalist dependency (see Jones 1995, 1999; Negrine 1996; Davis forthcoming). In terms of restricting access, PRPs go to great lengths to stop information being released, to hinder journalists' access to organisational figures, scupper exclusives and side-track investigative reporting. In fact, in the corporate sphere the most politically effective use of public relations appears to have been in restricting mainstream reporter access and quashing negative stories (Tiffen 1989; Ericson et al. 1989; Davis 2000c, 2002).

Another significant form of access might be referred to as *access by proxy*. It is quite clear that those working in public relations believe that it works most successfully when working invisibly. For all types of source, that means media–source relations can be most effective when there is no direct access and/or reporting of a source at all. This is certainly a feature of lobby reporting at Westminster. As Davis (2002) has also documented with reference to resource-poor groups, many such organisations have found it advantageous to use third parties, promote public policy changes, and damage oppositions rather than appear directly in the media themselves. In terms of third parties, MPs, 'experts', the 'alliance with science' and the great British public (in the form of opinion polls) have all been used to put forward the opinions of non-official organisations (Wilson 1984; Hansen 1993a; Davis 2000b). In terms of public policy approaches, both unions and pressure groups (Wilson 1984; Kerr and Sachdev 1992; Manning 1998) have succeeded in gaining positive media coverage with strategies that focused on the needs of the public rather than on their own private interests. The third common form of access by proxy involves seeding negative stories. Journalists, given the basic research or directions for a negative story, can then produce a piece that achieves all the aims of the original source. Stories of 'incompetent ministers', 'political sleaze', 'corporate greed' and 'union extremism' frequently begin their runs, not with investigative journalism, but with rival source supply.

These additional observations lead one to conclude that there is not a simple balance sheet that links media access (or appearances) with favourable media coverage. One cannot simply tally up government, corporate and other source levels of access in order to ascertain who is being more favoured by the media. For example, non-appearance and little obvious media access may be the intention of a source. Frequent appearances in the media are equally likely to be instigated by rival sources and journalists, and can often result in poor media relations and unfavourable coverage. Media access by certain sources is often utilised for the benefit of others. Research on public relations therefore reveals that media–source relations are rather more complex than previous work on sources and news production has assumed. Just as those relations are more complex, so too are the benefits brought by PR to sources.

Conclusion: the Winners and Losers in Britain's Public Relations Democracy

Bearing all these factors in mind, who in Britain over the last two decades has benefited most in the new public relations democracy? The evidence presented suggests two somewhat contradictory trends. Certain powerful sources are using PR to secure their long-term favourable media relations in sections of the national media. At the same time, however, 'resource-poor' and 'outsider' sources have also used public relations to gain more frequent and favourable coverage. How is this possible?

First of all it is probably fair to say that the long-term dominance of British political elites has been significantly enhanced – but only at a certain cost. Such sources, particularly those in government, have made ample use of all the key resources outlined above. In terms of economic and human resources, governments have employed PR operations that are literally a hundred times larger than alternative sources. They clearly also come top in terms of 'media capital' and have traditionally had very strong natural affinities with news producers. So, even if such sources have been in conflict or the focus of negative coverage, they are still likely to have extended their dominance as news sources over the period. At times of national crisis (e.g. wars or large-scale industrial action), the concerted use of PR to exploit all types of resource advantage has resulted in a virtual monopoly of official source supply. The same is true when political elite consensus has been reached on a number of social and economic issues. However, there have also been certain long-term costs relating to public trust and journalist cynicism. Public support for politicians, party memberships and voting levels have all declined in the period in question. Indeed, the recent 2001 general election recorded the lowest voter turnout since universal suffrage was introduced.

The play of these factors has been rather different for the corporate sector in Britain. Businesses have maintained their superior economic resources, human resources and public relations expertise. At a time when British politics has become very 'pro-business', and the British press have largely supported such shifts, this would suggest significant improvements in business source–media relations have been connected to PR. However, those improvements have worked in less direct ways than expected. Because of a lack of mainstream media–source affinity, business source dominance of news has only been truly effective in the specialist financial news media. In terms of generating favourable mainstream media coverage and public respect, businesses have not done especially well. Corporate PR has in fact benefited the business sector most by keeping corporations and their practices out of the public eye – while simultaneously keeping the focus of economic responsibility on government. Indeed, the 1980s in Britain might be seen as a period in which corporate and government PR effectively privatised a number of economic policy debates and established several areas of unchallenged consensus. Thus, at the present time, privatisation and private enterprise are considered more beneficial than state control. Low inflation, engineered by interest rates and reduced public spending, are essential for the economy. Increased corporate regulation, taxation and accountability, as well as strong unions and interventionist government, are considered harmful. The strength of the economy is more important than social welfare because a strong economy supports better welfare. And so on.

In contrast, the 1990s might be seen as a period in which alternative interest group PR began to break into established elite discourse networks and to use the media to bring policy debates more into the public sphere. This has been more so in the 1990s because public relations professionals and methods have become more widely disseminated. Their successes might be due to several factors. First, superior elite media access and messages have often been cancelled out by competitor elites and/or the fact that they were acting, consciously or not, as third-party endorsers for weaker sources. Second, resource-poor groups have begun utilising alternative resources and advantages, such as voluntary labour and quicker communications operations. Third, such groups have shown that they can have potentially strong media–source affinities. Many have thus linked their campaigns with the needs of 'the public' and/or attacked 'greedy' and 'incompetent' corporate and government elites. Fourth, they have formed and maintained their own journalist contacts by improving media relations and supplying regular research and stories to them. Several have worked hard to cultivate reputations associated with expertise, calm authority, forward thinking and public awareness. They have thus succeeded in using PR to disrupt established reporting patterns and alter levels of media (cultural capital) significantly.

However, despite the grounds for pluralist optimism laid out in this chapter, liberal ideals regarding news production and source access cannot be said to have been cumulatively strengthened by all these developments. The fact that journalism is so dependent on public relations material considerably undermines the ideal of an independent fourth estate media. Several groups and constituencies in society lack even the most basic resources required to gain access. Dramatic media victories by pressure groups and unions using PR have been irregular and, in any case, do not always translate into meaningful changes of government or corporate policy. Infrequent successes by such groups cannot in any way be compared to the multiple daily decision-making processes that are dominated by government and/or business PR or that fail to find coverage. Of additional concern, to outsider groups in particular, are the ideological shifts required to gain regular, favourable coverage. As different groups develop media-oriented strategies, so policy agendas get altered and risk being trivialised. A focus on personal corruption or company ineptitude comes to replace discussion of the effects of privatisation or global warming. Just as pressure groups risk incorporation into the state, the more established they become, so campaigning organisations risk losing sight of their goals as they attempt to adapt to the media politics of middle England.

CHAPTER SUMMARY

- The profession of public relations has expanded tremendously in Britain over the last two decades, most significantly in the corporate sector. It is now the norm for large and medium-sized organisations, of all descriptions, to use PR on a regular basis.

- The influence of public relations on news production and media–source relations has increased as news has become subject to increased competition and editorial resources have been cut.

- Four types of resource have been identified which affect a source's ability to use PR. These include: economic capital, media capital, human resources and media–source affinity (this last includes bureaucratic and newsworthy considerations).

- Different types of source have used varied combinations of such resources to influence their media–source relations and in different ways.

- The state and political parties have successfully utilised PR to increase their long-term media access advantages and to manage difficult media relations.

- The corporate sector has benefited from PR, in political terms, by restricting mainstream media coverage and controlling specialist financial news sections.

- Public relations has also been adopted by 'outsider' and 'resource-poor' campaigning groups. They have also successfully used it to overcome their poorer media–source relations.

PART III

SOURCE FIELDS
Dominant Interests

CHAPTER 3

'A Good Day to Bury Bad News?': Journalists, Sources and the Packaging of Politics

Bob Franklin

On 10 October 2001 British newspapers published a leaked email drafted by government special adviser (spin doctor) Jo Moore, within minutes of the attack on the World Trade Center in New York on 11 September. The email, addressed to her colleagues in the Press Office suggested, 'it's now a very good day to get out anything we want to bury' (*Daily Telegraph*, 10 October 2001: 2). Many journalists, politicians and members of the public expressed their outrage at such apparently cynical and opportunist attempts to manage the news: seasoned journalistic voices offered more phlegmatic appraisals. 'Spin of this kind isn't new,' suggested a distinguished political columnist. On the contrary, 'it is as old as politicians in a jam. Proclaim bright triumphs from the rooftops and slip out the garbage via the back door . . . it's what these advisers are there for' (Preston 2001: 17). An anonymous reader's letter from a retired press officer in the Government Information and Communication Service (GICS) during a previous Conservative administration, confirmed that

> this kind of news manipulation was standard practice . . . On the day of the appalling Dunblane shootings, my colleagues and I were instructed by our chief press officer to release any 'bad' news stories for the very reason that they would be overlooked or 'buried' in the next day's coverage of events. (Guardian, *10 October 2001: 23*)

As if to underscore the routine and unexceptional character of Moore's news management suggestion, her email carried the standard heading 'Media Handling'.

While this incident attracted widespread media attention and justifiable public opprobrium, the significant revelation in this story was not the moral misjudgement and culpability of an individual government spin doctor, but the extent to which politicians' determination to set the news agenda and to use media to inform, shape and manage public discourse about policy and politics, has become a crucial component in a modern statecraft which emphasises what I have elsewhere described as the 'packaging of politics' (Franklin 1994, 1999a,

1999). This packaging of politics rests on a particular understanding of the relationship between journalists and their political sources, which is characterised by collaboration more than conflict. This is not to deny that on occasion the relationship may become extremely combative and conflictual. But the typical pattern is a relationship in which the two parties are judged to work in complementary, if not collusive, ways. Mutuality of interests drives and sustains the relationship. Journalists and politicians, in Blumler and Gurevitch's phrase, have become 'mutually dependent' and 'mutually adaptive' actors, shaping and regulating each other's behaviour and jointly controlling mechanisms for resolving conflicts between them (Blumler and Gurevitch 1981). Political columnist Simon Hoggart employs a graphic metaphor: journalists and sources inhabit 'the shared media and politicians' snakepit, in which we slither all over each other, hissing with hatred, but hopelessly knotted together' (*Guardian*, 1 June 2001: 15).

But I wish to suggest that this relationship is highly variable and hope to illustrate some of the resulting complexity by exploring two case studies. The first examines the changing relationship between journalists and the New Labour government following its successes in the 1997 and 2001 elections: this relationship has already attracted considerable scholarly attention (Barnett and Gaber 2001; Franklin 1998, 1999; Ingham 2001). The second case study considers relationships between local journalists and political parties in the constituency setting during the 2001 UK general election: the literature exploring local political communications is relatively underdeveloped, although there are recent welcome additions (Larson 2002). In the national setting, political sources typically dominate the relationship illustrating neatly Gans's assertion that while 'it takes two to tango . . . sources do the leading' (Gans 1979: 116). But in the local setting this relationship is reversed. While political sources may in certain circumstances be highly successful in shaping political news coverage, this success is always achieved within parameters defined by local journalists, who prescribe ahead of the election the quantity and character of coverage that the news outlet is willing to provide.

Negotiating the Final Draft of Political News

Sun columnist Richard Littlejohn entertains few doubts about his role as a journalist: even fewer about his relationship with politicians and political sources. 'The job of someone like me,' he claims, 'is to sit at the back and throw bottles.' Politicians are among his favourite targets. He believes they are well resourced to defend themselves. 'They employ an entire industry,' he suggests, 'often using public money, to present themselves as favourably as possible and I certainly don't see it as my job to inflate the egos of little men' (*Guardian*, 22 February 1993). But while some might cherish this image of the journalist as 'watchdog', everyday relationships between politicians and media are typically less confrontational. Each group has interests and needs which can be achieved most readily in co-operation with the other. Expressed broadly, politicians require access to the media to convey political messages to the public, while for their part journalists must enjoy at least a minimal co-operation from politicians to guarantee a credible and well-informed political journalism. In brief the relationship between journalists and their political sources is an exchange relationship in which 'insider' political information and opinion is traded for coverage in news media (Ericson et al. 1989). The relationship is symbiotic, serves divergent needs for each group, but unites both because of their over-lapping fundamental purposes. Recognition of this mutuality of interests has drawn the two groups closer together until they have become 'inextricably linked' (Blumler and Gurevitch 1981: 473).

Within this broad framework of 'co-operation', however, conflict remains central and routine: indeed, two features of the relationship ensure that conflict is endemic. The first expresses journalists' and politicians' divergent perceptions of the fundamental purposes of political communication. For journalists, the relationship provides opportunities to educate, enlighten and inform readers and viewers about political affairs; for politicians the purpose is to persuade voters to their point of view (Blumler and Gurevitch 1981: 485). The ambitions of information and propaganda seem destined to collide: and routinely. A second source of conflict is a consequence of the relationship being governed and regulated by mutual recognition of a set of 'agreed' rules and conventions which trigger confrontation if either party 'breaks' those rules. Consequently, a jour-nalist who publishes an embargoed story, makes public use of an 'off-the-record' statement, or identifies a source, places the relationship at risk. Similarly, if a politician 'leaks' a major story to another journalist, disavows a statement made previously to a journalist, or refuses a journalist an interview, the relationship begins to break down. But it is in the interests of both parties to negotiate and repair any breaches to re-establish a viable way of working together – a process described as 'mutual adaptation' (Blumler and Gurevitch 1981: 472). Understood within this framework, political news has become identified as the product of a process of mutual construction by politicians and the media. According to Mancini, 'the final draft of the newspaper article or TV news broadcast is the result of a long process of negotiation between journalists and politicians' (1993: 34).

The process of mutual adaption is driven by a strategic complementarity of interests. The media perform invaluable functions for politicians and their sources. Media coverage, for example, may help politicians to create and main-tain a high public profile: what Mancini dubs politicians' 'quest for fame' (1993: 37). Media reporting may also prove vital to politicians' efforts to promote public awareness and support for particular policy initiatives – essentially an agitprop function (Franklin 1999: 22). More strategically, political sources use journalists to evaluate or anticipate public reaction to particular policy pro-posals. In the UK, politicians routinely use the parliamentary lobby to 'test the water' (Kellner 1983: 279). If public reaction is adverse, politicians can disown the policy, denouncing the original story as a mere press rumour.

Political sources, moreover, routinely set the news agenda to create a favour-able climate of opinion about particular policy debates and issues. Sources' growing preoccupation with 'spin' is evident. In the two years following the 1997 election, the Labour government issued 20,000 press releases; an 80 per cent increase on the 1992 Major government (Cohen 1999b: 15). Politicians also use media for unequivocally propagandist purposes. In its first year in office, Labour spent £165 million on advertising, while the launch of 172 new campaigns during the first three months of 2001 (just ahead of the general election), cost £62 million and made the government the largest purchaser of advertising in the UK: ahead of Unilever (2nd) and BT (3rd) (Watts 2001: 13). Finally, the media are on occasion considered capable of fulfilling even more significant functions for politicians. Schatz, for example, argues that the reason for televising the German Parliament, following the collapse of the Nazi regime in 1945, was to popularise the Bundestag and re-establish a democratic way of life in Germany (Schatz 1992: 234).

Politicians and their sources fulfil a smaller but no less significant range of functions for journalists. First, the activities of politicians constitute a regular source of stories for journalists working in both the national and local press, which are significant both for their quantity and news value. Second, politicians, both as individuals and via institutions like the lobby, provide a major source of political news for journalists: 'politics', claims McNair 'is the staple food of journalistic work' (2000: 43). Third, politicians are the central actors on political programmes. It is politicians' appearances, moreover, which lend the pro-grammes authority and credibility. Spin doctors are conscious of this 'credential-ising function' and discipline journalists by withholding comment or denying access to politicians when journalists previously have been critical of them. Finally, Mancini claims that in Italy, friendships with politicians can result in promotion for journalists and broadcasters (Mancini 1993: 37).

In summary, while politicians and the media may pursue different goals, this occurs within an agreed framework that offers potential benefits to both groups. Each group requires the other, no matter how reluctantly, to prosecute its own interests and purposes. Politicians' and journalists' mutual reliance prompts a continual adjustment or 'adaptation' of their relationship to ensure continuity, despite the conflict and co-operation that characterise them. This adjustment and adaptation mean that considerable diversity is possible in the particular form that this relationship may assume.

Journalists and New Labour: an Over-managed Relationship under Stress

Since 1997, the Labour Party has imported its election-winning media operation into government. This 'Millbankisation' of government (Gaber 1998: 10) has involved: the centralisation of communications at No. 10; a more assertive rela-tionship with journalists; and the politicising of the Government Information and Communications Service (GICS). This centralisation of communications control has impacted critically on journalists' relationships with political sources, whether special advisers or civil service press officers working in the various Whitehall departments: relationships have become noticeably more adversarial.

Centralising Relations with Media

Centralising communications at No. 10 under the control of the Prime Minister's Press Secretary Alastair Campbell (more recently the Director of Communications) has been the key priority in Labour's communications strategy. The intention has been to establish the government as the key and primary definer in media discussions of policy, to ensure the consistency of the government line and to minimise any media articulation of dissenting voices. Central control is strict but largely effective. The Mountfield report on government communications suggested that:

> all major interviews and media appearances, both print and broadcast, should be agreed with the No. 10 Press Office before any commitments are entered into. The policy content of all major speeches, press releases and new policy initiatives should be cleared in good time with the No. 10 private office . . . the timing and form of announcements should be cleared with the No. 10 Press Office.

The government's 'communications day' begins with a 9 am meeting attended by senior communications staff including Alastair Campbell, Jonathan Powell the Prime Minister's Chief of Staff, specialist advisers from the Treasury and the Deputy Prime Minister's Office as well as representatives from the Cabinet Office and the Chief Whip's Office (MacAskill 1997: 8). The meeting tries to ensure congruence between strategy and presentation and consigns specific individuals to resolve any particular presentation problems arising that day (Mountfield 1997: 8). Labour's determination to stay 'on message' requires that nothing is left to chance. The policy 'message' must be carefully scripted, meticulously rehearsed, universally endorsed by party and government, centrally co-ordinated and favourably presented in the news media.

A number of new (post 1997) institutions are entrusted with key roles in orchestrating relationships between politicians and journalists. The Media Monitoring Unit (MMU), for example, prepares a daily digest of news media content and identifies potentially problematic issues for consideration ('rebuttal') at the morning communications meeting held prior to the 11 am lobby briefing. The Strategic Communications Unit (SCU), established in January 1998, is responsible for 'pulling together and sharing with departments the government's key policy themes and messages' (Select Committee on Public Administration 1998: para. 19), i.e. keeping sources 'on message'. The SCU liaises with the expansive media management organisations in individual departments to co-ordinate government policy messages but also to prevent ministers and special advisers 'forming their own Baronies' (Williams 2000: 10). The SCU also drafts ministerial (including prime ministerial) speeches and inserts common phrases and soundbites to illustrate the consistency of the government's 'message'.

The key task for the SCU is to co-ordinate the media presentation of events and stories for the coming week. The Unit prepares a weekly diary of events known as 'the grid' which it presents each Thursday to the heads of information in the various Whitehall departments. The purpose of the diary is to prevent unhelpful clashes between departments' release of news, to ensure that positive developments are not overshadowed by 'bad' news and, on occasion, to 'slip out' any bad news on what is broadly a good news day for the government. The grid is based on the routine returns from departments about forthcoming news events. A memo from the head of the SCU to heads of information in departments, dated 9 November 1999, outlined the new centralised protocols for developing co-ordinated media coverage:

> From now on for each major [news] event we will be using a planning document (copy attached) for which the relevant Downing Street press officer will be responsible. As you can see it sets out the key messages that should be communicated by the event, how they link to the government's overall message, and the methods we will be using to get wide coverage in the run up, launch and follow up to the event. *(Cited in Williams 2000, Annex H)*

A senior press officer claimed the SCU had been highly influential in shaping relationships with journalists. 'By organising the diary so strictly', he suggested, 'the SCU has played a critical role in the government's efforts to dominate the news agenda' (cited in Williams 2000: 15).

This centralised structure regulating relationships between politicians and journalists has prompted perhaps predictable tensions in Labour ranks, but also between special advisers and civil servants working in the GICS. In March 1998, for example, Harriet Harman (then Secretary of State for Health) was chastised by Campbell for giving media interviews without his approval: a leaked fax demanded she explain 'why the interviews with the *Guardian*, *Woman's Hour* and *World At One* were not cleared through this office' (*Guardian*, 30 March 1998: 5; Jones 2001: 145). More recently and spectacularly, special adviser Jo Moore and Head of Information Martin Sixsmith, both working in the Department of Transport, 'resigned' after a 'feud' for communications supremacy flared up between them. Each began to brief journalists against the other, prompting 'mixed' and contradictory 'messages', which in turn caused embarrassment for No. 10 and triggered journalists to question the capacity of 'Downing Street's once fabled spin operation . . . to offer consistent explanations' of events. Such questions 'sealed the fate' of both and underlined the centralised communications control exercised from No. 10 (*Guardian*, 16 February 2002: 13).

Carrots and Sticks: Sources' Changing Relationships with Journalists

Labour's uncompromising news management strategy offers journalists and broadcasters 'tough' choices. If they accept the government line, they will be rewarded with the occasional minor 'exclusive', but the 'awkward squad' who are critical will have their bids for interviews denied and will no longer receive telephone tips about 'breaking stories and exclusives' (Gaber 1998: 14). In short, the government is playing an old-fashioned game of carrots and sticks (Ingham quoted in *Select Committee on Public Administration*, 1998: 9–14). *Guardian* editor Alan Rusbridger describes how this game was played out in the run-up to the 1997 election. Campbell 'used to ring up to cajole, plead, shout and horse-trade' Rusbridger claims.

> Stories would be offered on condition that they went on the front page. I would be told that
> if I didn't agree, they would go to the *Independent*. They would withdraw favours, grant
> favours, exclude us from stories going elsewhere . . . Now we have almost no contact. *(Cited
> in Oborne 1999: 184)*

But sticks are more commonplace than carrots. In October 1997, Campbell
circulated a strident memo to all Heads of Information in the GICS arguing that
media handling must become more assertive. 'Decide your headlines', he
insisted, 'sell your story and if you disagree with what is being written argue
your case. If you need support from here [Downing Street] let me know'
(Timmins 1997: 1). For journalists writing against the government line, the
'handling' has become rough! Journalists are privately bullied, publicly har-
angued and excluded from off-the-record briefings. There are 'very few journalists' whom Campbell 'has not attempted to abuse or humiliate' (Oborne 1999:
181). Labour spin doctors, moreover, have 'never hesitated to destabilise
journalists by going behind their backs to their bosses' (Oborne 1999: 182). The
most celebrated such occasion involved Andrew Marr, a close ally of Labour and
at that time Editor of the *Independent*. Marr wrote an article critical of Labour's
European policy, prompting Campbell to contact David Montgomery, then Chief
Executive of Mirror Group Newspapers, which owned the *Independent*, and
insisted that Marr be sacked (Cohen 1999a: 153–4). Campbell told Marr 'you are
either with us or against us' (McGwire 1997: 11).

What Seymour-Ure (1968) describes as 'press–party parallelism' is influential
here, with relationships based on shared political commitments more likely to be
congenial. Consequently, Campbell displays a particular courtesy during lobby
briefings to *The Times*' correspondent Philip Webster and Trevor Kavanagh of
the *Sun* (both owned by Murdoch's *News International*): Campbell's golden rule
'is that he leaves the *Sun* well alone' (Oborne 1999: 181). But George Jones of the
critical *Daily Telegraph* (favoured by previous Conservative administrations)
finds himself in 'the wilderness' and 'starved of the oxygen of information
which alone can sustain the dedicated political reporter' (Oborne 1999: 174).

Broadcast journalists, especially those at the BBC, fare little better. Some are
thoughtfully ambivalent about the effectiveness of Labour's media management
style and the consequences for their journalistic independence and professional
integrity. Sky's Adam Boulton acknowledges with admirable honesty,

> The trouble is that the government is operating at a level of news management that is way
> above the level of British politics. I do not blame Alastair for that. As far as Alastair is
> concerned, it is all fair in love and war, as long as it's in favour of Tony. On a good day, you
> can see an intelligent, honest administration at work. On a bad day I feel soiled, when we
> end up seeing the press conniving in our own manipulation. *(Quoted in Toolis 1998: 31)*

Boulton's final remarks not only underscore the closeness of journalists' relationships with their political sources but also signal the extent of 'crossover'
between the two groups in terms of their professional roles and career histories.

Jones neologises the term 'journo-politicos' to describe the new generation of
policy advisers who have been at 'the sharp end of the hard sell' which has

characterised New Labour's approach to the media. These hybrids – whose background is in 'media, publicity or politics' and whose 'success is judged in terms of their effectiveness in political presentation' – symbolise the degree to which the roles of journalists and politicians have become fused as 'demarcation lines have become blurred' (Jones 2001: 68–9). For their part, journalists are increasingly being appointed to senior posts in the GICS, or to jobs as special advisers to ministers and thereby metamorphosing into government sources. The political editor of the *Mirror* claims that 'Blair's government is stuffed with journalists' (Routledge 2001: 34), while the appointment of a succession of senior BBC staff to government posts has prompted one description of the BBC as 'a regular target for the Downing Street raiding party' (Jones 2001: 79). Similarly, politicians and government sources are increasingly behaving like journalists. In the first two years of the Labour government, 166 articles were published with Tony Blair's by-line: only 13 less than *Sun* columnist Richard Littlejohn (*Independent*, 8 June 1999). The great majority of these articles were written, of course, by Campbell and ex-tabloid journalists Philip Bassett and David Bradshaw, who now staff the SCU.

Crossing the Line: Politicising the Government Information and Communications Service

In government, Labour has access to the resources and services of the GICS, staffed by 1,000 civil servants whose press and public relations activities are governed by a code of conduct (The Whitehall Red Book) designed to guarantee their political impartiality. 'Press officers' according to the Red Book, must 'establish a position with the media whereby it is understood that they stand apart from the party political battle, but are there to assist the media to understand the policies of the government of the day' (Cabinet Office 1997: para. 11). By contrast, special advisers are 'not bound by the usual requirements that civil servants should be . . . impartial' (Select Committee 1998: xv). The Select Committee on Public Administration, investigating concerns that the Labour government might be politicising the GICS by ignoring these distinctions, concluded that there 'is a very fine line between the promotion and defence of government policy and the promotion and defence of the ruling party's policies' (Select Committee 1998: xv). Since 1997, however, civil servants have expressed growing concerns that this 'line' is too frequently crossed. Senior information officers have warned about the 'creeping politicisation of the GICS' with significant consequences for their relationships with journalists (1998: 80). The government has responded by arguing that it wishes only to 'modernise' the GICS to ensure 'it is equipped to meet the demands of a fast changing media world' (Mountfield 1997: para. 2). Four developments have triggered civil service concerns; each has been influential in recasting source relations with journalists.

First, the government has appointed unprecedented numbers of special advisers whose main priority is press relations and the promotion of government policy. The 32 advisers appointed by John Major's government were increased to 60 in the first year of the Labour government at an additional cost of £600,000 (a 44 per cent increase over Conservative expenditure) (Franklin 1998: 11). There are currently 81 advisers with 26 based at No. 10 – three times as many as under the Major administration (Jones 2001: 5).

Second, in the first year of the Labour government, 25 Heads of Information and their deputies, from a total of 44 such senior posts, resigned or were replaced: the Select Committee on the GICS described this as 'an unusual turnover' (Select Committee 1998: xviii). The reasons informing these staff changes were varied but included 'the desire of ministers for information officers to be less neutral than they thought was compatible with their regular civil service terms of employment' (Select Committee 1998: xviii). The retired Head of Information at the Northern Ireland Office spoke of a 'culling' of Heads of Information and their replacement 'by "politically acceptable" temporary bureaucrats': a process he labels the 'Washingtonisation' of the civil service (Select Committee 1998: 86). By 2002 none of the original 44 Heads of Information remained in office.

Third, this growth of special advisers has created a 'two-tier structure of information' in which the advisers have become the dominant partners over civil servants (Select Committee 1998: ix). Advisers are chosen by ministers: they are close and trusted friends. By contrast, Heads of Information are an inheritance of government and judged to be rule-driven and unduly 'impartial' in their relationships with journalists. Consequently, the significant communications tasks are allocated to the adviser, leaving the civil service press officer with more routine day-to-day matters. GICS officers suggest that the 'enormous increase in the power of the special adviser' is 'widely acknowledged'. In one department, the arrival of the minister's 'workaholic mouthpiece' meant 'every single press release, and there were to be a lot more of them, had to be cleared by a special adviser' (Williams 2000: 27–9).

Finally, the most significant change at the GICS has been the need to 'get on message', i.e. to propagandise for government. In October 1997, Campbell sent a memo to Heads of Information confirming that the central task of GICS publicity was that the 'government's four key messages' must be 'built into all areas of our activity'. Labour is 'a modernising government', a government 'for all the people', which is 'delivering on its promises' with 'mainstream policies' which are providing new directions for Britain (*Financial Times*, 9 October 1997: 1). Some information officers have preferred to resign before complying with central dictates which so thoroughly eschew their professional commitments to neutrality and recast their relationships with journalists. Many senior press officers have

privately expressed their uneasiness at being expected to switch to a more aggressive approach where seizing the agenda and occupying the front pages is apparently more important than the content, where events and announcements are relentlessly pushed rather than being left to find their own level according to their news value, and where those media outlets or individuals which did not adhere to the 'on-message' approach are penalised by intimidatory tactics and the threatened withdrawal of access and facilities. (*Select Committee 1998: 1–82*)

Reporting Election News:
Journalists and Sources in the Local Setting

The activities of local journalists and local politicians in the constituency campaign for the UK general election 2001 reveal different facets of the relationship between journalists and their sources.[1] Both groups have evident interests in shaping and reporting the electoral agenda. For parties the ambition is to manage electoral news in ways that present their candidates and policies to maximum electoral advantage. For journalists the purpose is to provide readers with informed, engaging and impartial coverage of a significant community event. A study of election campaigning and press coverage across four consecutive general elections (1987, 1992, 1997 and 2001) in ten selected constituencies in Yorkshire, found that while relationships between journalists and local parties were often viewed as intensely conflictual, there was mutual and growing acknowledgement of collaboration and 'working together' to generate election news (Franklin and Richardson 2002). Indeed, in the context of election reporting, the relationship locally had become so routinised and closely regulated via a series of pre-election meetings which established agreed ways of working, that it constituted nothing less than an institutionalised quinquennial ritual from which election reporting emerged as a wholly collaborative product.

The Same Routine: Journalists and Sources Organise Election Coverage

When the election is called, local newspaper editors arrange meetings with candidates and party officials to establish and agree the consensual conventions that will dictate coverage. But editors also wish to convey the specific part which they envisage parties will play in the election coverage. This includes identifying the kinds of stories they want the parties to 'deliver' as well as the extent of coverage the paper will provide. The news editor on a local evening paper explained the very clear basis on which the relationship between journalists and politicians rests: editorial space in exchange for insider news and information.

> We write to them [the parties] and set out what we hope to achieve, what our aims are, *what we are promising them and what we expect from them.* Just basics really: then we speak to them. Me and the Editor have been here now for a couple of elections and two of the MPs were sitting MPs so in the past we've had the meeting in the office here. We asked them if they wanted to come in this time and they said 'Are you doing the same routine, because we know it so that's OK.' We talk to them regularly enough so there isn't a need to sit down and have a formal meeting. But there's always some candidates chosen about six months before the election, who are new to the area, so we have them in at that stage.[2] *(Emphasis added)*

Consequently, for experienced journalists and party press officers, relationships during an election have a well-established feel: it is the 'same routine'. Everyone knows the 'rules'. Only newcomers require induction into the agreed ways of working. The complicity of the two communities in generating election news is clear.

With journalists and politicians in broad agreement about the kinds of story that will win coverage, the parties begin their media-based campaigning. Throughout the election each of the three major parties issues press releases to local newspapers and radio stations informing them about specific events involving their candidate for that day. The time and location of events, as well as the details of possible photo opportunities, are clearly specified. Press releases are written in a journalistic style and constructed in the form of a news story, but they also incorporate the particular 'spin' that the party wishes to place on the event. Parties claim that local journalists, who are typically underresourced and hard-pressed to meet editorial deadlines, will often accept these well-crafted press releases which, with the minimum of revision, can be published under the by-line of a local journalist or 'political correspondent'.

Research studies from previous elections reveal that issuing press releases, or 'information subsidies' as Gandy (1982) described them, is a highly effective marketing tool for securing coverage. A comparison of the press releases issued by the Labour Party in one constituency during the 1992 general election, with the local newspaper's election coverage, revealed that 29 press releases generated 28 stories in the newspaper. The paper published at least one story based on a press release each day of the campaign: on three days all coverage of the Labour Party derived from party sources. Journalistic revision of press releases was minimal. A third of the stories simply replicated the release verbatim: a further fifth made modest revisions and published between 50 and 75 per cent of the original text of the press release. Local journalists were sceptical about press releases, claiming that they usually 'spiked them'. However, one local journalist conceded that 'the Labour Party was well geared up, they had some good press releases, some good copy, so they got a decent share of the coverage' (Franklin 1994: 166–72).

But parties' news management activities begin long before the onset of the actual campaign period. They constitute a continuous and ongoing party function and underscore the routine and regular nature of journalist/source relations: in 'peacetime' as much as during elections. A press officer interviewed after the 2001 election claimed:

> We began about six years ago, about two years before the 1997 election. The candidate had just been selected and wasn't well known in the constituency. So the priority was to get coverage every week in the run-up to the election. So we would meet up and decide on story lines and most weeks we would get three or four stories in the local paper. During the recent election [2001] we had a good story in every day of the campaign.

Journalists and Sources Report a 'Local' Campaign

In 2001, parties promoted the 'localness' of their candidates and placed the importance of local issues at the heart of their media campaigns. Parties achieved considerable success in winning coverage for these concerns but their achievements largely reflected the close congruence between media and source ambitions to stress the local. For their part, local journalists express a perennial professional concern with local issues. In interviews, journalists invariably defined a 'good election story' as being synonymous with a 'local election story'. A journalist working on a weekly paper was explicit:

> I would say that a good election story is something that affects people locally. A local issue . . . Anything to do with the local hospital, the re-development of the supermarket in the town centre, these are all local issues and important issues for MPs to be involved with.

Parties also made unprecedented efforts to stress local themes in their press releases in 2001: within the Labour Party this emphasis was a concerted strategy developed by the party centrally. A regional officer confided:

> I don't know whether I should tell you or not, but there was a determined effort by the national party. It is definitely the case that in the 246 seats that we won for the first time in 1997, we were all following the same plot: being local. The candidate had to be a local person, who knew and understood the nature of the constituency, of the people and their problems, their issues and their successes. It was definitely something that we were trying to emphasise that this candidate has demonstrated over the last four years that they were local and had got stuck into tasks that people around here wanted to be done.

The commitment of both journalists and party sources to 'go on the local', as one editor expressed it, certainly generated an unprecedented local focus in election coverage. In 1987, for example, 44.7 per cent (533) of election items were local rather than nationally focused: by 1997 the balance between local and national aspects of campaign coverage had moved to a position of near balance with 49.7 per cent (620) of reports favouring a local emphasis. But in 2001, 58.6 per cent (733) of local press coverage focused on local issues and concerns. The parties' efforts paid off in a flurry of newspaper coverage stressing the local credentials of the candidates. In many cases local journalists' reliance on a party press release was evident. An incumbent Labour MP, for example, confessed in a carefully crafted soundbite:

> I could not think of living anywhere else. I've lived here all my life (she can just about see the house in New Bond Street, where she was born, from her office window), and I can't see me leaving . . . There is no place like Halifax.

On the facing page a journalist described how the same candidate 'met up with a couple of ladies who she had worked with at [a local] hospital many moons ago. (Does she know everyone in Halifax? It sometimes seems she does)' (*Halifax Courier*, 17 May 2001: 4–5). An opposition party candidate seemed similarly aware of the need to eulogise everything 'local'. 'I have lived in the constituency for more than 25 years', she claimed, 'and I can't imagine being MP for anywhere else. I love representing local people' (*Halifax Courier*, 18 May 2001: 4).

Mutual Reliance and Media Dominance: the Local Paper as Kingmaker

But despite this undoubted success of party press officers and political sources in shaping election coverage, the great majority of journalists and all party sources believed it was the local newspaper which remained dominant in their relationship. The mutual benefits to be derived from the relationship are also acknowledged by both groups. 'It's definitely a relationship with two sides', a party official acknowledged:

> The newspaper doesn't want to have nothing to report, but equally the MP wants good coverage. Neither side wants to fall out with the other too much but MPs certainly need newspapers more than the other way round . . . I think newspapers are in the driving seat. It might be just the way I feel but it has always seemed to me that we are at their mercy: completely at their mercy. It doesn't matter whether you come up with the best story and the best picture in the world. If they don't feel like covering it, then they won't . . . They have the upper hand. If you want to have news reported in a local paper then you have got to work with the people that are there. They can be as horrible as they like. And you just have to let them be.

A different press officer was unequivocal.

> I would go so far as to say that the local paper is a kingmaker. I spent a long time fighting that campaign and worrying about why it was so hard, why it was so awful. And I came to the conclusion that it was in large part due to the local newspaper. So that is how important they are. They actually have the ability to potentially win and lose elections.

This perception of relations between party sources and journalists is shared by the latter and reflects the local monopoly situation which most local newspapers enjoy. The editor of a daily paper denied any suggestion of partisanship in the paper's reporting but acknowledged the paper's potential to be influential in electoral outcomes.

> We don't fly the flag for any political party. We don't think it's right for us to do that because we have a local monopoly. It was 'The *Sun* Wot Won It' and it could happen here. Obviously we would be in a position to influence an outcome here. Without boasting, it's just a fact. But it's a fact you have to appreciate and a responsibility you have to accept.

One local journalist denied any influence to political sources and party spin doctors in shaping election coverage: the very idea seemed incredible. There was one Conservative candidate, she suggested, who 'used to bully journalists and I could tell he was trying to lead me into a certain direction. You have got to be careful. But what have we got to lose? What have we got to lose by not following their agenda? Nothing!'

This phenomenon of local media dominance presents the mirror image of the relationship between news media and political sources which prevails nationally.

Feeding off Each Other: Journalists and Sources

The suggestion in this chapter has been that the relationship between journalists and their political sources is best understood as essentially collaborative rather than conflictual: the relationship is symbiotic and characterised by mutual reliance between the consenting partners. Journalists and political sources are engaged in what has been described as an exchange relationship, where the commodities to be bartered are 'insider' political information and access to editorial space which sources can use to disseminate messages congenial to a particular candidate, policy or ideology (Ericson et al. 1989). The relationship, however, is volatile, complex and highly variable, with sources and journalists enjoying different and shifting fortunes in diverse settings. Consequently, Bernard Ingham, while acknowledging the reliant and collusive character of the relationship, as well as the prospect (if not certainty) of conflict, suggested that journalists and their sources live in 'a permanent and natural state of tension'. Their relationship is 'essentially cannibalistic. They feed off each other but no one knows who is next on the menu' (Ingham 1990).

This chapter has illustrated some of this complexity and diversity by high-lighting two case studies to illustrate the dominance of sources in the national setting. It has also shown how in the context of the constituency campaign during recent general elections, local journalists and news media have illustrated their ability to set the limits within which political sources operate and might achieve success. The key variable in shaping who is 'next on the menu' in this 'cannibalistic' relationship is the communication resources which each can muster and bring to the exchange.

The prominence of local newspapers in their relationships with party and other political sources reflects the monopoly which they enjoy in their circulation areas (Franklin and Murphy 1998: 18–19).[3] Sources have access to only this single outlet for their messages and consequently, as the party official quoted above complained, 'They have the upper hand. If you want to have news reported in a local paper then you have got to work with the people that are there.' A research study in West Yorkshire illustrated the crucial impact of structures of local news media organisation and ownership on the relationship between sources and journalists. The leader of a local metropolitan authority, for example, aided by his press officers, routinely influenced the reporting of local politics in the two local daily newspapers by withholding information from one paper while offering monopoly access to 'exclusive' and 'insider' political news to the other. The conditions of publi-cation, which detailed not only the content of reports but their positioning within the paper, were clearly specified. Such conditions of newspaper duo-poly favour politicians and political sources who can exploit rivalries and market competition between newspapers to their advantage. Where a local newspaper enjoys an editorial monopoly in reporting the local political scene, however, the balance in the relationship shifts and the newspaper is able to assume a more controlling and sometimes critical posture towards political coverage (Franklin 1991: 17).

But local political communication networks are in flux and two recent developments have contributed to the empowering of political sources. First, the number and quality of journalists employed in the local press are declining, reflecting falling circulations and profits in competitive local markets. A senior editor expressed her 'deep concern' about the lack of specialist political reporters:

> We always had people who came into journalism because they were interested in politics. But now . . . the reporters are not specialist enough to write about politics. There isn't the money to get senior journalists . . . So you've got an uphill struggle in reporting an election not only to inform your readers but to inform your colleagues.

For their part, political sources are increasingly aware that local papers possess highly variable journalistic resources: weekly free newspapers are 'pasted up by a single sub in an afternoon' while a daily newspaper will employ a greater number of journalists and perhaps a specialist political correspondent. Sources shape their media strategies accordingly. A regional press officer acknowledged:

> A lot of it is to do with resources . . . when we train press officers we tell them that the more stuff you can give to an overworked journalist the better, because they don't really have the time to go through it. So yes, in terms of the weeklies we just gave them press releases which they reproduced . . . The *Hebden Bridge Times* and the *Todmorden News* more or less print anything you give them as you give it them. But it was the daily newspaper which was the one which was really difficult.

A second development supportive of sources' relationships with journalists is the increasing incursion of national news sources into local communication networks. Regional and local newspapers provide particularly 'accessible' sites for the placing of articles featuring prominent national politicians' by-lines (although ghosted by press officers and special advisers). Oborne recalls the 'spectacular stunt' in 1998 when Alastair Campbell 'managed to foist an identical exclusive by Tony Blair on more than a hundred regionals, each distinguished only by an individual paragraph which acknowledged the local audience' (Oborne 1999: 199). Some journalists recognise the growing influence of political 'spin' in shaping local journalism. The 'spin' emanates increasingly from national news sources like the Government Information and Communications Service, the lobby, the Central Office of Information and the press sections of individual government departments. One editor claimed this 'management and manipulation of news' resulted in journalists 'being used'.

By contrast, in the national setting, sources are increasingly assertive in their relationships with journalists: again the organisational structures of news media are significant. Nationally, there is a significantly greater plurality of news media with 20 daily and Sunday newspaper titles, 24-hour television news channels, news programmes on national terrestrial and satellite channels, combined with an expansive number of national radio services with stations like BBC *Radio 4* and *Radio 5 Live* focused largely on news coverage. Consequently, there is a plethora of journalists for sources to entice with 'carrots' or to cajole with 'sticks'. Sources are perfectly positioned to play off journalists in rival news organisations and strike ready bargains about the 'placing' of exclusives in targeted newspapers for particular readerships and audiences.

Developments in new technology and government deregulation policy, moreover, have created a multi-channel broadcasting ecology which not only strengthens sources' ability to manage news coverage and function as gatekeepers regulating politicians' appearances on news media, but also allows sources opportunities to target specific messages at narrowcast audiences on minority channels. Journalist Nick Cohen summarises some of these concerns and raises others which empower sources:

> The explosion in the number of channels and stations gives senior politicians and their minders the ability to refuse interviews to presenters or journalists who are out of favour. The state has a thoroughly politicised propaganda machine which can swamp reporters with recycled news, diversionary announcements and leaks to the boys and girls who won't bite the hand that force feeds them. *(Cohen 2001: 18)*

In common with the local press, moreover, Cohen argues that 'journalists whose budgets have been slashed . . . don't have the resources to investigate or the time to produce considered work' (Cohen 2001: 19). Evidently in the national setting it is currently sources who are the 'dominant' partners in their relationship with journalists, while locally roles are reversed. But these relationships are volatile and constantly shifting. The mutually collaborative character of the relationship spawns diversity: access to communications resources generates complexity and variety in the relationship between sources and journalists. Both continue to feed off each other but, to cite Ingham's metaphor, the menu of the day is constantly changing.

CHAPTER SUMMARY

- The relationship between journalists and political sources is changing, reflecting a growing commitment by governments, parties, interest groups and individual politicians to the 'packaging of politics' for media presentation and audiences'/voters' consumption.

- Following Ericson et al. (1989), the relationship between journalists and sources is understood as an exchange relationship in which 'insider information' is traded for access to editorial space in news media. Consequently the relationship between journalists and political sources is essentially symbiotic and consensual although, within this overall framework of collaboration, the prospect for conflict is not merely possible but routine.

- Two case studies illustrate the complexity and diversity of the relationship. Nationally, the Labour government's relationship with journalists reveals the dominance of sources. Locally, the analysis of relationships between journalists and parties in the context of reporting the general election in 2001 illustrates the reverse: the dominance of local news media and journalists in their relationships with sources.

- Since the 1997 election, New Labour's strategy for managing relations with journalists has involved: the centralisation of government communications at No. 10, a more assertive relationship with journalists, and the politicising of the neutral civil service staffed Government Information and Communications Service.

- Evidence from the longitudinal study of journalist/source relations in the general election campaigns of 1987, 1992, 1997 and 2001 suggests that while party sources are successful in shaping election coverage, this success is achieved within parameters established by local journalists and news media.

- The key variable in forming the specific character of the journalist/source relationship's particular setting is the character of the communication resources which each can bring to the exchange.

Notes

1 This section draws on the findings of a series of studies of local press reporting of the general election in ten selected West Yorkshire constituencies in 1987, 1992, 1997 and 2001. Each study addressed three broad questions. First, to what extent and with what success do local parties try to influence reporting of the constituency campaign? Second, how do journalists and editors respond to these party news management initiatives? Finally, what is the eventual press coverage of the election like? Each study has involved analysis of newspaper contents of all newspapers circulating in the sample constituencies, combined with semi-structured interviews with party sources and press officers, journalists and editors.

2 Unless otherwise stated, all cited interview materials are drawn from interviews conducted in June and July 2001.

3 In the context of the constituency campaign during a general election, radio and television are regulated by the various Representation of the People Acts which limit sources' potential for influencing the news agenda and predisposes them to focus their attentions on the 'unregulated' print media. This reinforces the dependency of sources on the local newspaper.

CHAPTER 4

Journalism under Fire: The Reporting of War and International Crises

Philip M. Taylor

Public knowledge about foreign events, including wars and international crises, is heavily dependent upon the mass media. If the media provide our 'window on the world', then how translucent is the glass? How much actual public understanding is there of the ways in which the media interact with, and report on, international events? And to what extent are the public generally aware of the dangers of inadequate or distorted impressions being created by the reporting of complex crises in 'faraway' countries? These questions have become even more crucial since the terrorist attacks of September 11, 2001 and the subsequent launch of 'Operation Enduring Freedom', the media coverage of which has been at best confused in terms of relating the complexities of what is 'a new kind of war'. Are we to see a new kind of war reporting emerge or will new events become mediated through old patterns of news coverage?

The premise of this chapter is that understanding the relationship between war, conflict and the media is essential for an informed democratic citizenship. Citizens have the right and, indeed, the responsibility to participate in political life; to do this effectively, they need to have full and accurate information and a clear understanding of the issues involved. Only then can informed decisions be made to support or oppose foreign policy decisions that are made by governments on their behalf with life-or-death consequences. The performance of the news media in being able to achieve this role effectively thus becomes a critical issue; it is what makes the news media significant within the democratic political process. However, their traditional role as informers, educators and entertainers has undergone significant change during the course of the last ten years. Their environment today is one of intense competition, deregulation and rapid technological change within a global market. Even more recently, they are facing competition from various 'new media', especially specialised news services on the Internet, which are bound over time to increase in credibility as alternative sources for foreign news events. And, thanks to the portable digital camcorder, we are also seeing the rise of what may be termed the 'citizen journalist', who is often present when professional journalists are absent, as was the case with the recent (July 2002) footage in Los Angeles of a white police officer beating up a black teenager, or the roadside footage of Charles de Gaulle airport in Paris when Concorde crashed. All this in turn has created new factors shaping the way in which world events are reported, distorted – and misreported. The degree to whether these developments help or hinder an informed public may prove vital to the preservation of democracy itself.

Perhaps we expect too much of our media in this role within the political body politic. If we look at some of the operational constraints of working within the media, we begin to realise that there is a limit to what can be done. For example, time is an important issue. The broadcast media in particular have very little time to present complex issues. Moreover, the arrival of 'real time' reporting since the 1980s has changed the nature of news gathering, especially the pressure to meet deadlines that were once measured in days and hours and are now required in minutes or live 'as it happens'. So whereas once a reporter would verify facts from a number of different sources before going to print or on air, we now see television journalists saying things like 'rumours are circulating that . . .' or 'one can only speculate that . . .'

Space is a further issue. In traditional broadcast packages on the nightly news, there is a limit to what can be done by radio and television reporters who usually have only three-minute slots in which to summarise complexity. In newspapers and current affairs magazines, there is more space – and longer deadlines – but in the most popular tabloids, foreign events are frequently condensed into 'the world in brief' because of a perception that the public are no longer as interested in international affairs as they once were – except perhaps at times of crisis or war. This means that news of wars can frequently burst on to our television screens without warning – and hence without the context necessary for public understanding of how such wars erupted.

The general decline in media interest in international events between the end of the Cold War and the terrorist attacks on the United States in 2001 also meant that many journalists have had to re-learn old lessons very quickly about war reporting (eight have been killed in Afghanistan to date, excluding Daniel Perle) while many also struggled to grapple with the complexities of the 'war against global terrorism'. As this particular story has gradually fallen off the front pages following the overthrow of the Taliban, and as the 'war' itself moved into the shadows of the intelligence, financial and legislative realms, it may well be that media reporting of a war against a non-state actor – namely an international terrorist organisation – will continue to be patchy, erratic and confused. Time indeed will tell.

Access to the battlefield – or increasingly the 'conflict space' – is another crucial issue. Sometimes reporters themselves have only limited access to information in what are, after all, very dangerous situations. For example, it is official Anglo-American policy never to discuss military events involving Special Forces, often not even after their deployment has long ended. This is why we saw only patchy coverage of the war in Afghanistan against the Al Quaeda movement. Moreover, governments have increasingly developed elaborate mechanisms for shaping, and perhaps even distorting, the media coverage of events. Indeed, it was this aspect of the relationship between the public, the media and government propaganda which prompted some of the earliest communications scholars, such as Harold Lasswell (1927, 1935), to investigate this phenomenon with particular initial reference to wartime. The public rely on the media, to use Walter Lippmann's phrase, to form the 'pictures inside their heads', to help them make sense of a complex and confusing world. In turn, governments want to ensure that those 'pictures' are of such a nature that public support – rather than opposition – for their policies will follow. Hence those who appreciate the significance of controlling time, space and access to frame the way in which events are reported have the best chance of controlling the news agenda.

Theory vs. Practice

The best way, therefore, to understand this topic is, on the one hand, to examine the operational aspects within the profession of journalism that shape the way in which war and crisis reporting takes place and then, on the other, to examine 'external' aspects that shape the nature of the media coverage. This is because there are increasingly official forces in the form of, for want of a better phrase, 'strategic communications' agencies that work hard to shape the global media agenda, particularly in wartime. In other words, if we use the media as our window on the world, we must be under no illusions that there are forces at work attempting to draw a curtain over it to obscure our view.

It is no coincidence, for example, that the development of modern military censorship is inextricably connected with the advent of the modern war correspondent. Prior to the Crimean War (1853–6), newspaper reports of victory or defeat in battles tended to be written by participating soldiers as 'official eye witnesses'. As such, they can be read rather like official regimental histories, with triumphs accentuated and defeats minimised. But when a civilian – William Howard Russell of *The Times* – was despatched by his editor to cover the British Army's performance in the Crimea, including the infamous 'Charge of the Light Brigade', the public face of battle was changed forever (Knightley 1975). This was because Russell was appalled at what he saw. His revelations about the conditions in which British troops had to fight, their lack of equipment, even the poor quality of their leadership, were backed up by hard-hitting lead articles by *The Times'* editor, William Delane, and they caused a sensation in Britain. As a result, the idea was born in the military mind that censorship of the media was one way to guarantee media – and thereby public – support. Concomitantly, there emerged the notion within the military establishment that the civilian reporter was not only dangerous but also potentially treacherous.

For the next century and a half, relations between the military and the media evolved into a series of compromises unique to each conflict but with an underlying set of rules governing the relationship (Taylor 1987, 1995, 1998; Fialka 1992; Young and Jesser 1995; Carruthers 2000). It must be borne in mind that this relationship evolved against the backdrop of the communications revolution, including the arrival of the mass media (popular press, radio, cinema and television), increased democratisation and military accountability, and of Total War and Cold War. All these developments brought with them greater public interest and involvement in the waging of inter-state warfare. In the words of French Prime Minister Clemenceau, war – especially modern industrialised warfare fought on a mass scale involving mass slaughter in a mass media age – had become too serious a business to be left to the generals. Each conflict, of course, brought its own special demands and innovations, but the inevitable presence of growing numbers of journalists on battlefields required the military to take more seriously what would now be termed 'media management'.

The Military Perspective on Censorship

In its earliest manifestations, the media 'problem' was tackled straightforwardly via censorship. It may seem a platitude to reiterate that battlefields are extremely dangerous places. What happens there would appal and repel most people, especially civilians caught up in the fighting or those watching from afar. Even professional soldiers, intensively trained for combat, sometimes crack under the pressure of its actual experience. After the Crimea, however, it would be fair to suggest that, thanks to the war correspondent, warfare in the eyes of the public would never be the same again. The military, who knew and feared this, especially if increased scrutiny resulted in an increase of popular anti-war sentiment, embarked upon their long road of censorship or, as they now prefer to call it, 'security review'. Their time-honoured justification for this is made in terms of preventing valuable information from falling into enemy hands and thereby jeopardising the safety of the troops. But the fact remains that their political masters were also motivated essentially by a large degree of damage limitation – not merely on the battlefield itself but also amongst the watching civilians far beyond it.

In fact, the authorities need not have worried. For example, during the First World War, journalists (who were turning out to be every bit as patriotic in support of the nation at war as the man in the street) quickly discovered that the slaughter not only needed to be rationalised (cf. Pick 1993) but that it also had to be rationed. The reality of modern industrialised warfare was so stark, the boredom so numbing and the killing so brutal and large-scale, that reporters found that they had to negotiate between the conflicting pressures of the public's increasing right – and need – to know on the one hand, and what it would tolerate as an 'acceptable' face of warfare that would preserve public support – and continued media consumption – on the other. As a result, war correspondents became not merely observers of conflict but mediators of its horrors. In the process, they also became participants in the wider propaganda struggle for the crucial public support for its continuation – or otherwise.

In more recent times, this issue took a different twist during the war in former Yugoslavia in the early 1990s. Former BBC correspondent Martin Bell suggested that because editors found much of the television footage from Bosnia too horrific for public transmission on grounds of 'taste and decency', a distorted image of what was actually happening in Bosnia was being conveyed. This 'self-censorship' on the part of the broadcasters resulted in a 'sanitised' image of a war that was far more brutal than the public realised. Bell suggested that one result of this was a general public disinterest in the first European war since 1945, and he linked the lack of international intervention to this situation. Bell called for a 'journalism of attachment' to counter apparent public indifference to the horrors taking place in Bosnia. His critics – who were many – suggested that he was calling for journalism to become an instrument of anti-war propaganda.

The Media Perspective and Causes of Tension

It is not only the military who have a problem with negotiating the realities of war with public support for this organised violence. The media must also share some responsibility. But in wartime, the question is: responsibility to whom? They have a responsibility to the military, in that their reporting should not jeopardise the lives of soldiers by disclosing information that might assist their adversaries. The BBC World Service is still remembered with resentment by the UK military for having broadcast the news of the British attack on Goose Green during the Falklands War prior to the actual attack, but it was government briefers who released this news to the media. The media also have a responsibility to tell 'the truth'. The question facing journalists, therefore, is how much of 'the truth' should and can be told. Today, thanks to the speed and global reach of their reports, courtesy of new communications technology, there is also the question of how quickly this can and should be done.

Here we need to distinguish between reporters in the field and editors back at base. Journalists in the field quickly understand the need for 'operational security', especially once it is explained to them that publicising such details as numbers and locations of troops would not only endanger the soldiers' lives but also their own! But wars are Big Stories and news organisations compete for the best, the most exciting, coverage. Journalists are highly individualistic, competitive, disrespecters of authority – all qualities that stand in direct contrast to those valued by the military. When their worlds collide, there is perhaps bound to be trouble – and a need for compromise.

The military are traditionally in the business of secrecy, the antithesis of the reporter's primary objective: publicity. As Martin Bell put it, 'our instinct is to publish and be damned, theirs is to censor and be safe' (Bell 1995: 30). In open, democratic societies this inevitably creates a tension. In the authoritarian and dictatorial regimes, there is less of a problem because where the media are state-controlled they can simply be expected to serve as the mouthpiece of their governments. But in countries like Britain and the United States (especially in the latter case where freedom of the press is enshrined in constitutional legislation) the media are more problematic. In Britain, for example, broadcasting was initially considered to be a medium of such potential abuse that a heavily regulated monopoly was created in the form of the BBC. Whereas its founding Director General, John Reith, could speak of the 'brute force of monopoly' as a means of ensuring state responsibility towards serving the British public's need (rather than, in its early years, right) to know, a significant consequence of this paternalistic approach to the new working-class electorate and audience was the emergence of a 'public service tradition' that engendered a 'national' rather than 'party political' approach to reporting events. In other words, if the BBC reported one side of a dispute, it felt obliged to 'balance' the story by reporting the other or opposing point of view.

In wartime, this creates significant problems. Prior to the Second World War, the BBC established an unrivalled reputation for 'balanced reporting' and credibility by adopting this method – which was put to excellent use during the Second World War when it developed what would become its World Service. Yet the very fact that journalists felt obliged to report both sides of a story contrasted with the nation's expectations that the media behave in a patriotic manner, that journalists should help the home nation and not the enemy, and support 'our boys' in the field. This was why Churchill referred to the BBC as the 'enemy within the gates'. Perhaps, as a former war correspondent himself (from the Boer War), he should have understood better the military–media dynamic. Despite his views, however, the British opted for a censorship policy of news rather than views. And because the flow of news from a battlefield could be largely controlled by the military, there was a good chance that any views formed beyond the battlefield back at the editorial office would largely echo the military agenda.

A great deal of military control can be exercised by providing or preventing journalistic access to and from the battlefield. All copy was scrutinised by military censors in the field – in the same way as they checked letters from the troops back home – and any offending material was removed. This was easier when most media outlets were written media. But with the advent of the cinema, film footage had to be scrutinised in the same way – even a road sign in the background of an otherwise innocuous sequence might aid the enemy if the footage fell into its hands. The problem was compounded further with the advent of radio, with its potential to report live from the battlefield. All such reports were therefore recorded and scrutinised prior to transmission. Extrapolate forward to live television, mobile phones and the Internet and you can begin to understand that military censors have had an increasingly difficult task as new communications technologies have provided journalists – and now citizen journalists – ever more channels for information flowing out from a combat zone.

As one veteran correspondent quipped: 'whenever you find hundreds of thousands of sane people trying to get out of a place and a little bunch of madmen struggling to get in, you know the latter are newspapermen' (cited in Rosenblum 1993: 1). Today we would add radio and television correspondents. But we would only see this happen if the editors had decided that the story was newsworthy. If insurance can be secured for the journalist, the operational constraints of what can be reported need to be constantly borne in mind when evaluating their 'first rough drafts of history'. How much access to the fighting did the journalist have? Is it possible to convey anything more than a 'snapshot'? What was going on beyond the reporter's line of vision? The BBC's John Simpson has put it thus:

It is rather like an account of a football match written from a seat near one of the goals. Whenever the play was down at my end, I had a superb view of it. But when it moved to the far end of the pitch, I only knew what was happening when I heard the crowd roar. *(Simpson 1995: xv–xvi)*

Equally, if two or more journalists are present at the same event, they will not necessarily report it in the same way. The emphasis, manner, tone and insight which each journalist brings to bear on a given story are highly dependent upon the personality, experience, education and location of the journalist. The journalist also works for, or on behalf of, a news organisation which has particular institutional interests and emphases that may affect the editorialisation of the story – or indeed whether the story gets covered at all.

These are some of the internal factors shaping the reporting of war. It should not be forgotten, however, that 'the media' are a very heterogeneous body. A tabloid journalist will have different perspectives to a reporter from a broadsheet; a radio reporter has different needs to a picture-hungry television journalist; and a public service broadcaster will have a different approach to someone from a commercial station. The one thing they have in common is 'the story', but their approaches can vary considerably. It is this potential diversity which worries governments who would prefer that their national – and now international – media all sing from the same song sheet. This is why they try to orchestrate the opera of war.

Official Wartime Propaganda

Since 1914, governments of all persuasions have attempted to resolve the problem of sustaining popular support in wartime by establishing institutions for the manipulation of information reaching the public via the media (Sanders and Taylor 1982). During the First World War – a 'Total War' in which the gap between the domestic and fighting fronts narrowed substantially – the press corps were carefully husbanded in what became the first modern paradigm for the military–media relationship. Journalists were confined largely in lavish castles away from the fighting ('chateaux warriors') while the new silent film cameras were invariably denied access to areas in which the death and destruction were taking place. Elaborate official propaganda machines worked hard to sustain public support over four long years by trying to regain the traditional distance between the fighting and civilian fronts which communications and the media now threatened to compress. The war correspondents who occupied the ever-shrinking space in between were thus seen as potential enemies within the military gates rather than as allies in the service of democratic freedoms – itself a relatively novel concept at the time of the Great War.

But if the idea was to project an image of war quite different from its brutal realities, then in the long run this once again failed, since the Great War holds a unique – and perhaps undeserved – place in the twentieth-century psyche as one of futility and unnecessary sacrifice (Fussell 1975; Ekstein 1989). That war, perhaps more than any other, is said to have marked an 'end of innocence' about the real nature of war, a 'rite of passage' to a more realistic public perception of what modern weaponry can do to real people. However, such an impression could not have been gleaned at the time from the media, whose record of patriotic jingoism and the demonisation of adversaries through atrocity stories was unparalleled up to that point (Haste 1977). If there was a new realisation, it came subsequently as an *ex post facto* rationalisation for the enormous sacrifice and loss that had taken place, the tragedy of which had touched almost everybody.

However, from this anachronism a myth was born, namely the assumption that a sanitised version of war via the media helps to sustain public support for it. Moreover, can we place any credence on the converse assumption, now so prevalent among critics of the media, that if only the 'reality' of war could be shown, public support would be undermined? Those with a fondness for counterfactual history often suggest that if television cameras had been present on the Western Front, then that brutal conflict would not have lasted as long as it did. Yet this misses two fundamental points. In the first place, the military authorities would never have let cameras anywhere near the fighting. And second, it assumes that 'the camera never lies'.

But there is also a third and much more significant issue. Despite the growth of pacifism towards the end of the Great War and the postwar traumatic horror of the war's losses and consequences, the public and the media in the victorious powers for the most part continued to support the war. The Allies did not experience the internal collapse of Austria-Hungary or the revolutionary uprisings in Germany and Russia which contributed so much to the defeat of those nations. The point is that in the national wars of the twentieth century, the media tend to be every bit as patriotic as the public they are serving. They are not uncritical in this support but when 'our boys' are fighting, the instinctive reaction of media and public alike is to support them.

The actual record of media coverage of military involvement is however quite different from myth. It is in fact more one of co-operation than conflict. This has been largely forgotten – mainly as a result of the American experience of the Vietnam War, to which we shall return shortly. But it is an undisputed historical fact that the media have helped the prosecution of national wars – 'wars of national survival' – during the twentieth century far more than they have ever hindered them. And the reasons for this lie not just in the development of ever more sophisticated methods for controlling and manipulating the media. Whereas in authoritarian regimes the state-controlled media are straightforward mouthpieces of government policy that can therefore be expected to support a war effort automatically, in free societies – even during wartime – such control has its constitutional or legal limits. This makes the record of democratic media support for national wars in the twentieth century all the more remarkable, and begs further examination.

Much has already been written elsewhere about the processes by which first the press and then subsequently the mass media came to constitute a 'fourth estate' in the body politic of democratic nations. At the micro-level, however, there are still remarkably few academic studies of reporters in the field. Fortunately, there are numerous memoirs by journalists describing conditions in the field, especially during times of war. Military memoirs can sometimes reinforce the impression that the military–media dynamic has always been characterised by tension. However, General Alexander, who took command of British North African forces in 1942, felt differently:

> My own opinion is that the press correspondent is just as good a fellow as any military officer or man who knows a great many secrets, and he will never let you down – not on purpose – but he may let you down if he is not in the picture, merely because his duty to his paper forces him to write something, and that something may be most dangerous. Therefore he must be kept in the picture. *(Cited in Royle 1987)*

Indeed, the record of most war correspondents in the Second World War is one of wholehearted support for the war effort – whatever side they were on. In Britain, for example, despite strict censorship procedures, the number of occasions on which the media clashed with the government in six years of Total War was remarkably few (Taylor 1987). And when American correspondents after Pearl Harbor likewise encountered bad news, they often failed to report it 'not because disclosure might help the enemy in playing to Allied weakness, but simply because it reflected negatively on the Allied performance' (Voss 1989: 24). Hence General Eisenhower could refer to the 500-strong press corps attached to his command as 'almost without exception . . . my friends' (Challener 1970). This is where patriotism and propaganda coincide, and in wartime the record of the journalists' profession as patriots and propagandists is every bit as noteworthy in democracies as it is in authoritarian regimes. The difference is that in one, the media volunteer to serve this role and in the other, they are compelled to do so. The system of voluntary censorship adopted in Britain and the United States in the Second World War did not however extend to combat zones, where field censorship of what modern war does to real people was particularly tight (Roeder 1993). The military might argue openly that this is essential to prevent relatives and friends being offended by the sight in the media of their loved ones in anguish, but the legacy of historical iconography – the element of public morale – also survives in this process. Hence only enemy dead were shown in cinema newsreels and even then in not too much detail. But the bigger picture also suffered. On D-Day 1944, censors accompanied 558 accredited print and radio correspondents on to the five Normandy beaches 'checking that not one of them wrote or radioed dispatches that would help the enemy or dismay people at home'. However, of the 700,000 words filed on the first day none really captured the horror of the reality: even 'the much loved Ernie Pyle . . . was laconic: "Our men were pinned down for a while, but finally they stood up and went through, and so we took that beach and accomplished our landing"' (cited in Evans 2001). This is a far cry from the more authentic depiction in Steven Spielberg's feature film, *Saving Private Ryan*, made 50 years later. Therefore the degree to which the news media are capable of portraying the realities of war while it was happening and hence adversely affect morale and promote anti-war sentiment remains largely to be seen. It has, quite simply, never happened.

This is not to deny that the news media have proved quite successful in conveying a *sense* of the fighting. But just as the military fear what would happen to public morale if the 'whole truth' were known, so also do the media fear the risks of alienating their customers if the 'whole truth' were told. It is here that interests of the war reporter and the soldier in the field coincide, although it is rarely acknowledged as such – perhaps because the military mind rarely grasps this and because the news media dare not acknowledge it. There is almost an institutionalised mutual suspicion, which belies the historical facts.

Vietnam: the 'Uncensored War'?

In the United States, the Vietnam War is pivotal in this debate, as the first 'television war' in which the mass public could observe modern war in all its lack of glory. Television stands accused of having stripped away the delusions of the past about the nature of real war, the American 'end of innocence', and of thereby completely changing the operational considerations of military commanders when they deploy their troops into battle during the information age.

Vietnam was the first military defeat in the history of the United States. Defeated nations try to come to terms with why they lost. How could a Third World nation like North Vietnam defeat (or not be defeated by) the most powerful military power on earth? Many senior military and political figures were convinced that the answer couldn't possibly lie with political or military failings. So a scapegoat was found – the news media, and particularly television which was at that time reaching near universal social penetration and was becoming the most trusted source of news and information. There emerged a widespread belief that television had conveyed the brutal realities of modern warfare into the living-rooms of middle America and, in the process, had undermined popular support for the war. The lack of restrictions on journalists covering the conflict in what Daniel Hallin (1986) has termed 'the uncensored war' meant that they could travel to anywhere in the battle zone, film anything they saw and say anything they wanted. The result, especially after the so-called turning point of the Tet Offensive in 1968, was critical coverage night after night fuelling anti-war sentiment – a 'stab-in-the back' theory reminiscent of rationalisations for defeat in Germany after the First World War.

There are many problems with this theory. Before 1968, the media were generally felt to have been supportive of Washington's line and largely accepted what they were told about the course and causes of the war. With Tet, however, a more sceptical note began to creep in as journalists realised that what they were being told did not conform to what they were actually seeing. For example, Walter Cronkite, the CBS anchorman and one of the most respected journalists in the United States, went to Saigon to see the Tet Offensive for himself. The sight of North Vietnamese troops attacking the American Embassy compound in the South Vietnamese capital, Saigon, came as a great shock, especially to President Johnson who is said to have decided not to stand for re-election as a result. But does this automatically mean that the US lost the war as a result?

It is too easily forgotten that American troops were not withdrawn from Vietnam until 1973. This was *five years* after Tet, a period just as long and as significant as US involvement in Vietnam before it – and a period longer than American involvement in the Second World War! It is surely inconceivable that any democratic government could sustain a war effort for such a length of time without public support. Johnson's successor, President Nixon, actually extended the war into Laos and Cambodia – and he was re-elected in 1973. Certainly, public protests in the United States against the war enjoyed a high media profile, and disquieting images of little girls running naked down dirt-tracks covered in napalm or of executions of Vietcong suspects certainly cast doubts over the morality of US involvement. But at no time between 1963 and 1973 did public opinion polls indicate that opposition to the war was a majority sentiment. Indeed, it could be argued that the news media stand accused of treachery after 1968 by actually doing a better job than they had done before that date, when they had uncritically accepted what they were being told by political and military spokesmen.

What this phenomenon of the 'Vietnam Syndrome' illustrates is a crisis of confidence on the part of successive US administrations about their ability to control the media agenda. When the news was bad, in time-honoured tradition, they shot the messenger. We also need to consider this debate within the context of media effects. We still have no watertight evidence that the media possess the capacity to convert pro-war sentiment into anti-war behaviour amongst a mass audience. This measure of uncertainty needs to inform all the academic debates about the impact of the media – from the effects of televised violence, advertising, the impact of 'cultural imperialism' and indeed of war reporting.

Vietnam Antidotes: from the Falklands War to Operation Desert Storm

With Vietnam myths very much in mind, the British government led by Prime Minister Margaret Thatcher was at first inclined to exclude the news media altogether from the Royal Navy Task Force that was deployed in 1982 to liberate the Falklands. In the end, under pressure from those very Fleet Street editors who provided her with such media support, Mrs Thatcher relented. However, only 29 journalists and crew were authorised to accompany the troops – and they were all British. The foreign media were to be supplied by the Reuters correspondent. Several factors influencing the subsequent news media coverage quickly became apparent. First, the media were totally dependent on the military for access to and from a war zone fought 8,000 miles from home. This was not just physical access but, in this final era before accessible mobile communications such as mobile phones and fax machines, access to communications as well. There were numerous examples of journalists requesting access to the military communications equipment only to be told that these facilities were locked up in military use. The result was that journalistic copy was often delayed – and one ITN report took longer to reach London than Russell's dispatches from the Crimea had done 130 years earlier! Slow or 'cold' news, even in the early 1980s, was to London editors no news at all – which was good from the traditional military point of view which now positioned Vietnam as the twentieth-century Crimea. But was this good for the democratic public back in Britain?

Once again, the military need not have worried. The tabloid press in Britain was unhesitantly patriotic, with famous *Sun* headlines such as 'GOTCHA!', 'UP YOURS, GALTIERI' and 'ARGIE BARGIE'. The BBC, starved of 'hot' news from the Task Force, combined with its public service tradition of reporting both sides, was accused in Parliament of being 'unacceptably even-handed' by using such phrases as 'the British forces' rather than 'our boys' and by carrying footage from Argentinian television. Public support, as well as media support, for the conflict remained high.

One further aspect of the Falklands War deserves mention. The 29 journalists who accompanied the Task Force underwent a phenomenon known as 'bonding' with the troops whose sea-borne accommodation they shared (Morrison and Tumber 1988). By the time the Task Force reached the battle zone, there was a greater sense of mutual identification amongst people who shared the same bread, bunks and beer for weeks on end. And so when naval censors asked the BBC's Brian Hanrahan not to mention how many planes he had seen leave the aircraft carrier – ostensibly for reasons of operational security – he was happy to oblige by using the now famous words, 'I counted them all out, and I counted them all back again'. No clues there as to the location of the ship but a successful mission with no losses was clearly good for morale back home. There were examples of micro-censorship. Phrases such as 'horribly burned' were cut from copy prior to transmission and the word 'cleared' was used instead of 'censored'. In short, the entire experience was an attempt by the military to present a one-sided view, and a highly favourable view, of a war with little actual bloodshed. As one public relations officer told an ITN reporter: 'You must have been told you couldn't report bad news before you left. You knew when you came you were expected to do a 1940 propaganda job' (Badsey 1995: 57).

The Americans watched the Falklands conflict with considerable interest. From their observations was born the idea of 'military pools', which were eventually the recommendation of the Sidle Commission established to investigate what went wrong with the military–media relationship in Vietnam. In the meantime, when US troops invaded Grenada in 1983, the Reagan administration decided to exclude the news media altogether, protesting that events had moved so quickly that there had been no time to organise safe transport for the press corps. The resultant media blackout enabled the US military to conduct its operations without any prying eyes, while back in Washington speculation ran riot in an information vacuum. That vacuum could only be filled by official reports, including official footage shot by combat cameramen, and released when it suited Washington – which usually meant a considerable time after the event. By the time the chorus of media protest was assuaged by allowing some journalists into the combat area, the fighting was all but over and the military mission achieved. It was the low point of US military–media relations in the post-war era.

It was probably also the last time that such tight control of media access could be achieved. The arrival over the next few years of new communications technologies like the fax machine, mobile phone and portable camcorder meant that censorship of copy, audio and audio-visual reports would be harder and harder to achieve, especially once journalists were able to afford to connect these technologies to satellite equipment that would soon be small enough to carry in the overhead luggage compartment of a commercial airliner. By the time of the Gulf War of 1991, some of this equipment was available, especially satellite equipment, which meant that, for the first time, war would be fought out in 'real time' – in other words live from the battle zone.

The Gulf War of 1991

As a result of the military–media rows after Grenada, the 'Mobile Reporting Team' (MRT) – or 'pool' – had emerged as a compromise. Put to the test for the first time in the US invasion of Panama in 1989, the pool was a small group of reporters selected to accompany troops into battle at short notice. Media guidelines were agreed with editors and reporters in advance of deployment, so that journalists understood properly the 'do's and don'ts' of what they could report. The select band of pool reporters were then expected to share their copy with colleagues, which ran against the grain of journalistic competitiveness for a 'scoop' but was better than no access, Grenada-style, at all. Pool reporters would inevitably bond with the soldiers they went into battle alongside, and so supportive copy could be expected that did not provide the enemy with valuable information about their location and strength – now even more important in an age of instantaneous global media coverage. From the military's point of view, this seemed the ideal solution to the Vietnam Syndrome, especially once the system was put fully to the test in Operation Desert Storm.

To make certain, the American pools did not allow satellite equipment. Instead, reporters in their pools were expected to submit copy and pictures to their 'minders' (Public Affairs Officers) for scrutiny prior to delivery to Forward Transmission Units (FTUs) who would relay the material back to the hordes of journalists back in Riyadh (the so-called 'hotel warriors') for transmission to the rest of the world. The pool reporters wore uniforms and, through the phenomenon of bonding, could largely be expected to be co-operative. Indeed, what is remarkable about the Gulf War – probably the most widely reported in history – is just how few instances of field censorship were reported subsequently by the pool reporters. In the British pool, journalists were briefed by General Smith about the entire battleplan a week prior to the launch of the ground war – and none revealed the secret. Moreover, once the land war began after six weeks of intensive bombing, the ground forces moved so rapidly that there was no time to simply stop the MRTs to enable them to send their copy back to Riyadh. As a result, and despite all the sophisticated communications equipment, the ground war went virtually unreported until after it was all over, 100 hours after it had begun.

The US-led coalition had initially imposed a news blackout on the ground war but quickly broke it once it was realised that the news was all good. Even so, watching global audiences were not seeing battle footage; instead they were watching live pictures of press conferences held in Riyadh's hotels. The presence of so many journalists – three times the number that were present at D-Day – at those conferences does beg the question: what was the point of being there? After all, the military had learned to use *live* television to address the global audience directly, actually by-passing the traditional mediation role of journalists and thus dominating the agenda of world public opinion. The answer, of course, was that this process looked better, looked more accountable, more democratic even, if it was done in front of an audience of journalists from the free world. The military had learned that you must never lie knowingly to a journalist because that would jeopardise the credibility of the source. But that did not mean that the military told the whole truth. And as the old saying has it, if you ask stupid questions, you will get stupid answers. Or to put it more soberly, if journalists unversed in military jargon or military strategy don't know the right questions to ask, they will only get the answers they deserve. Most of the 1,500 journalists in Riyadh were not specialised defence or foreign correspondents: this provided the military with another opportunity to dominate the news media agenda with their own. One need only recall that the footage of precision-guided bombs and missiles hitting (not missing) their military (not civilian) targets – which was a dominant image of the Gulf War – was supplied by the military, not created by the media.

There was one loophole in this system. In Baghdad, journalists from coalition countries were permitted to remain in the capital. Saddam Hussein tried this unique experiment in the hope that western journalists would be able to report massive devastation and civilian casualties that would appal world public opinion and, in turn, put pressure on western governments to stop the bombing. Saddam also believed in the Vietnam Syndrome. But his experiment backfired; the coalition did not bomb Baghdad intensively, preferring instead to use precision-guided (or 'smart') missiles and bombs – and these invariably hit their intended targets. And because the coalition did target largely military or political rather than civilian installations, western journalists in Baghdad found that they were not being escorted to these sites because their resultant pictures would have provided the coalition with valuable intelligence about 'bomb damage assessment'. In other words, if the coalition was targeting civilian buildings – as Iraqi propaganda maintained – then the Iraqis would have been quick to show the world such attacks.

There were really only two occasions when such an opportunity arose. The first was the bombing of an alleged 'baby milk plant', which the coalition maintained was a chemical weapons installation. When journalists were escorted to this site, they noticed a recently painted sign – in English – with the words 'baby milk plant', although they could find no signs of chemical weapons construction. Although there remains much controversy about this incident, the best evidence to resolve the issue is circumstantial. If the Iraqis before and after the incident were reluctant to escort western journalists to military sites, then why begin now? The second incident was a precision-guided bombing attack on the Al Firdos installation in a Baghdad suburb. Around 400 deaths occurred – mainly women, children and old men. Western journalists were escorted to the scene of devastation and were told that no censorship restrictions would apply that day. The coalition maintained that it was a military bunker and thus a legitimate target, whereas the Iraqis protested that it was a civilian air raid shelter. The pictures that were beamed around the world of the dead seemed to confirm the Iraqi position.

It was, from the point of view of media performance and western public support for the war, the defining moment. Reporters in the field filmed the horrendous scenes of what real war can do to real people, while editors back at base wrestled with issues of 'taste and decency' as to how much of the devastation should be shown without offending the audience. Different news organisations took different decisions, and the degree to which explicit pictures were shown varies from country to country. In Britain, the BBC decided not to show all that was available to them ('self-censorship'?) but was still attacked the next day for carrying 'Iraqi propaganda', with the *Daily Mail* labelling it the 'Baghdad Broadcasting Organisation'. The news of 400 civilian casualties was certainly bad for the coalition, whose official spokesmen claimed that they didn't know why so many people had been present in the 'bunker'. The *Sun* came to the coalition's defence by suggesting that Saddam had deliberately placed civilians in a military bunker for propaganda purposes.

This incident brought into sharp focus many issues for the relationship of war and the media. There was the tendency to shoot the messenger – in this case television – for the bad news it carried. Even in the United States, CNN was accused of 'treachery'. Second, there was really no way that non-specialised reporters could evaluate fully whether the installation was either a bunker or a shelter, and so they merely reported the claims of both sides. But because the television reports did carry horrendous scenes, despite the fact that they had been 'sanitised' by many news organisations, the sheer horror of what had happened could not be denied. How much should television have shown? Editors had to walk the line between reporting the horror without showing all of its gory detail for fear of offending or alienating its audience. Indeed, this line is extremely thin for, on the night of the bombing, the BBC received more complaints about its coverage of the attack than at any other time of the war. Viewers know that real people die in wartime – but they don't want it to be shown in detail in full technicolour, especially in prime-time when children might be watching (Morrison 1992).

This brings us back to Martin Bell's arguments about how much should be shown. Show too much and there is a danger that audiences will either become alienated or desensitised over time to the horrors of real war; there is a danger of 'compassion fatigue' (Moeller 1999). Show too little, and audiences – as Bell suggested – might not realise just how serious a situation had become, resulting in public disinterest.

Real War and Media War: Journalism under Pressure

Once a conflict breaks out, it is not always apparent to the casual observer that in fact two wars have really broken out – the 'real war' and the 'media war'. In real wars, real people die. In media wars, however, the realities of war, such as death and destruction, are both distant and distanced from a non-participating mass audience by the very mediating role of the media. Real war is about the sounds, sight, smell, touch and taste of the nasty, brutal business of people killing other people. Media war is literally a mediated representation of that reality but which is ultimately a third party or audio-visual 'snapshot' of it.

This is why academic analysis of media performance in war and crises is invariably critical. Because the watching public relies so heavily upon the media for news, information and interpretation of complex events, and because the media generally are unable to provide the breadth and depth of objective and balanced reportage valued by scholarship, scholarly analysis of media per- formance is rooted more in frustration about what the media *should* be saying, or are not saying, as distinct from what it is possible to say. Scholarship, however, enjoys the luxury of time for reflection and consideration which is denied journalism, especially now that profession is so technologically driven. This leads to accusations about the media having 'dumbed down', how their business is now 'infotainment' and to such charges that contemporary wars like the Gulf War 'did not happen'. The media in turn respond by attacking media scholar- ship for not being 'in the real world'. The pressure on journalism continues, and the very real danger of an understanding gap opens up.

This chapter has attempted to bridge that gap by outlining what can be done by journalists operating in circumstances that are not always fully appreciated by watching civilians far from the danger zones. We expect our free and democratic reporters to tell the truth, when in fact the 'whole truth' can rarely be told – at least at the speed we have come to expect of modern news gathering. Many reporters and their supporting crew members die every year in pursuit of this quest to feed the public's 'right to know', whereas some research indicates that many members of the public do not want to know what is happening if it upsets them (Morrison 1992). This is the real challenge for modern journalism – and for the media scholarship that puts so much effort into rewriting those first rough drafts of history.

The war against international terrorism provides even fresher challenges. As it slowly sinks in that this is indeed a 'new kind of war' – an asymmetric conflict between a global coalition led by the United States against a non-state actor – and that the war will not just be fought out on the military front, will the news media rise to the challenge? On many 'fronts', notably in the area of intelligence, the media will be denied access and therefore will not be able to tell the story. Much of the effort will be in the realm of private diplomacy, which is difficult for the media to report beyond men in suits turning up to meetings in big limousines. On the financial and legislative fronts, specialised knowledge will be required to understand their complexities. Further military operations will require journalists to relearn many of the lessons of their predecessors about reporting from the field. In a conflict that may take years to wage, will the media be able to sustain their interest and hence their coverage, never mind the considerable expense involved in foreign news gathering? Or will they merely choose to rely upon government versions of events, as expressed through their growing number of strategic communications activities?

CHAPTER SUMMARY

- Media performance in the coverage of war and conflict is a critical issue for healthy democracy.

- Understanding the limits of war journalism, of what can be covered, is as important as understanding official efforts to manipulate the image of what is actually going on.

- The military–media relationship is often far more one of co-operation than conflict, despite the experience of the Crimean War and the myths surrounding Vietnam.

- There is a crucial difference between 'real war' and 'media war'.

- The war on terrorism presents new challenges for understanding how new types of conflict can be covered.

CHAPTER 5
The Political Contest Model

Gadi Wolfsfeld

The competition over the news media is a major element in modern political conflicts. The Pro-Choice and Pro-Life movements in America, the Serbians and the Muslims in Bosnia, Amnesty International, Russia, Chechnya, Al-Quaeda and the American government all compete for media attention as a means to achieve political influence. Each antagonist attempts to promote its own frames of the conflict to the news media in an attempt to mobilise political support for its cause. If we can understand the rules of combat and the factors that lead to success and failure in the arena, we will be one step closer to understanding the role that the news media play in such conflicts.

The focus in this chapter will be on the role of the news media in *unequal political conflicts*. These include all public confrontations between a government and at least one other antagonist in which the state (or one state) has a significantly superior amount of coercive resources at its disposal. Many conflicts fall under this category: protests, terrorist acts, riots, rebellions, revolutions and all-out wars between powerful countries and weaker ones.

The term 'antagonist' refers to any group, institution or state involved in an ongoing conflict with another group, institution or state over a political issue. I shall refer to the more powerful antagonists as the *authorities* and to the weaker ones as *challengers*. I adopt the term 'challenger' from Tilly (1978), who makes a distinction between two types of 'contenders': those who have low-cost access to resources controlled by the government (*members*) and those who do not (*challengers*). The present discussion does not therefore deal directly with the competition between political parties that takes place during and between elections. While many ideas developed here can be applied to that realm, the number of studies about the media and elections far exceeds those that look at the more intensive conflicts.

The theoretical model presented here is called the *political contest model*. The thrust of this model is that the best way to understand the role of the news media in politics is to view the competition over the news media as part of a larger and more significant contest among political antagonists for political control. I want to put the politics back into political communication. Many of those who have studied this issue have made the same mistake as beginning protest leaders. They have been so blinded by the radiance of the news media that they have lost sight of the more powerful political forces that lie beyond them. The model rests on five major arguments, discussed below.

1   The political process is more likely to have an influence on the news media than the news media are on the political process

The political process has a major impact on the press because of various inter-actions:

- Political power can usually be translated into power over the news media.
- The political culture of a society has a major influence on how the news media covers conflicts.
- The news media are much more likely to react to political events than to initiate them.
- Political realities often determine how antagonists use the news media to achieve political goals.
- Political decisions have a major influence on who owns the media and how they operate.

This does not mean that news media do not also influence the political process. They help set the political agenda; they can accelerate and magnify political success and failure; they can serve as independent advocates for victims of oppression; they can mobilise third parties into a conflict; and they are central agents in the construction of social frames about politics. The press serves as a powerful catalyst for political processes and it is therefore essential to better understand how this catalyst operates. This cycle of influence, however, usually begins within the world of politics.

2   The authorities' level of control over the political environment is one of the key variables that determine the role of the news media in political conflicts

Political conflicts are characterised by moves and counter-moves as each antagonist tries to initiate and control political events, to dominate political discourse about the conflict, and to mobilise as many supporters as possible to their side. Those who have success in these areas also enjoy a good deal of success in the news media.

The news media's role in these conflicts is directly affected by the outcome of this struggle. When authorities succeed in dominating the political environment, the news media find it difficult to play an independent role. When, on the other hand, the authorities lack or lose control, it provides the news media with a much greater array of sources and perspectives from which to choose. This offers important opportunities for challengers to promote their own frames to the press.

3   The role of the news media in political conflicts varies over time and circumstance

This contention emphasises the need to develop a dynamic approach to the study of this issue. Those who attempt to find a single unified role for the news media in political conflicts are wasting their time. When covering political violence and terrorism in wars such as Vietnam and the Israeli war in Lebanon, the press was accused of being virtual saboteurs who undermined military effort through biased anti-government reporting. Social movements, on the other hand, often accuse the press of being an instrument of government propaganda. Similar accusations were levelled at the press during the Gulf War and to a certain extent in the Falklands, Grenada and Panama.

The role of the news media in conflicts varies according to such factors as: the political context of the conflict; the resources, skills and political power of the players involved; the relationship between the press and each antagonist; the state of public opinion; the ability of the journalists to gain access to the conflict events; and last but certainly not least, what is happening in the field. All of this is beyond variations in the antagonists' control over the political environment mentioned above. Thus, not only does the role of the news media vary across conflicts, it can also change within the course of a single conflict.

4   Those who hope to understand variations in the role of the news media must look at the competition among antagonists along two dimensions: one structural and the other cultural

The best way to learn about the rules of combat is to watch the battle. Antagonists compete over the news media along two major dimensions. They compete over access to the news media and they compete over media frames.

The model uses two dimensions of analysis, each of which contributes an important perspective on these struggles. The *structural dimension* looks at the extent of mutual dependence between the antagonists and each news medium to explain the power of each side in the transaction. This offers important insights about which political actors are most likely to gain access into the arena. The *cultural dimension* of analysis focuses on how norms, beliefs and routines all have an influence on the construction of media frames of conflict. This second dimension serves to remind us that political contests are also struggles over meaning in which success within the news media can lead to higher levels of political support.

5   While authorities have tremendous advantages over challengers in the quantity and quality of media coverage they receive, many challengers can overcome these obstacles and use the news media as a tool for political influence

The literature on this topic presents mostly one side of this picture. It is a story of gloom and doom in which powerful governments can exploit the dependence of the news media to drown out alternate frames and agendas. Authorities have routine access to the news media; they also have the staff, skills and resources to take full advantage of that access.

There is, however, another part of the story that is just as important to tell. Challengers can and do compete with the authorities over the news media. Some of these opportunities emerge from the political blunders of the powerful, while others can be attributed to outside events. The news media keep a large stock of anti-authority frames for those antagonists who have the resources and skills to use them. Researchers should focus their attention on the exceptions as well as the rules.

When taken as a whole, these five arguments suggest a process that is neither linear nor constant. The competition between authorities and challengers over the news media is as fascinating and unpredictable as politics itself. In some ways the central arena resembles the modern sports facility that can be converted into several structures, each designed for a different type of event. Sometimes the arena is used for lavish spectacles in which officials show off their most colourful costumes and weapons. At other times it is a place for fierce contests in which challengers and authorities square off in brutal combat. And at yet other times it becomes a theatre in the round, putting on tragic morality plays about the plight of the oppressed and the need for social change. The goal of this model is to better explain the political, social and situational factors that dictate how and when the arena is transformed.

This chapter represents an abbreviated version of the full model (Wolfsfeld 1997). The goal is to provide a brief outline of some of the major structural and cultural principles that form the basis of this approach.

The Structural Dimension: the Contest over Access

The relationship between political antagonists and the news media can be described as a 'competitive symbiosis' (Wolfsfeld 1991) in which each side of the relationship attempts to exploit the other while expending a minimum amount of cost. Each side has assets needed by the other to succeed in its respective role (Blumler and Gurevitch 1981). Political activists and leaders rely on the press to get their message across to a variety of publics and the press relies on the antagonists for information and events that can be turned into news. It is this exchange of information for publicity which explains an important part of the relationship between the two systems.

There is a formula that clarifies this part of the relationship between antagonists and the news media. The initial principles are based on exchange theory (Blau 1964; Grossman and Rourke 1976) and/or power dependency theory (Ball-Rokeach and De Fleur 1976; Emerson 1972; Reese 1991). The relative power of either side – a given news medium and a given antagonist – is determined by the value of its services divided by its need for those offered by the other. Power is a question of relative dependence; who needs whom more at the time of transaction. As noted, while some aspects of this relationship remain fairly constant, others change over time and circumstance.

Presidents of the United States, for example, have a tremendous amount of news value and journalists are willing to 'pay' a lot to receive information from them. There are many ways in which the press accommodates Presidents. The news media are much more likely to allow Presidents free air time to make speeches to the nation than other political actors; more likely to quote them directly in news reports; more likely to treat them with respect in interviews;

and more likely to station journalists permanently with the explicit purpose of collecting information from the President.

Presidents, however, must also accommodate the press. They need the media to promote their image and their policies. This adaptation comes in many forms that range from the staging of media events to the creation of an informational infrastructure that facilitates the distribution of information to reporters. The amount of need will vary within different political contexts. Presidents' dependence on the news media often rises at election time, for example, because of their increased need to send information to the public. This increased dependency will be reflected in a more conscious attempt to carry out newsworthy behaviour and to give public speeches with the appropriately placed soundbites.

The notions of value and dependence also determine which challengers gain access to the news media. Here then is a second struggle over access: the contest among challengers. Once again the choices made by the news media will depend on the relative value of the information being offered by the various actors, while the willingness of each actor to adapt to the news media will depend on their need for publicity.

There are four major factors that increase the inherent news value of antagonists: their level of political and social status; their level of organisation and resources; their ability to carry out exceptional behaviour; and their level of control over the political environment.

Political and social status can be defined as the formal and informal standing of an actor, group, organisation or country within a particular political and social system. When elites plan strategy, make decisions or carry out policies, it is considered news. The news media consider elites inherently newsworthy and rely on them as their major sources of information (Bennett 1983; Paletz and Entman 1981; Molotch and Lester 1981; Entman 1989; Gans 1979; Reese et al. 1994; Shoemaker and Reese 1991). The ways in which status increases demand can be easily illustrated by simply considering 'who chases whom'. While high-ranking officials, politicians and celebrities are constantly surrounded by journalists awaiting their every statement, those with lower status move about in relative anonymity and must make special efforts to obtain publicity.

Antagonists with a high level of organisation and resources are in a better position to create news because the creation of major events is organisationally expensive (Alinsky 1971; Bennett 1983; Gans 1979). The ability to produce a major demonstration, for example, demands organisation, people and money. In addition, actors with resources are more likely to be considered inherently newsworthy even before they act, due to assumptions about their potential for political impact. A mere threat of a strike by a large union is considered news, as are rumours that the government may send troops to quell political disturbances, or that a major international power is contemplating economic sanctions against a 'rogue' state.

The third major factor that increases the news value of an antagonist is the degree to which they carry out exceptional behaviour. The word 'exceptional' carries two different meanings that provide important insight about the construction of news. Behaviour can be considered exceptional in the sense of being either unusually important or unusually deviant. There are indeed two gates for entering into the media arena: the front gate is reserved for those regarded as exceptionally eminent, while the rear is intended for the exceptionally weird.

Challengers are often forced to carry out exceptionally strange or violent acts as a substitute for their lack of status or resources. Dissidents may burn an American flag, dress up in weird costumes, or even carry out terrorist attacks to obtain access to the central arena. Leaders of smaller countries may choose to give an especially provocative speech or make threatening moves to gain an international platform for their demands. In the fall of 1994 for example, Iraq set off a mini-crisis with the West by moving troops towards the Kuwait border. CNN immediately sent Peter Arnett back to his old stomping ground to produce stories about how painful UN sanctions were to the country. Until then, Iraq's pleas for attention had been ignored. Iraq moved the troops, and it got the coverage. Such actions serve as a crude but effective battering ram for breaking down the gates of the central arena.

Challengers must pay a heavy price for this type of entrance: they must remain in costume. Weaker antagonists only remain newsworthy if they remain deviant and this widens the gap between the haves and the have-nots. The Hippies of the 1960s are remembered primarily for their outlandish costumes and war paint; the most memorable photographs of the Black Panthers have them holding guns; the PLO was long linked with the pictures of the masked terrorists taking hostages at the Munich Olympics; and the concept of the early women's groups as radical 'trouble makers' remains etched in the collective memory of many Americans. Having gained access to the media, such groups must then fight an uphill battle for legitimacy.

Dependence on the News Media

One cannot calculate the total level of power without also considering an antagonist's level of dependence on the news media. The greater the need for the services offered by the news media, the more vulnerable the antagonist is to being influenced by the news media, hence the weaker its bargaining position compared with competing antagonists. Dependency leads to adaptation.

There are two major factors that lead to an increase in media dependence. The first is a lack of alternate access to political influence. A major reason for turning to the news media is to gain access to political decision-makers. The press, however, is a rather crude and even dangerous communication channel. Those who have more direct access to such decision-makers can work privately and have less need for media attention.

The second factor that influences dependence is the need for external support. This is the other major service the news media provide for political antagonists: access to third parties (Gamson and Wolfsfeld 1993; Schattschneider 1960). The need for public support varies among antagonists and over time. Social movements, for example, usually depend on the public because their goals are long term and broad based (Gitlin 1980). Labour unions, on the other hand, can frequently avoid turning to the press. They clearly look for public support during a strike but at other, less intensive times union leaders will prefer to work directly with authorities (be they private or public) and to stay out of the public eye.

The interests of political leaders also vary among issues and circumstance: public mobilisation is essential for some policies and less important, or even detrimental, for others. As the need for public support rises and falls, so too does the willingness of antagonists to change their message, tactics and behaviour to meet the needs of the media. Thus, dependence on the media is determined by the need for an antagonist to send its message 'up' (to major decision-makers) and 'out' (to the public).

The Principle of Cumulative Inequality

It is now obvious why so many observers have stressed the advantages which political power brings to those seeking media attention. It is possible to summarise this axiom by referring to the principle of cumulative inequality. This principle states that those who most need the news media are the ones who find it the most difficult to obtain them; the rich get richer and the poor remain poor. The major reason for this Catch 22 is the already stated correlation between political power and all of the factors that lead to a higher news value and a lower dependence on the news media. Political power leads to political and social status, organisation and resources, the ability to carry out exceptional behaviour in the positive sense of the word, more direct access to political decision-makers, and less need for external support to achieve political goals.

There is also a clear correlation among these factors that goes beyond their relationship with political power. Organisation and resources bring status and status facilitates access to decision-makers. Easy access to the news media becomes simply another indicator of wealth and power. The politically power-less find themselves in the same trap as all members of the underclass: they lack the clout to gain resources and they lack the resources to gain clout.

Political power and power over the news media are not, however, perfectly correlated. The discussion turns to dealing with this important gap.

Control over the Political Environment

From here, the playing field begins to level. The authorities' amount of control over the political environment, I shall argue, is the key situational variable that determines whether the news media will play an independent role in a political conflict. It is one of the most important wild cards which ensures that conflicts between authorities and challengers over the news media remain genuine contests.

Many communication scholars treat the political world as a given, and con-centrate almost exclusively on variations within the news media. The political world is seen as something more stable and solid, even static. Nothing could be further from the truth. The political world is in a constant state of flux, and as political scientists have learned over the years, it is painfully difficult to predict.

The ability of the antagonist to control the political environment can be understood in terms of three variables: the ability to initiate and control events; the ability to regulate the flow of information; and the ability to mobilise elite support. Each of these factors increases the ability of an antagonist to dominate public discourse about a particular issue. While the news media constitute the central area of the public space devoted to politics, they are not the only place where politics occurs. Politics happens in the legislature, in the courts, in the streets, on the battlefield and in discourse among elites, journalists and the public. Those who dominate these forums will have little trouble dominating media discourse.

Here, too, authorities enjoy important advantages over challengers. They can bring their status, organisation and resources to bear within all these forums. After all, this is what political power is all about. But there are definite limits to their power. Their inability to maintain full control over the political environment provides considerable opportunities for challengers to make significant inroads into the political process and the news media.

There are, then, two parts to this story. The first, which is better known, is that political power brings important advantages to those who want to achieve exposure in the news media. Political power brings status, organisation and resources, the ability to carry out exceptionally important behaviour and a reduced level of dependency on the press. The second, less familiar, part of the story is that despite these obstacles, challengers can and do compete. Authorities are never in full control of the political environment and these gaps provide important gateways for challengers to enter. The ability of the challenger to compete successfully with more powerful antagonists will depend to a large extent on their ability both to create and to exploit these opportunities. Some measure of success in this area will come to those challengers who can initiate and control events considered newsworthy, who find innovative ways to circumvent the powerful's control over the flow of information, and who make serious inroads among political elites.

The Cultural Dimension: the Contest over Meaning

The transactions between antagonists and the news media are more than a business deal. They are a set of cultural interactions in which antagonists promote their own frames of the conflict while the news media attempt to construct a story that can be understood by their audience. The most useful way for researchers to deal with this aspect of the relationship is to focus on the interpretive frames constructed by the news media about political conflicts (Bennett 1990; Gamson 1989, 1992; Gamson and Modigliani 1989; Gamson et al. 1992; Gamson and Wolfsfeld 1993; Gitlin 1980; Ryan 1991; Scheufele 1999; Wolfsfeld 1991, 1993). Here, we shall adopt the definition of frames proposed by Gamson: 'A central organizing idea for making sense of relevant events and suggesting what is at issue' (1989: 35).

Many political conflicts centre on disputes over frames, as each antagonist attempts to market its own package of ideas to the mass media and the public. It is important to examine the level of correspondence between the frames adopted by the media and those offered by each of the political antagonists in order to better understand this competition.

The news media's professional focus on events means that they usually employ the shallowest level of frames. The rhetoric of antagonists, on the other hand, is more symbolic; leaders attempt to communicate on a deeper level. This is one reason why so many antagonists find it difficult to promote their frames to the news media: the news media are interested in current affairs, not ideology. Links to deeper frames can be found, however, in editorial pages.

The frames at one level usually suggest a deeper frame and this is why the choice of media frames is so important. Consider, for example, the different levels of frames employed by the American public and the news media in the early stages of Vietnam. One could speak about the deepest level of framing by focusing on the notion of PEACE THROUGH STRENGTH, a long-time principle that suggests that aggression must be met with force. The next level of framing might be the COLD WAR frame, which can be considered an application of the first principle to the conflict between the Soviet Union and the West (Hallin 1986). A more specific frame that deals with Vietnam could be labelled the FALLING DOMINO frame, which suggests that the struggle in Southeast Asia is a struggle against the spread of communism in that part of the world. Finally, one could talk about the framing of a particular event or campaign such as the Gulf of Tonkin incident, which was framed as an UNPROVOKED COMMU- NIST ATTACK ON AMERICAN FORCES (Hallin 1986). Media frames that focused on communist attacks and the threat to the rest of Southeast Asia evoked deeper, more powerful frames.

While media frames are generally based on frames that are available in the surrounding culture, they are also designed to serve the specific needs of jour- nalists. The news media construct frames for conflicts by attempting to fit the information they are receiving into a package that is professionally useful and culturally familiar (Gamson et al. 1992; Gans 1979; Gitlin 1980; Tuchman 1973; Wolfsfeld 1993). The process is best understood as one in which journalists attempt to find a narrative fit between incoming information and existing media frames. Thus, the construction of media frames is neither 'frame-driven' nor 'events driven'; rather it is an interactive process in which journalists look on their cultural shelf to find a thematic package that is best suited for the events they are covering.

A good deal of the information about political conflicts used by the news media comes from outputs generated by political actors. Outputs refer to all actions, information and interpretive frames produced by political antagonists. These outputs are not always created to influence the news media nor are they all planned in advance. The notion of incoming information refers to the sum total of data about antagonists and the conflict that is available to the press, including outputs. The success of antagonists in promoting their frames to the news media will depend on their ability to ensure that the incoming information and events offer a good narrative fit with their preferred media frames.

The political power of any antagonist has an important effect not only on the struggle over access, as discussed earlier, but also in the battle over meaning. Political power provides a large arsenal of weapons that can be used in this contest. The same factors that increase the politically powerful's level of access to the news media also increase the professional and political resonance of their outputs.

The relationship between political power and control over media frames runs through several paths. The first has to do with the distinction between 'front gate coverage' and 'back gate coverage', alluded to earlier. Antagonists with political power are much more likely to gain access to the news media through the front gate as legitimate players in the political process, rather than through the back gate reserved for social and political deviants. Those with political power and resources are more likely to be treated with respect by the news media (Blumler and Gurevitch 1986; Paletz and Entman 1981). Assumptions about the inherent importance of such groups, and their ability to produce acts that enhance their legitimacy, lead to more dignified frames. Antagonists with less political power are more likely to come to the public's attention through what Gans (1979) has called 'disorder news'.

A second reason political power leads to cultural advantages has to do with the creation of news beats. Beats not only provide routine access to particular sources, they also serve as a means of cultural inculcation. Just as a social scientist spending a good deal of time in a particular culture runs the risk of over-identification, journalists – who are selected for a particular beat because they have the appropriate education and background – often adopt the language, customs and perspective of the host culture (Molotch et al. 1987). Editors are very aware of the dangers of reporters 'going native' and often try to rotate them.

Journalists who cover the Pentagon offer a good example of this phenomenon, and one that is particularly relevant to the issues at hand. Most of the major media outlets are given offices and facilities within the Pentagon complex. This allows journalists the luxury of being close to the scene of action and to exploit the technological infrastructure established for the dissemination of information. However, when journalists spend so much time within the military environment the line between expertise and co-optation becomes blurred.

I am reminded of an interview I conducted in the Pentagon with a senior reporter from a major television network. He maintained that he had trouble understanding the complaints by other journalists about the difficulty in obtaining information from the Pentagon during the Gulf War. He argued that he had no such trouble and that he could operate independently during the war. His claims of independence sounded somehow discordant with the scene of the interview. His office was located inside the Pentagon, where he was on a first name basis with the officers in the surrounding departments. The pictures on the wall were typical battle scenes, his bookcase was filled with books about the military, including many publications by the Pentagon, and both his sweater and his coffee cup carried the emblem of the Joint Chiefs of Staff.

It is rare for challengers to be considered sufficiently valuable to be designated for a beat, and thus they usually have fewer opportunities to socialise reporters into their own culture. More often editors will assign one of their less experienced journalists to cover an unconventional story or even assign a different journalist to each such event. There are, however, exceptions to this rule. In the coverage of Tiananmen Square, for example, journalists spent a considerable amount of time with the protesting students and had very few contacts with Chinese officials. This may be one reason why so many reports adopted the students' perspective of the conflict (Shorenstein 1993). A similar process occurred during the protests in Israel over the evacuation of the Sinai town of Yamit (Wolfsfeld 1984a, 1984b); journalists and protest leaders spent a good deal of time working together and a symbiotic relationship developed which went beyond the normal source–reporter relationship. Goldenberg (1975) offers yet another example by showing how the *Boston Globe*, in response to a successful mobilisation by resource-poor groups, changed some of its news beats to give more coverage to these activists.

Another important reason for the relationship between political power and success in the cultural domain can be explained by examining those production assets that increase an antagonist's ability to plan, execute and package information in ways that are easier to absorb by the news media. Effective public relations demands knowledge, experience, talent and money. Professional spokespeople – sometimes described now as 'spin masters' – are experts in intercultural communication who translate political information into news-speak.

Challengers can rarely afford to hire such professionals and usually do without official spokespeople or depend on spokespeople who are much less knowledgeable and experienced. The communication between the challengers and the news media becomes more difficult and the culture gap more telling. Those challengers who do mobilise some of these resources will be in a much better position to compete with the authorities in the cultural realm.

The ability to control the political environment is another benefit that political power brings to those who want to promote their frames to the news media. Each of the three elements said to be important for determining the quantity of news coverage also has an influence on the quality of coverage. The ability to initiate and control events allows one to prepare the story carefully in advance; the ability to regulate the flow of information allows one to take control of the story line; and the ability to generate consensus among elites assures that most frequent sources will all be telling the same story.

Political power in western countries, however, is a variable rather than a constant; it is limited rather than absolute. The political process is a dynamic one and the ebbs and flows of political control provide many opportunities for challengers to promote their frames to the news media. Some of these opportunities emerge from the political failures of the authorities, others arise out of the actions of outside forces or unplanned events, and yet others from the actions of the challengers themselves (Staggenborg 1993).

The fact that the authorities are never able to take absolute control of events, the fact that their best-laid plans often go astray, provides important opportunities for challengers to promote alternate frames to the news media. The best way to understand the relationship between events and the promotion of ideological frames is to suggest that certain events give advantages to certain frames. When journalists have to choose between alternate ways of placing the events within a context, some frames make more sense than others. The nuclear accident at Three Mile Island gave important advantages to ANTI-NUCLEAR frames (Walsh 1988); the decision by 'Bull' Connor to use attack dogs and fire hoses on civil rights demonstrators gave advantages to CIVIL RIGHTS frames (Garrow 1978); the IRA attacks on London civilians offered advantages to the

TERRORISM frame; and the collapse of the Soviet Union offered important advantages to those promoting ANTI-COMMUNISM frames.

In each case the events serve as vivid demonstrations of some underlying political claim. The resonance of such events is plain to see. One side is attempting to ride the wave for all its worth, while the other finds itself speaking in terms of 'damage control'. Having defined the context of the event, journalists look for other sources and stories that fall under the same heading.

Challengers who are able to produce outputs that resonate within the professional and political culture of important news media can compete with their more powerful adversaries. The news media maintain a large store of anti-authority frames that can be taken down and applied when circumstances warrant. The POWER CORRUPTS frame described above is just one example of such a construction. The fact that leaders are considered inherently newsworthy is a dual-edge sword. From a journalistic perspective, a negative story about someone in power is often valued more highly than a positive one. Challengers often perform symbolic judo by turning the celebrity of authorities to their own advantage. Thus, under varying circumstances, journalist culture can either reinforce political power or set limits to it.

Ryan (1991) provides an example of a much less established challenger who was able use journalistic norms successfully to promote their frame to the news media. The New Bedford (Massachusetts) delegation to Nicaragua was organised with no staff and few resources to protest against the US government's role in Nicaragua during the 1980s. Ryan talks about the careful planning that went into the media campaign of the New Bedford delegation, which allowed them a good deal of success in passing their frame to the news media:

> Interest was the strong suit for the New Bedford group. The delegation itself was a good story: amidst the rumors, lies, and self-serving misspeakings of Washington bureaucrats, a group of average Americans, with no political axe to grind, had ventured into a war zone and come back to speak the truth as they had seen it with their own eyes. *(Ryan 1991: 34)*

Their presentation to the news media had all of the elements of a good news story that resonated with existing media frames of conflict. It included human interest (delegates crying during the press conference), good visuals (pictures of victims taken during the trip) and cultural resonance (ordinary citizens had gone to see for themselves). The New Bedford group was also very conscious of the need to present a well-structured frame of the Nicaraguan story that could compete with the dominant frame that was being promoted by the Reagan administration.

The government was promoting EAST–WEST CONFLICT frame as a way of describing what was happening in Nicaragua, and this well-known concept was given a good deal of play in the news media. Nevertheless, the New Bedford challengers put forth a HUMAN COST OF WAR frame, and this also resonated well within journalist culture; it was a familiar media theme and one that had a good deal of cultural resonance within the general society. The fact that both frames were very familiar to the news media facilitated genuine competition between the two interpretations.

While many challengers are forced to enter the media through the back door, others are able to promote a more sympathetic frame to the media. The principle of political resonance tells us something important about which challengers will be most successful in their attempts to promote competing frames to the mainstream news media. Groups whose members appear to come from the elite, whose goals are more reformist than revolutionary, and whose actions fall into what the news media regard as reasonable dissent, will find it much easier to promote their frames to the media than those who violate these norms.

Many challengers are interested in significant changes and they face several dilemmas. How can they tailor their message to resonate within the political culture of the mainstream media without altering them beyond recognition? If they do attempt to promote a more moderate frame, how can they remain newsworthy? How can they achieve both political resonance and journalistic resonance?

One option is to work for long-range change in the society, which will then lead to changes in media frames. The ways in which the news media relate to political movements are especially likely to reflect such changes in political context. Consider changing media frames about the women's movement in the United States (Danielian 1988; Tuchman 1978). The fact that media frames about this movement changed so radically from the mocking notion of 'bra-burners' to the current level of legitimacy is more than anything else an indicator of the changes that occurred in the general society. The concept of sexism may have been reinforced and popularised by the news media, but the creation of the term and its cultural resonance are better traced to changes in the American political culture.

In a similar vein, some scholars have suggested that the environmental movement in the United States initially had trouble obtaining media coverage because the press did not have any ready-made categories for dealing with this issue (Strodthoff et al. 1985). The American news media no doubt played a role in raising public consciousness about this issue, but there were larger political processes at work that affected the political culture of the press.

Social movements can be important here. As Gamson (1988) shows, until the 1970s there were no anti-nuclear power frames appearing in the American news media, because such frames were so rare within the general society. This helps explain why a serious nuclear accident that occurred in 1966 in the Fermi reactor, 30 miles south of Detroit, was barely mentioned in the American press. Later, environmental and anti-nuclear movements played an important role in changing the nature of media discourse about this issue by successfully promoting anti-nuclear frames to compete with those being promoted by the authorities. This led to a very different framing by the news media of the subsequent accidents at Three Mile Island and Chernobyl, and in the more general discourse about this issue.

Promoting Frames Internationally

Opportunities also exist for international challengers to promote their frames to the outside news media. Authorities will find it much more difficult to promote their frames of conflicts to the news media of other countries owing to differences in political culture. International challengers may in certain circumstances find that their frames resonate much better abroad than they do at home. The political implications of this process may depend on the relative power of each country involved. The key for challengers is to find political resonance within the news media of the most powerful third parties they can find.

When the United States is not the authority in question, the American news media become a critical target for both sides in the conflict. Antagonists will often attempt to package their messages in ways that resonate within the American political culture. The use of signs, speeches and materials in English employed by international challengers and the conscious use of symbols that resonate within western societies tell us something about the search for third party help. The student demonstrators in Tiananmen Square quickly realised the importance of the American news media and adapted their media strategy accordingly (Shorenstein 1993). A good deal of their attention was devoted to mobilising the American television networks to their cause by using the appropriate signs and interviews. When the Chinese authorities decided to suppress the protest, they prevented the American cameras from covering the event.

When the United States is directly involved in a conflict, on the other hand, foreign challengers will find it especially difficult to find any sympathy within the American news media. They may be able to promote their frames successfully to other countries but the realities of power in the international community suggest that this may not prove important. To compete successfully against the American authorities within the United States, challengers may have to find domestic sponsors for their frames.

Thus, there are two major factors that set important limits on the ability of authorities totally to dominate media frames. The first is that they often lose control over the political environment and this offers important opportunities for challengers to promote alternate frames to the press. Second, there are many influences within the professional and political culture of the news media that work against the authorities. Those challengers who can overcome the obstacles of entrance to the central arena will be given a genuine opportunity to fight.

These then are some of the basic principles of the political contest model.

CHAPTER SUMMARY

- The competition among antagonists over the news media takes place on two levels: a contest over access and a contest over meaning. The contest over access is best seen as an exchange of services: antagonists who can provide the news media with the most valuable information and events are granted publicity in return. The competition over meaning is more complex. Journalists attempt to find a narrative fit between existing cultural frames and ongoing events.

- Authorities, it is argued, have important advantages in both areas: political power can often be translated into power over the media. Not only are the powerful more likely to gain access to the news media, they are often in a position to influence how they and their policies will be covered. Nevertheless, challengers sometimes do emerge victorious. They either create or exploit events that provide them both access and sympathy.

- The fact that it remains an open (albeit unfair) contest is what makes this line of study so intriguing. Researchers who hope to understand such competitions are advised always to begin by considering the nature of the political and professional environment in which the news media are operating. They should then move on to consider the amount of status and resources that each antagonist brings to the table.

- Finally, scholars need to consider the professional and cultural resonance of each antagonist's messages and actions. Armed with such a scorecard, observers will be in a much better position to understand the rules of the game as well as the most likely outcomes.

PART IV

SOURCE FIELDS
Challengers

CHAPTER 6

Non-governmental Organisations and the Media

David Deacon

It is only recently that questions have opened up about the potential influence of non-governmental organisations (NGOs) in media terms. For a long time the only story deemed worth telling was how capitalist media values operate systematically to delegitimise non-official sources. For example, Roland Barthes once dismissed the media appearances of trade unions and other pressure groups as 'a small inoculation of acknowledged evil' (quoted in Fiske 1987: 39). Even when commentators acknowledged the political importance of non-governmental organisations, many underplayed the significance of media and communication issues as catalysts for these changes (e.g. Rose 1988; Coxall 1986).

In this chapter I review recent research on NGOs and the media that suggests these generalisations are increasingly difficult to sustain. A substantial part of this discussion will examine media issues involving specific kinds of NGOs operating in a particular political context: namely, trade unions, charitable and voluntary organisations and 'Quasi-Autonomous Non Governmental Organisations' (aka 'quangos') in the UK.[1] Although this focus may limit the generalisability of some of the observations, this specificity is needed to avoid introducing new overgeneralisations.

Defining Non-governmental Organisations

The main problem in making undifferentiated observations about NGOs relates to the sheer variety of organisations that the label encompasses. NGOs are conventionally defined as formal, 'non-statutory', non-profit-making organisations. This means that any general discussion about them includes charities, trade unions and other cause-based organisations, as well as mainstream political parties and many professional and corporate interest groups. It is also often asserted that NGOs are 'resource-poor' organisations. This is far from an absolute rule. For example, some of the largest charities in the UK are now multi-million pound concerns and make considerable strategic investments in communication and publicity.

An added complication is that it is proving increasingly difficult to make neat distinctions using the not-for-profit and non-public criteria when identifying NGOs. Trade unions have the strongest claim for qualifying as NGOs. Their role is to represent the collective interests of labour against capital, and their credibility depends on their ability to demonstrate their independence from the market and the state. Additionally, their power rests on their capacity to recruit and mobilise an extensive membership, which requires formal, organisational structures.

The case is less clear with voluntary organisations. The last 30 years have witnessed significant retrenchments in state responsibilities for welfare provision across Europe. Public welfare systems are often said to be in crisis, due to spiralling costs and 'a crisis in values', in which state intervention is claimed to exacerbate the dependencies and inequalities it was intended to resolve. In this context, the voluntary sector has been 'rediscovered' by politicians and academics from across the political spectrum. In Britain, one of the main effects of this transition has been to alter the terms of statutory financing of the sector. Many voluntary organisations now enter into contractual agreements with government for the delivery of key services, and this has blurred the boundaries between voluntary and statutory provision.

The status of 'quangos' as NGOs is by far the most dubious (a fact acknowledged by the reference to *quasi*-autonomy in the acronym). The term is used for organisations that are appointed by government to fulfil various services whilst operating 'at arms length' from the state. As such, they balance on the cusp between official and non-official sectors and perform diverse functions, such as providing services, advising policy-makers, monitoring and regulating other institutions, upholding the interests of certain social and cultural groups, encouraging the private sector, and promoting pro-social values. Matters are complicated by the fact that there is disagreement as to which organisations should be classified as quangos.[2] Furthermore, although most quangos have their remits defined by statute (which means they can hardly claim to be 'non-statutory'), other organisations have transformed into quangos over a period of time. But the 'quangoisation' of pre-existing organisations is not a one-way process of agency capture in which the statutory sector claws-in organisations. In some cases it can mark a repositioning of an organisation towards the non-statutory sector. Finally, some quangos are required to be profit-making, thereby technically breaching the 'not-for-profit' principle. For the purposes of this discussion, however, it is these uncertainties that make quangos useful for comparisons with other NGOs.

Before commencing this comparison I have some general points to make about why interest has grown in the agenda-setting power of various non-official organisations.

New Conditions: New Perspectives

The developing literature on the sociology of news sources has transformed the way in which the politics of media access are theorised. By decentring media professionals in analysis of news creation, numerous studies have exposed more unpredictability than many critical perspectives previously allowed. This has prompted a re-evaluation of even sophisticated models of elite-media hegemony, such as the 'primary definition' model, which acknowledges the relative autonomy of journalists, but claims the pressures and routines of news production, together with journalists' professional ideals of providing authoritative and objective accounts, lead to a 'systematically structured *over-accessing* to the media of those in the powerful and privileged positions' (Hall et al. 1978: 58).

It is now argued that the power of 'primary definition' cannot be seen as an automatic expression of the power structure, but is dependent upon successful strategic action by sources. Conflict within political systems, journalistic acuteness, dissent between elite figures, and astute political interventions by other sources, can all combine to open up media debate in unpredictable ways. Non-official news sources inevitably attract more attention within this new analytical framework (Schlesinger 1990: 81).

To some extent this change in perspective has been necessitated by social changes that various NGOs have helped to accelerate. Berry (1984) describes the emergence of an 'interest group spiral' and 'advocacy explosion' in US domestic politics during the late twentieth century. Meyer and Tarrow (1998) identify similar processes in dissimilar terms with their discussion of the 'movement society' and the broad expansion of 'contentious politics' across many democratic systems. These changes have been linked to the widening of educational opportunities and concomitant 'rise of sophisticated citizenry' (Mazzolena and Schulz 1999), and emergent environmental, material, social and ideological conflicts within, and between, capitalist societies (Blumler and Gurevitch 1996: 126–7).

The extent of interest group proliferation varies across political systems and there is disagreement as to whether these developments are positive. Some claim the spread of interest groups has revitalised pluralist democracy, while others see this change as a mixed blessing. One thing that is accepted is that as public policy networks and processes have become more complex and unpredictable, and as the political role and social functions of non-official groups have expanded, so publicity and communication issues have become ever more significant. Blumler describes the emergence since the 1970s of a 'media centric model of pressure group activity' (1990), in which organisations have become far more 'publicity minded' and acutely conscious of the significance of the role of mainstream media. This reflects the emergence of a 'communications dependent society' in which 'the publicity system of many advanced democracies has become a power-brokering sphere' (Blumler and Gurevitch 1996: 127).

With these general trends in mind, we turn to the case studies to consider how evident they are, and what forms they take, in more specific contexts. Each case study shares the same structure to facilitate comparison.

Trade Unions and the Media

Trade union influence in the UK has sharply declined since the 1970s due to deindustrialisation, the growth of the service sector, widespread unemployment and casualisation of labour, the effects of globalisation and the anti-union policies of successive governments. Between 1979 and 1994 aggregate union membership fell by more than 5 million, reducing the density of employees with union membership from 58 per cent to 38 per cent (Martin et al. 1996). This fall has reduced the resources available to unions and 'their legitimacy in the eyes of both employers and government' (Marsh 1992: 243). Any analysis of current communication strategies within the sector needs to bear this broader context in mind.

Media Coverage

During the 1970s, when unions were at the apogee of their power in the UK, numerous analyses of news reporting emphasised how these sources were symbolically marginalised and delegitimised (e.g. GUMG 1976, 1980). Trade union coverage was shown to focus on unions' involvement in industrial conflict and ignored their engagement in constructive policy initiatives (e.g. health and safety at work). This conflictive frame emphasised the negative public consequences of industrial action, and failed to provide comprehensive explanations of the origins of industrial disputes. In quantitative terms, state and elite trade union sources received privileged media access over employers and ordinary trade unionists. In qualitative terms, the language of trade union reporting was also said to undermine the status of union voices when they appeared.

These accusations offended many influential media personnel (Eldridge 1995: 7–8), and in the 1980s several 'revisionist' analyses appeared that challenged this critical orthodoxy. Two influential examples are Harrison's (1985) attack on the work of the Glasgow University Media Group, based on a re-analysis of their original source material, and Cumberbatch et al.'s (1986) assessment of broadcast coverage of the 1984–5 industrial conflict in the mining industry. In broad terms, these and related studies exonerated broadcasters and other journalists from the accusations of systematic bias in their coverage of trade unions and industrial relations. Where imbalances in coverage were identified, they were explained as the consequences of the pressures of news gathering, rather than journalists' conscious or unwitting prejudices.

These revisionist arguments provoked a series of sharp exchanges (see Sparks 1987; Cumberbatch et al. 1988). This debate was not helped by some points of confusion as to what exactly the media were being accused of by their critics. For if the counter-response of the revisionists has often seemed unconvincing in their rebuttals of the critics' original evidence (Goodwin 1990), their studies exposed some epistemological confusions within some of the original critiques. For example, the Glasgow studies at once relied upon notions of objectivity and impartiality to attack journalists, 'while dismissing such claims as inherently ideological' (Stevenson 1995: 28).

More recent research has tended to negotiate a position between the extremes of critical outrage and revisionist sanguinity. This is partly owing to a shift in research emphasis towards investigating the dynamics of news creation directly by examining the links between journalistic practices and trade unions' communication strategies. Such insights have been largely absent from most critical and revisionist accounts, which were highly dependent upon textual analysis (Cottle 1993a).

Trade Unions as News Sources

The value of this new approach is illustrated by Davis's (1998) study of media reporting of the British government's proposals in 1992 for privatising the postal service. These plans were opposed by the Union of Communication Workers (UCW), who instituted a concerted PR campaign against the plans. Davis's content analysis shows that although UCW sources came to be treated more positively or neutrally than either government or management sources as the dispute unfolded, the union received considerably less coverage than their political opponents. At face value, this suggests that the recruitment of mainstream media support to the anti-privatisation cause was due to elite divisions within the party of government and the vehemence of public antipathy. The union benefited from wider political developments, it did not instigate them.

By linking analysis of media reporting to an analysis of the union's communication strategy, Davis shows that the union played a vital role in galvanising public, party political, professional and expert opinion, which in turn had a significant effect on media framing. By commissioning polls and lobbying influential opinion leaders, the union 'bypassed the need for institutional legitimacy and direct access. Instead they gained a voice by using the legitimacy and access possessed by other sources: the public, "economic experts", politicians and assorted "neutral" user groups' (Davis 1998: 182).

Other similar studies of the influence of unions' communication strategies have produced more modest appraisals of union power in this respect. Negrine's analysis of media reporting of the pit closures in Britain in the early 1990s shows that, despite a transient period of intense public and media support for the mining unions, the issue quickly dropped off the media agenda, leaving them 'marginalised to the fringes of the political process' (Negrine 1996: 124–5). This allowed the government to prosecute its plans unhindered. Another study of media coverage of the 1989–90 ambulance drivers' strike also tells a story of limited success (Manning 1998: ch. 8). By comparing the health unions' campaigning strategies with the terms of media reporting, Manning shows that they had some initial successes in recruiting mainstream editorial support for their cause, but were less successful in influencing the terms of media debate even during these early stages. As the dispute intensified, the unions' influence weakened, as journalists were presented with a range of news angles that invited less favourable coverage.

Manning also concludes that the difficulties experienced by the health unions in this dispute reveal problems that confront media and PR activities in the sector. Apart from financial constraints, the structure of unions can inhibit their effectiveness in managing media coverage effectively in a pressurised political context. Trade unions are supposed to have a 'bottom-up' political structure, in which the leaders act as the conduit for the collective wishes of the membership. Also many have a diverse, federated structure, with local branches exerting a degree of autonomy in their local operations. Although these may reflect admirable political ideals and practices, they do not always offer a promising basis for effective media relations. To remain 'on message', an organisation requires a high degree of centralised control, which does not sit easily with the traditional internal practices of the union movement. These fault-lines tend to open up during periods of intense political pressure, increasing the 'porosity' of these news sources and muddling the messages they seek to convey.

Manning's study identified two ideal types of union structure. On the one hand, there are unions where press and publicity functions are marginalised and trapped within a civil service style hierarchy. On the other hand, there are organisations that permit a higher degree of integration for their media and PR operations with their leadership. These differences in part reflect the 'dilemma of incorporation' that unions have had to confront in response to the changing political realities they face. In the period of his research, Manning found a stubborn residue of suspicion within certain unions towards the media, that readily characterised journalists as class enemies, working at the behest of state and capitalist interests.

More recent empirical work suggests that these recalcitrant tendencies may be reducing. In his 1997 survey, Davis found that two-thirds of unions employed at least one media or publicity person and only 9 per cent saw their organisation as having no PR function. Fifty-seven per cent employed other lobbyists or press cuttings agencies and 77 per cent said their communication budgets had increased during the 1990s, half of those substantially. Where Manning and Davis agree is on the underlying reasons for the increasing emphasis on media and publicity activities in the sector, in particular the steep decline in union membership and the spread of a 'new political realism' across the Labour movement. Thus, the embrace of promotionalism in this context is not an act of assertion, but of defence: attempting to avoid marginalisation in a changing political and economic context.

Journalists' Perspectives

In accounting for what they saw as the concerted bias of the mainstream media against unions, the Glasgow University Media Group emphasised the social background of journalists and their middle-class values. It is noticeable that these kinds of biographical explanations are sidelined in studies that do analyse the 'specificity of professional practice' (Stevenson 1995: 33), and replaced by an emphasis on the role played by professional values and news-gathering practices in producing a constrained and selective account of union activity. Here again, Manning's research offers valuable insights, not least in demonstrating that one of the harsh new realities unions have to confront is a shift in the designation of editorial responsibilities within news organisations. Whereas in the 1960s and 1970s 'labour' and 'industrial' correspondents were elite specialist correspondents, through the 1980s and 1990s their number and prestige diminished in the face of the rise of financial correspondents. This is at once an expression of macro politico-economic shifts and a compounding factor in these processes.

It is also clear from Manning's work that journalists' perceptions of the political role and characteristics of trade unions frame their utilisation as news sources, and accounts for the emphasis on their conflictive rather than constructive roles. To use a distinction developed by Peter Golding and myself (1994), trade unions are used as 'advocates' by journalists – i.e. organisations whose interventions are framed by the interests of the constituencies they represent. As news discourse is inherently conflictive, this can enhance their news value in political disputes, but the perception of unions' partiality prevents their deployment as 'arbiters' in news coverage. Arbiters are experts used by journalists to adjudicate 'objectively' over public issues or the actions of others, and their interventions can have a crucial impact on framing media treatment of specific subjects. Thus to influence the terms of media debate at this level, as Davis demonstrates in his case study, trade unions often have to recruit the support of external experts to validate their arguments, and it is often necessary to maintain a degree of public dissociation between the union and the expert, for fear that any links may erode the perceived authoritativeness of the latter's proclamations. This trend contrasts with common strategies deployed within the voluntary sector, where publicists strive to encourage a situation of *association* between the work of a voluntary organisation and the views of significant public figures. Moreover, as we shall see, some voluntary organisations are permitted to speak as arbiters in their own right.

The Voluntary Sector in the News

In contrast to the union sector, the voluntary sector in the UK has expanded exponentially over the last 30 years. Volatility in patterns of public and corporate giving and major changes in the source and structure of statutory support for the sector, however, have meant that voluntary organisations are having to compete for a shifting, and in some regards, shrinking financial pool. At the same time, broader quandaries have emerged about the appropriate political and social function the sector should fulfil. Whilst successive governments have encouraged an expanded role in service provision, they have been less enthusiastic about an increase in these organisations' political influence. This is at variance with a growing consensus within the sector that organisations should adopt a more active campaigning approach. It also increases the potential for conflict, as political advocacy can lead groups into an oppositional stance to the institutions that support them.

All of these factors have intensified communication issues in the sector, and have led many to expand and professionalise their public communication and marketing activities to meet these challenges. Between 1988 and 1993 the aggregate annual expenditure on voluntary sector-based advertising increased from £18 million to £35 million, and this pattern has continued apace. Studies have also consistently demonstrated that this development in paid public communication activities (advertising, mailshots, etc.) has been very uneven, suggesting a widening gulf between the leading charities and the rest (e.g. Pharoah and Welchman 1997).

One possible solution is for less well-resourced agencies to focus their promotional efforts on attracting mainstream media coverage. But, here again, voluntary organisations confront uncertainty, owing to changes in the broader media environment. For example, the growing pressure on public service broadcasting has created worries about how well voluntary groups will fare in a market-led media system.

Media Coverage of Voluntary Organisations

Research into media reporting of voluntary organisations has identified several broad trends in media coverage of the sector (Deacon 1999; Deacon et al. 1995). Coverage tends to cluster around general and non-contentious areas of voluntary and charitable activity (e.g. children, animals and health) and to neglect organisations working in minority or contentious issue domains (e.g. the 'black voluntary sector'). Voluntary organisations receive more coverage for their deeds (fundraising, doing good works, etc.) than for their political interventions (raising topics, adjudicating upon the views or actions of others, providing information, etc.). When voluntary sector sources are included as commentators, their most common role is a 'signalling' one: highlighting issues and concern for public debate rather than directly engaging in the cut and thrust of political argument. This funnelling in the representation of voluntary organisations is more apparent in some media sectors than others. The national tabloid press and local press, in particular, seem more likely to focus coverage around fundraising initiatives and other 'good works'. In contrast, national TV and radio news give greatest prominence to the political interventions of voluntary agencies as 'signallers' and 'critics'. However, unlike much union reporting, instances of direct media criticism are rare. Finally, scant attention has been paid to the broader political questions raised by the expanding role and importance of the voluntary sector in Britain (e.g. concerns about ensuring appropriate levels of public accountability in what is now a multi-billion pound sector, and the implications of a transition from a grant- to contract-based system of statutory sector funding). The overall picture that emerges is of limited but indulgent media treatment, based on a somewhat antiquated impression of the sector (Brindle 1999: 44).

Voluntary Organisations as News Sources

Research into communication and media strategies in the sector confirm an increasing, but perhaps more uneven, emphasis on public communication to that noted in the union sector. For example, a recent survey of voluntary organisations (Deacon 1996) found that less than one-third of organisations had designated press and/or publicity officer(s), which is a significantly lower proportion than Davis found in his survey of trade unions. Just over half had distributed a news release or organised a press conference in the preceding year, and a small majority conducted any form of formal media monitoring. Moreover, these activities were all significantly linked to organisations' material resources. Organisations with paid employees, the largest annual budgets, and a national sphere of operations were more likely to produce formal publicity material, engage in news management, recruit external marketing expertise and monitor media output. The survey also revealed that these organisation types reported significantly higher and more diverse levels of mainstream media coverage, and a greater appetite for more. Collectively, these findings suggest that the media are exacerbating rather than reducing the communication gap between the well resourced and the rest.

However, the survey also suggested that the money–coverage link can be disrupted by other factors. Voluntary organisations that reported most regular parliamentary and central government contact also indicated the highest levels of media contact. Moreover, when 'governmental proximity' was controlled, resourcing factors were no longer consistent predictors of media contact. For example, organisations with paid staff that had the most regular central government contact were more likely to have gained media exposure than groups dependent on volunteers who had equivalent contact. In contrast, 'governmental proximity' retained a statistically significant link with media contact, even when the availability of paid employees was controlled.

Second, 'campaign-focused' organisations (as distinct from those principally concerned with 'caring/service/advice', 'self-help' and 'other functions') reported most contact across all media sectors and were more likely to feature as 'commentators' in hard news coverage. But they were no more professionalised than other organisations in their communication work, spent no more on publicity activities, and only shared a broad enthusiasm for media attention. Where they did differ was in the motives they ascribed to their publicity-seeking via the media. These proved to be significantly more externally orientated and 'issue' based. The same principle applied to the better resourced, professionalised organisations, who also displayed consistently broader communicative agendas than smaller organisations. But multivariate analysis showed that 'organisational resources' and 'campaign orientation' had independently significant links with media contact.

The fact that financial factors alone do not account for differences in media contact shows that strategic actions can at least partially offset the logic of capital. It also highlights the need to consider the mediating role of news professionals.

Journalists' Perspectives

In interviews, journalists emphasised two criteria that influenced whether voluntary agencies receive coverage: 'topicality' and 'generality'. 'Topicality' is mainly used to test the value of voluntary sector information in 'hard news' terms. As the sector was not identified by national journalists, in particular, as a significant leadership arena in its own right, voluntary organisations have to conform to news agendas determined by other powerful agencies and events. One consequence of this is that voluntary organisations working in areas that become topical in the news agendas might suddenly find the media very receptive to their views.

The criterion of 'generality' reflects journalists' concerns about audience maximisation and is more of a 'soft news' test. It creates a preference among journalists for a 'big charity' with demonstrable widespread support, which deals with issues of a general and non-contentious nature.

Aside from news value judgements, journalists' views were also framed by an additional tier of judgements about credibility. News reporting in the main strives to be an authoritative discourse. With the voluntary sector, the issue of authoritativeness is less clear-cut than it is with other NGOs, even unions (which have a demonstrable constituency and an elected mandate), as anybody can set up a voluntary group and make inflated claims for their work.

Journalists appeared to make clear distinctions when assessing the credibility of voluntary organisations, and these influenced how and whether organisations were reported. Furthermore, these judgements operated as a filtering mechanism, leading to the exclusion of voluntary agencies seen to lack credibility. This helps explain the uncritical tone of voluntary group coverage. In most cases a 'critique by exclusion' operated in which organisations deemed to have questionable motives or dubious competence were ignored rather than castigated: their lack of intrinsic news status militating against any sustained media attack.

The issue of credibility also influenced those occasions when voluntary agencies were invited to comment on issues in the news. Journalists often welcomed the partiality of organisations prepared to make critical interventions on broader matters of public policy, which explains the greater media prominence of campaign-focused organisations, who were most orientated to external debate and therefore most likely to provide the controversial news-bites upon which journalists depend.

Journalists made clear distinctions as to which organisations' views could be taken on their own merits, which required further corroboration or balancing, and which should be completely ignored. On this point, many news professionals drew sharp distinctions between campaign-orientated groups and other types of voluntary and charitable agencies, particularly service providers. Campaign groups were seen to lack the involvement and support of an identifiable client group, which, in the journalists' eyes, lent authority to the views and opinions of those organisations that possessed such a base.

For this reason, campaign-orientated groups were considered more useful as 'advocates' rather than 'arbiters': a source of controversial reaction, rather than informed comment. In contrast, the views of caring and service-providing organisations were often given greater credence, because they were seen to be based on practical experience rather than political opinions. By the same token, the greater the range and representativeness of an organisation, the more authority was attributed to its views, because this increased the breadth of interests it could claim to represent. Official links with, and recognition by, government also served to enhance estimations of an organisation's political credibility.

This demonstrates how different factors work interactively to fashion patterns of inclusion and exclusion, and the prevailing importance of media logic. The predominant portrayal of voluntary organisations as 'doing good works' in a 'soft news' context, rather than as engaged political actors in a 'hard news' context, is partly bound up in journalists' uncertainties about the authoritativeness of many voluntary agencies as commentators on public matters, but also reflects the reticence or inability of many voluntary agencies to engage consistently with the media in this more controversial context. Furthermore, the research shows that newsworthiness is not just determined by the efficient distribution of publicity, but also the nature of the messages being produced. Smaller organisations appeared not only least able to invest in formal press and publicity work, but also to have the most instrumental and limited communicative agendas, which also acted to inhibit their appeal to news professionals (who repeatedly criticised the failure of many voluntary agencies to extrapolate their messages effectively and to stress their broader significance).

This latter point highlights an essential problem with the suggestion that mainstream media coverage can somehow compensate for growing divisions in public communication paid for and initiated by organisations themselves. Ironically, by seeking to use media publicity for instrumental purposes (fundraising, volunteer recruitment, etc.), organisations inadvertently prepare the basis for their exclusion.

Of course, these are tendencies rather than deterministic trends. Strategic actions and effective political networking can compensate for limited financial resources and enable smaller organisations to win considerable media exposure. But there are limits to how far agencies are in control of their own media destiny. Astute media-centred campaigning may gain organisations prominence as 'advocates' of a particular viewpoint or interest group, but it cannot enable them to win status as 'arbiters' in news. This role is conferred by the news professionals and rests on their judgements about the political status and cultural capital of specific organisations. And in this respect, as in many others, the well resourced, the widely known and the well connected enjoy conspicuous and considerable advantages.

Quangos: Publicity by Appointment

As with the voluntary sector, the quasi-governmental sector has expanded considerably over the recent period. According to one estimate, quangos now control a collective budget of £60.4 billion in the UK: representing a third of all public expenditure and a 45 per cent real term increase since 1979 (Weir and Hall 1996). These changes have prompted debate about their broader democratic and constitutional implications. To whom are these public bodies accountable? Is their 'arms-length' relationship a smoke screen for enacting government policy beyond parliamentary and public redress? Do they represent a more efficient and independent means for conducting public business? Who gets appointed to these public bodies, and on what basis?

The mid-1990s witnessed intense political debate about the role of quasi-government in Britain. Central to this debate were allegations about endemic secrecy that was claimed to prevent any effective monitoring of quangos' activities, not least by journalists. Many of these assertions were based on two connections that were taken as axiomatic. Because quangos' political authority is not bestowed by the public, they were assumed to lack any incentive to care whether public or other non-state sources knew of their activities or held them in esteem. Furthermore, as there were few official requirements for quangos to be open about their activities, it was taken that these opportunities for inscrutability and secrecy were widely exploited.

There are grounds for suspecting that the matter is more complicated than has been suggested. For example, although quangos are not elected by the public, many fulfil highly significant public roles. Given this engagement, it seems implausible that all quangos can be oblivious of their wider political context. Furthermore, very few, if any, organisations operate in a state of complete secrecy. As Downing comments, 'Secrecy is not used as an impermeable shield blotting out all communication, but as a device to allow the pinnacle of the power structure to communicate how and when it prefers' (1986: 14). Recognition of this point shifts the focus away from a model of total disengagement towards one that is more attuned to analysing the terms of external engagement. Opening up these questions does not deny the validity of concerns about secrecy and freedom of information, it contextualises them – revealing them as part of the picture, rather than the entirety. It also enables us to appreciate how strategies of disclosure (publicity) can help protect the private realms of an organisation by assuaging or redirecting external scrutiny (Ericson et al. 1989).

Media Coverage of Quangos

Recent research suggests that quangos appear with greater regularity in mainstream media coverage than voluntary agencies, even though in aggregate terms they are less numerous than the thousands of voluntary and charitable organisations currently in existence (Deacon and Monk 2000). As with voluntary organisations, reporting was found to cluster around an elite band of executive and regulatory agencies, with other agencies receiving more variable and unpredictable exposure. Significantly lower levels of coverage were found in the national tabloid press, and this cannot solely be explained by the more limited news space available in these sectors. There was a paucity of coverage of 'advisory' quangos (despite their crucial significance in the formulation of public policy) and routine coverage of specific quangos concentrated on their public functions or external engagement with other political institutions and sources. There was comparatively little coverage given to the internal scrutiny of these bodies (e.g. the specific operations of the appointment process).

As with voluntary organisations, specific organisations were only occasionally subjected to direct editorial criticism or attack from other quoted sources. Routine coverage tended towards a neutral, even anodyne, treatment of quangos in action. This contrasted with media discourses about broader principles of quasi-government, which were entirely negative. In general terms, quangos were characterised as proliferating wildly, and as secretive, remote and unaccountable. Unlike media neglect of the broader politics of voluntary sector expansion, mainstream media attention to broader political questions related to the role of quangos has been episodically intense. Between 1994 and 1996 there was a concentrated episode of media interest in these issues, which has reduced considerably over the more recent period (and even though the 'quasi-fication' of government functions continues apace).

Collectively, these results point to inconsistencies in quango-related coverage. On an abstract level, journalists repudiate 'new managerialist' arguments that these bodies introduce greater efficiency and expertise to policy formulation and implementation, but these claims gain some implicit acceptance in specific treatment of individual quangos, which tends to emphasise the expertise of these bodies and their dissociation from the party political sphere.

Quangos as News Sources

As with unions and voluntary organisations, recent research suggests quangos' media and publicity activities have expanded over recent years. In a survey of British quangos conducted in 1999, 67 per cent said their investment in these areas had increased over the preceding three years (Deacon and Monk 2001). Additionally, there seemed greater levels of, and less variability in, formal provision for media relations than has been found in the voluntary sector. Three-quarters of responding agencies had staff with formally designated responsibilities for media and publicity, and the majority felt resourcing for this work was at least adequate. This suggests that the high level of media coverage of quangos is at least in part due to the actions of these quangos, an interpretation further supported by the finding that advisory bodies (which received the least media exposure) invested considerably less in media and publicity activities than executive agencies.

Therefore, the latest data challenge the common stereotype of quangos as almost pathologically introverted, but show some quangos have been more fulsome in their embrace of promotionalism than others. Just as Manning found with unions, in some quangos the media and publicity offices occupy a highly peripheral role, whereas for others their contribution is deemed integral. This in part reflects differences in the material resources available to different types of bodies (for example, many advisory bodies have no paid staff of their own and are serviced by a secretariat drawn from their sponsoring government department), but it also reflects the disposition of the most senior figures within the quango. As quangos are highly hierarchical agencies, the disposition of these key internal figures has a pervasive influence on the publicity orientation of individual organisations. Several interviewees claimed that a distinct culture change had occurred within their organisation following the appointment of a senior figure with a more receptive attitude towards media and publicity concerns.

When identifying the main audiences quangos sought to target in their publicity work, more cited 'the public' and 'customers/clients' than other elite professional or political sources (ministers, local government, business sector, etc.). Again, this seems to contradict the established view that these appointed bodies are more concerned about 'up-line accountability' to government than 'down-line accountability' to the public. However, additional comments made by senior PR personnel in interviews suggest that most quangos perceive accountability in different ways. Responsibilities to the public were consistently described in abstract terms. The public had an essentially canonical presence, as a collective that agencies felt responsible for, rather than beholden to. In contrast, accountability to government was described in precise contractual terms, which required the existence of other more direct forms of communication and consultation than that facilitated through public communication.

The implications of this distinction came through most clearly in agencies' discussions of their publicity motives. Here it is useful to introduce a further series of conceptual distinctions. First, between the use of publicity to facilitate internal scrutiny of organisations' operations (*internal accountability*) and to aid organisations' engagement with their broader political environment (*external engagement*). Second, within this latter category, between media and publicity use to promote the reputation of the agency itself (*organisation promotion*) and to advance issues, practices or values relevant to an organisation's public role (*role promotion*).

There was little evidence that quangos' publicity work was mainly driven by concerns about internal accountability, although the political furore surrounding accountability in the sector did seem to have had some impact on baseline information provision. Many quangos used publicity as a means of focusing attention away from excessive public scrutiny of their founding principles and onto their ongoing practice, not necessarily for any sinister reasons, but because excessive internal scrutiny of an organisation's remit and composition was seen to undermine their authority and frustrate their operational functions.

If publicity was geared mainly towards promoting quangos' external engagement, the importance of organisational promotion and role promotion tended to vary depending upon the audience an organisation was seeking to address publicly. Organisational promotion seemed least important in down-line communication to the general public, where the emphasis seemed to fall on instructing rather than impressing public opinion. Although this didacticism also infused public communication activities aimed at more specialised political and professional audiences, the more prestigious and influential the target concerned, the more organisational promotion shaded into the equation. This sensitivity seemed particularly acute with government sources.

These differences contrast with the media and publicity strategies of unions and voluntary organisations, which respectively place considerable emphasis on establishing a public profile and recruiting public support for their causes. This probably reflects the specific political characteristics of quangos. Because their political authority is not dependent upon public support, they can afford to be more self-effacing in down-line communication. But as appointed bodies, they need to be more mindful of their political patrons and other influential opinion leaders in their spheres of operations, for in hard political terms, these opinions matter very greatly. But even when seeking to impress, the quangos we analysed preferred to convey a dispassionate demeanour, mainly out of deference to the underlying ethos of 'arms-length' government, which is supposed to be characterised by selfless public service and political detachment. Again this offers a point of contrast with NGOs in the union and voluntary sectors, which often seek to press their claims through ardent and emotive appeals.

This is not to suggest that these organisations lack any meaningful autonomy in their operations or their communication activities. In fact, many quangos seemed highly self-determinate in public communication terms and saw public communication as an important means of demonstrating their independence. But this amounts to licensed autonomy, rather than absolute freedom. Government influence, in particular, tends to be exerted strategically, through the designation of quangos' roles and the appointment of senior personnel. Additionally, some agencies are permitted a longer leash than others in their public activities, reflecting the different structural relations between particular types of quangos and the centres of executive authority.

Journalists' Perspectives

Interviews with journalists confirmed that there is some confusion suggested in the content analysis findings in their attitudes towards quasi-governmental bodies. On an abstract level, most journalists were aware of recent critical debate about the expansion of 'the quango state', if somewhat uninterested in it (for most, it was seen as an old story that had run its course). The majority construed the term 'quango' as a negative rather than descriptive term and were reluctant to apply it to agencies that, in their view, provided valuable public service. When presented with a list of prominently reported quangos working in their subject area and asked which qualified as 'quangos', there were widely inconsistent responses. This suggests that although a professional consensus exists that quangos *per se* are somehow a bad thing, there is a singular lack of clarity as to the defining characteristics of quasi-governmental bodies.

Journalists were also asked to comment in detail on their relations with the quangos they frequently contacted in their news-gathering work. Very few voiced criticisms about these organisations' performance as information providers, most saw them as high-status organisations and very few could cite occasions where they had been directly refused information requested. Although this latter point may indicate a reassuring openness and accountability in quangos, it probably says more about the essentially reactive nature of news-gathering in relation to quasi-government. For example, most of the journalists we interviewed had only a vague awareness of various Freedom of Information proposals relevant to quangos, and most were not aware of their existing rights of access. It is also important to note how complicit these practices are with the promotional strategies of quangos, which seek to emphasise their external engagement rather than facilitate internal scrutiny.

Collectively, these comments suggest a contradiction in journalists' thinking about the authoritativeness and credibility of quangos. Whereas in principle they are readily characterised as 'advocates', cynically prosecuting the agenda of the state and other dominant interests, yet in specific instances they often gain a reputation as significant 'arbiters' in their policy areas. In these instances, the source of their legitimacy in part depends upon their effective communication strategies and general impression management (as is the case with unions and voluntary organisations), but also relates to their officially sanctioned status. 'Being taken seriously by government' can have a significant halo effect in media terms for voluntary agencies. The fact that this is a structural ingredient for quangos routinely serves to enhance their accreditation by media professionals.

Conclusion

These case studies demonstrate how publicity and communication issues have attained greater significance for NGOs over recent years, but also reveal the problems in overgeneralising in this area. The communication motives of different NGOs are to some extent dictated by the specific context of their operations, but there are also structural variations, reflecting the different political and economic roles of various NGO sectors. For example, as most quangos receive stable statutory funding, they will tend to place less emphasis on financial resourcing motives than do voluntary organisations, where dependency on public and corporate giving is high, and their financial state is generally more parlous. On another level, trade unions will tend to be more comfortable with open issue campaigning than voluntary organisations and quangos, partly because of their 'primary' political function, but also because they are not bound by conventions and regulations governing neutral public management and non-party-political charitable activity.

NGOs in different sectors tend to emphasise different types of communication motives depending upon their intended targets. When communicating with the public, unions and voluntary organisations generally prioritise 'role promotion' and 'organisation promotion', whereas with most quangos 'role promotion' is deemed more important than 'organisation promotion'. Conversely, in terms of government relations, quangos often place considerable emphasis on 'organisation promotion'. Again, this reflects the differing political contexts of each sector. Quangos' political influence is far less dependent upon public opinion than is the case for unions and voluntary organisations. However, their closer structural ties with government mean they have to be more circumspect in their dealings with official sources.

Finally, journalists' assessments of the news value and credibility of different NGOs have an impact upon how and when they are reported. In many respects, these appraisals are again highly context-specific, and link to the effectiveness (or otherwise) of the particular public communication strategies of individual NGOs. But structural variations can also be identified. Journalists' perceptions of unions' essentially political function mean they can only ever be cast as 'advocates' in coverage, however effectively they manage their media relations. With voluntary organisations and quangos, the situation is more flexible, offering some organisations the opportunity to be cast not just as participants in public debate, but also 'arbiters' in these areas.

CHAPTER SUMMARY

- Interest has developed recently in examining the influence non-governmental organisations can exert upon, and through, media discourses.

- This development is in large part explained by the proliferation of interest groups and spread of 'issue politics' in many political systems.

- There are difficulties in generalising about NGOs and the media relations because of the diversity of organisations that can be classified as 'non-governmental'.

- This chapter compares and contrasts media and publicity issues related to three types of NGOs in the UK: trade unions, voluntary organisations and quasi-autonomous non-governmental organisations ('quangos').

- A similar 'professionalisation' of media and publicity activities can be discerned in all three sectors, albeit for distinct and different historical reasons.

- Journalists' general conceptions about the characteristics of each sector have a significant impact on delimiting how, and how often, specific trade unions, charities and quangos are reported.

Notes

1 The voluntary sector and quango sections are based on research conducted at Loughborough University and funded by the ESRC (references: R000233193, R000236953).

2 The discussion here is based on an extensive definition of 'quasi-government' covering officially 'recognised' quangos (i.e. executive non-departmental public bodies, advisory non-departmental public bodies and tribunals) and 'non-recognised' agencies ('local public spending bodies', national health service bodies, 'next step' agencies, official regulators, nationalised industries and public corporations).

CHAPTER 7

Environmental Activism and News Media

Alison Anderson

This chapter focuses upon the strategies used by environmental pressure groups and activists to secure news access and representation. It explores the different techniques they deploy and their attitudes towards mainstream and alternative media. The environment provides a rich field of enquiry for exploring the relationship between news sources and the media. Indeed, this was the focus of some of the first UK empirical studies to explore the potential for non-official sources to influence news agendas successfully (see Anderson 1991, 1997). Over recent decades a few powerful environmental pressure groups have become significant players in the global policy-making arena and have become very well attuned to the demands of the news media. Alongside this there has been a proliferation of locally based grassroots networks, often possessing an ambivalent attitude to the mainstream media. In the UK activists have been involved in various anti-road actions and, more recently, in campaigns against the release of genetically modified organisms into the environment. These different groups face their own distinctive dilemmas concerning the development of media strategies and the use of alternative channels of communication.

Through case studies the chapter charts how and why different environmental groups and activists seek to secure media coverage and the reasons for their eventual news representation. The first case study involves Greenpeace and the furore over the intended sinking of the Brent Spar oil platform in June 1995. The second case study focuses upon the media portrayal of 'Swampy', the anti-roads protestor who gained media celebrity status in 1997 as a result of the campaign against a proposed new section of the A30 at Fairmile, Devon. In drawing upon these examples, we shall tease out some of the complexities that inform the way different environmental groups and activists seek to secure media representation. Despite sometimes competing against powerful institutional sources, environmental groups can gain considerable media access. However, the resulting media coverage is not necessarily on their terms and sources are constrained in several respects concerning how the issues are 'packaged'. The sheer amount of media coverage gained is, in itself, an inadequate indicator of success, since this depends upon how the issues are framed and the degree to which wider political objectives are realised.

Theorising Issues of Source Access

As mentioned in previous chapters of this book, it has commonly been claimed that the news media provide privileged access to official sources such as the government and the courts (see Hall et al. 1978). There are a number of empirical studies that lend support to this view. Undeniably powerful institutional sources generally enjoy advantaged access to the news media. Yet, during the 1990s a number of studies suggested that Hall et al.'s arguments need to be qualified in various ways to take account of the complexities of source–media interaction (e.g. Schlesinger 1990; Anderson 1991, 1993; Deacon and Golding 1994; Kitzinger and Reilly 1997). While Hall et al.'s theory of primary definers provides a very useful framework for identifying the structural relationship of powerful sources with the media, it underestimated the degree to which primary definitions are challenged and negotiated. The critique of Hall et al.'s theory of primary definers has stimulated a number of questions. These include:

- how the relationship between particular news sources and the media changes over time;

- the extent of inequalities of access both within powerful institutional sources and marginal sources themselves;

- the ways in which news media agendas may interact with those of political elites – on occasions where the media may be seen as acting as a primary rather than a secondary definer; and

- the strategies that marginal sources can best employ in order to influence news media agendas.

By empirically analysing the success or otherwise of the media strategies of politically marginal groups, we can learn a great deal about the institutional disadvantages that they have to contend with, as well as the factors that favour institutionally powerful sources in getting their messages across (Schlesinger 1990). It is important to recognise that non-official sources experience differing levels of access to the news media (Anderson 2000; Manning 2001). There are dangers in lumping a diverse range of groups into one category. We therefore want to distinguish between interest groups (such as the National Farmers' Union (NFU)), transnational pressure groups (such as Greenpeace International) and radical grassroots networks (such as Earth First!). Even within these categories there are important differences in terms of organisational structure and tactics. Until relatively recently the majority of research in this area has focused upon media organisations rather than source organisations. As Schlesinger observes:

> Once one begins to analyse the tactics and strategies pursued by sources seeking media attention, to ask about their perception of other, competing, actors in the fields over which they are trying to exert influence, to enquire about the financial resources at their disposal and the organisational contexts in which they operate, to ask about their goals

and notions of effectiveness, one rapidly discovers how ignorant we are about such matters – and this despite the undoubted importance of the contribution that production studies have made to the field. *(Schlesinger 1990: 62)*

Ericson et al. (1989: 262) point out that, despite studies such as those conducted by Gitlin (1980) and Goldenberg (1975) on resource-poor organisations, it remains an under-conceptualised area. As Schlesinger (1990) argues, orthodox approaches within this field have been media-centric, in that the bulk of their attention has tended to be directed towards how the news media use sources and has rarely considered the perspectives of the sources themselves. Case studies of environmental reporting reveal some of the complexities and contingencies that govern the accessing of different 'voices'. Interviews with environment correspondents and environmental pressure groups suggest that the situation, as applied to environmental reporting, which is the specific focus of this chapter, is more dynamic that Hall et al. would lead us to conclude (Anderson 1997). However, as Schlesinger makes clear, adopting a source-centred approach (through considering the strategies advanced by non-official sources) should not be seen as exclusively pluralistic. It makes just as much sense for researchers to attempt to address this from within a theory that sees the media as having considerable dependence upon the State. As we shall see, competing sources have differing levels of 'information subsidies' in terms of resources such as cost and time, which affects how far the media rely upon them on a routine basis. We shall begin by considering news strategies among organised environmental pressure groups before moving on to examine the ways in which grassroots activists secure news access and representation.

Ecological Activism among Organised Pressure Groups

Environmental groups adopt a variety of different strategies depending upon the nature of the organisation, the type of issues they wish to expose and the political context. One can locate the evolution of the environmental lobby within the broader context of the movement towards growing professionalism and political activism among pressure groups in general. Since the 1960s in the case of Britain there has been a significant increase in organised lobbying accompanied by the emergence of single-issue pressure groups with a more proactive approach to the media (Anderson 1997). Over past decades environmental demands have become increasingly institutionalised in Western Europe. During the 1980s and 1990s globalisation and the growing impact of new media technologies brought about a new emphasis on global marketing. Whilst there was heavy reliance upon dramatic media stunts during the 1970s, now there is more emphasis placed upon behind-the-scenes lobbying. Communication strategies are influenced by a number of different factors both internal and external to the organisation concerned. Four principal issues we shall discuss here are resource mobilisation, targeting, insider and outsider strategies and, finally, issue cycles and policy changes.

Resource Mobilisation

To some degree, success in defining a social issue as a problem is a reflection of the level of resources (members, time, financial base, media access) that an organisation commands. Goldenberg's (1975) study of resource-poor interest groups in Boston found they tended to experience much more difficulty in securing access to the news media than did official sources. Access to the press appeared to be closely connected with the perceived credibility of the group, which was in turn linked to the organisation's size, finance, public relations skills, expertise and geographical base. Here the concept of 'cultural capital' is relevant. In brief, this refers to the differing cultural competence, assets and skills possessed by news sources. However, resources alone by no means ensure that an environmental organisation is successful in attaining its goals. As Cracknell argues:

> getting coverage is only half the battle, getting the coverage to say what you want it to is another battle altogether . . . Environmentalists must not only have the resources to be able to produce their claims and command attention for them, they must also render their concerns in such a way that their case appears credible through the media. (*Cracknell 1993: 14*)

International environmental pressure groups like Friends of the Earth or Greenpeace have built up significant resource bases in recent years and in some senses operate as transnational corporations. However, whilst this may aid them in accessing the news media, effectively framing issues in their terms is much more difficult. Moreover, their opponents are typically huge transnational companies who have their own PR departments and spend considerable sums of money in promoting their 'green' image.

Targeting

Environmental organisations may target a number of different arenas in pursuit of their goals. These include the Houses of Parliament, the civil service, the European Union, industry, public inquiries, the academic community, political parties and the education system. Hilgartner and Bosk (1988) propose a 'public arenas model' in which they establish key fields in which claims-makers sponsor issues. In contrast to earlier organisations, contemporary groups tend to employ more radical campaign tactics and develop more proactive approaches to the media. Increasingly they employ skilled public relations personnel from journalistic backgrounds. Books such as Des Wilson and Leighton Andrews' (1993) *Campaigning* provide practical advice on things like putting a publicity plan together, producing press releases and campaign newspapers, and organising press conferences. Schlesinger and Tumber (1994: 39) identify a number of conditions that frequently affect a source's ability to reach its goals:

1   That the source has a well-defined message to communicate, framed in optimal terms capable of satisfying news values.

2   That the optimal locations for placing that particular message have been identified, as have the target audiences of the media outlets concerned.

3   That the preconditions for communicative 'success' have been assured so far as possible by, for instance, cultivating a sympathetic contact or fine-tuning the timing of a leak.

4   That the anticipated strategies of others (which may include support as much as opposition) are incorporated in ongoing media strategies. Support may be harnessed by coalition building. Opposition may, for instance, be countered by astute timing or discrediting its credibility.

5   That means exist for monitoring and evaluating the impact of a given strategy or tactic and for adjusting future action in the light of what is reflexively learned.

6   That some messages may be as much intended for private as public communication, thus operating on at least two levels.

Insider and Outsider Strategies

As Cracknell (1993) observes, it is useful to distinguish between two main types of strategy: insider strategies and outsider strategies. Briefly, insider strategies involve targeting government through the bureaucratic machinery and policy communities. Insider groups enjoy routine communication with governmental committees and actively participate in policy discussions, though often on a sporadic basis. Friends of the Earth has earned a reputation for political lobbying and campaigning through using educational arenas including the scientific community, as well as targeting the media. Outsider strategies, by contrast, seek attention through bringing about mass public concern through the media to try to force the government to change track. Greenpeace, for example, have often used these confrontational tactics in the past to generate mounting public outcry.

Issue Cycles and Policy Changes

Cracknell (1993) usefully distinguishes between 'focused' and 'diffuse' pressure. As he observes, media exposure may be particularly effective when the issue involves a clear-cut decision. In other cases, generalising an issue may lead to more interest from policy-makers since it can be harnessed to policy principles, and makes more use of their skills.

Over time targets may well change. Many pressure groups focus their attention on attracting media attention during the early stages and later on devote more of their energies to parliamentary activities. Strategic decisions involve weighing up the climate of public opinion, as well as considering political support and the stage in the life-cycle of the group.

Together, these four issues can be seen as governing the ways in which environmental pressure groups operate. Decisions about strategic action clearly reflect resource bases as well as the type of issue under debate, the life-cycle of the group and the weight of public opinion behind the issue. The following section focuses upon Greenpeace as an example of an environmental pressure group that has become increasingly attuned to the news values of large media organisations.

Greenpeace and the Brent Spar Affair

Greenpeace has become particularly sophisticated in using the media to exert pressure on the global market and in many ways acts like a transnational corporation. With approximately 30 offices worldwide, it operates at an international level and has its largest offices located in the UK, the Netherlands, Germany and the United States. The press desk operates on a 24-hour basis and the pressure group employs a range of professionally skilled staff with backgrounds in the media and public relations. Greenpeace communications, based in Amsterdam, possesses a full in-house photographic, video and film capability including a digital sound studio, three editing suites, a small television studio and footage archives. In addition, this incorporates compressed satellite encoders and decoders and three-dimensional computer graphics. Within environmental reporting there is also a tendency for the media to focus upon conflict and, as such, confrontational items involving 'goodies' and 'baddies' are seen as having particular audience appeal (Anderson 1997; Lowe and Morrison 1984). Greenpeace have become particularly adept at tuning into these news values. As Chris Rose, Campaigns Director at Greenpeace in 1990, observed:

> What Greenpeace are very good at is they've invented, if you like, a sort of morality play . . . You've got to have the pictures, it doesn't matter what they're talking about, you've got to have the pictures. So that takes Greenpeace straight out of the editorial system of gatekeepers . . . and it puts them in the same sort of news as the royal family/entertainment news . . . If you can't deal with it in those terms, and their formula, they can't really campaign on it, which is one reason they've stuck with boats on the high seas and are therefore not affected by things like trespass law. Issues are simplified, they're global problem issues and they're David and Goliath, a sort of pantomime I suppose. (*Cited in Anderson 1997*)

Previous studies have noted how Greenpeace has increasingly invested more energy in developing its science, as in the past it lacked credibility in the eyes of some journalists (for example, Anderson 1997). In the late 1980s Rob Edwards observed:

> The irony is that over the past few years Greenpeace has been making genuine attempts to beef up its scientific credibility. It has devoted more resources to research, to report writing, to conventional lobbying techniques. It has also sharpened up its advertising and begun direct mail shots. These changes have in turn annoyed some of the direct action traditionalists, who fear loss of purity and effectiveness. (*Edwards 1988: 18*)

A content analysis study conducted by Hansen (1993b) found that Greenpeace achieved a large amount of coverage in the UK press over the period 1986–91, and tended to be portrayed as a legitimate and credible actor. However, Hansen notes that:

> Greenpeace succeeds quite differently in getting coverage on different issues; in particular, it would appear that the more saturated the media arena is with a particular issue, the smaller the claimsmaking power of Greenpeace on that particular issue . . . The more detailed analysis of the ups and downs of issue coverage also indicated that Greenpeace's ability to gain coverage is closely related to its major campaign initiatives. *(Hansen 1993b: 176)*

This suggests that while Greenpeace is often successful in gaining campaign-related coverage, it is not routinely accessed by journalists in the same way that many official sources are. Instead, it tends to rely upon using graphic visual images to operate as 'signs' that generate public outcry and are intended to force an issue on to the political agenda. Claiming and securing legitimacy is a much harder task for an environmental group than simply gaining news media attention (Hansen 2000).

The above points are well illustrated by the Greenpeace campaign over the dumping of the redundant Brent Spar oil installation. In early 1995 Greenpeace obtained a copy of the plans of the multinational oil giant, Royal Dutch/Shell, to sink the Spar in the Atlantic Ocean. The protesters argued that Shell had not properly considered alternatives to deep-sea disposal and would establish a dangerous precedent. During the summer of 1995, Greenpeace activists occupied the oil installation, located roughly mid-way between Britain (Shetland) and Norway. It was not long before the German arm of Greenpeace proposed extending the occupation from a couple of weeks to months, with the objective of preventing Shell from removing it, and at the same time promoting the broader message of 'Save the Seas'. During May and June the campaign gained considerable momentum in Europe, particularly in Germany, where consumer boycotts of Shell petrol garages were co-ordinated by local organisations. Before this major stunt the issue of the decommissioning of redundant oil installations in the North Sea had attracted relatively little interest.

Greenpeace actions over the Brent Spar illustrate the increasing sophistication of major international environmental pressure groups, which have become particularly skilled in exploiting the power of the media and, in so doing, striking wider chords with the public. Initially it was the European news media that showed most interest in Shell's plans, but as politicians began to get involved, the UK news media woke up to the story. During the controversy national television stations in Britain relied very heavily upon raw footage of the events supplied by Greenpeace, since this saved them time as well as money – particularly during a period when news budgets were under some pressure. Greenpeace made considerable use of the latest advancements in media technology and provided the major news organisations with their own video news releases (VNRs), produced through pictures being scanned into a computer and then digitised images sent via satellite phone link to a news agency. Effective communication and co-ordination of activities through email and the Internet certainly demonstrated the benefit of having a rapid internal communication system.

In a dramatic about-turn in June 1995, Shell announced that they had decided to drop their plans for deep-sea disposal of the platform following considerable international pressure. However, this was followed by an announcement by Greenpeace in September that they had made an error in their estimation of the amount of oil on the platform. This was taken by some media practitioners as an apology for the whole of their case. It was followed by a backlash within the news media, particularly among senior television news personnel, as they expressed concerns that the images may have been manipulated by Greenpeace as they went through their editing suites. At the 1995 Edinburgh Television Festival a senior commissioning editor for Channel 4's news and current affairs commented:

> On Brent Spar we were bounced. This matters – we all took great pains to represent Shell's side of the argument. By the time the broadcasters had tried to intervene on the scientific analysis, the story had been spun far, far into Greenpeace's direction . . . When we attempted to pull the story back, the pictures provided to us showed plucky helicopters riding a fusillade of water cannons. Try and write the analytical science into that to the advantage of words. *(David Lloyd quoted in Rose 1998: 158)*

As Manning (2001) argues, this shows how an underlying scepticism about Greenpeace and its scientific credibility can rapidly reassert itself. The public apology from Greenpeace was followed by a period of intense media scepticism about Greenpeace; thereafter the organisation increasingly resorted to their web pages as a vehicle for getting their side of the story across. Indeed, Greenpeace were very quick off the mark in getting their web site functioning in sharp contrast to Shell, who were reactive. Finally, in January 1998 Shell announced their decision to bring the Spar ashore in Norway and build a new quay extension. Following this, in July 1998 all the governments of the North East Atlantic region agreed a ban on any future dumping of steel-built oil installations. There are, of course, questions raised about the impact of the sustained media attack on Greenpeace's credibility in the long term. Public opinion polls carried out both before and after the Greenpeace apology would seem to suggest on the surface that the organisation did in fact suffer little long-term damage in terms of expressed public attitudes (Rose 1998). Yet, as Hansen observes:

> It is one thing for environmental groups to achieve massive coverage for a short period of time and in relation to specific issues. It is quite a different task to achieve and maintain a position as an 'established', 'authoritative' and 'legitimate' actor in the continuous process of claims-making and policymaking on environmental matters. *(Hansen 1993: 151)*

One of the interesting features of the Brent Spar campaign was the effective utilisation of new media technologies by Greenpeace. The Internet clearly provides potential opportunities for organising petitions and co-ordinating actions across the globe, as well as increasing people's level of knowledge about the issues. Also, new media technologies provide the opportunity for greater co-ordination internally within environmental pressure groups; email was first introduced in 1988 in Greenpeace and it became one of the first environmental organisations to take advantage of such a system. Indeed, the Brent Spar case indicated the merit of having a very fast internal system of communication.

A tour around the current Shell web site illustrates how they have started to take communication with the wider public more seriously. The German boycott of Shell garages is said to have cost Shell Germany about 30 per cent of its normal revenue. Such companies have begun to realise that they can no longer afford to take a reactive approach and we are seeing a growing emphasis upon advocacy within the commercial sector (Bennie 1998). Since the Brent Spar turnabout in June 1995, Shell have spent millions of pounds on public relations, including producing CD ROMs for journalists and schools, and organising 'stakeholder' sessions with environmentalists across Europe. Grassroots environmental activists take a rather different approach to the media than organised pressure groups. The following section looks at the growth of this form of environmentalism and the characteristics of their approaches towards the media.

Grassroots Action and the News Media

Over recent years there has been a significant increase in localised grassroots environmental action across Europe (Doherty 1999b; Grant 2001; Rootes 2000). There are a number of ways in which we may distinguish between the more formally organised groups of the 1970s and the much looser grassroots networks of the 1980s. These networks do not have a fixed, fee-paying membership. Neither do they have a fixed leadership; instead leaders come and go. In fact, there is no recognisable hierarchical structure that characterises the more formally structured organisations. Also, they bring together a very diverse mixture of individuals who tend to favour direct action such as obstructing a bulldozer, as opposed to lobbying government, which is seen as ineffectual. Recently grassroots action has been mobilised within Europe over issues such as the genetic modification of food, and specific road building programmes. The growth of grassroots protest can be seen as one aspect of a wider phenomenon that is often referred to as 'DiY' culture. DiY stands for 'Do it Yourself' and refers to individuals' frustration with the alienating forces of globalism, together with the perception that the existing political structures are ineffective in terms of instigating fundamental social and economic change. According to Derek Wall:

> DiY culture has come to include diverse forms of cultural reproduction, using increasingly sophisticated mass-marketed items of cultural capital including photocopiers, hand-held videos, small presses and cameras. DiY media has acted as both a supplement and an alternative to the conventional mass media, which is often hostile to radical movements. Activists might take lightweight video cameras on 'actions', producing video cassettes that could be circulated to publicise movement activities and, simultaneously, discourage violence from police or security workers who do not wish to be filmed. *(Wall 1999: 160)*

One of the few books to provide an 'insider' account of some of the participants within this protest culture is George McKay's (1998) *DiY Culture*. This provides an interesting, mainly biographically based, account of the roots of this counterculture. Of course, we need to be aware that, like all insider accounts, the analysis is inevitably open to the charge of subjectivity.

Grassroots networks face a number of dilemmas in their relationship with the news media. These may broadly be summarised as involving the following: clash of cultural values, generating attention and commanding legitimacy, hostility to the mainstream media and the use of alternative channels of communication. We shall briefly discuss each of these in turn.

Cultural Values

The dominant values and lifestyle choices held by individuals involved in grassroots actions often openly conflict with those of the news media and the wider social structure. This can considerably strain the relationship between journalists and source. Gamson and Wolfsfeld (1993) provide an interesting analysis of power transactions in media–movement relations. They argue the relationship between social movements and the media tends to be based upon unequal power relations since social movements are more dependent upon the media than the media are on social movements. Additionally, they observe how movements often have different cultures which conflict with mainstream media and political cultures.

While this may apply in the case of many organised pressure groups, it is less applicable when considering looser grassroots networks. It is questionable as to whether they are always more dependent on the media since they often develop their own alternative media. Yet it is important to acknowledge that when the mainstream media do seek coverage, looser grassroots networks are often at a disadvantage since they tend to have no pre-identified spokespersons.

Commanding Legitimacy and Generating Attention

In order to bring about changes in the policy arena, it is necessary not simply to generate media publicity about an issue, but to cultivate 'legitimacy'. There is often an underlying conflict between the need to generate attention about an issue and, at the same time, to be seen as a legitimate source (Cracknell 1993).

Some grassroots networks eschew a credible public image and focus their attention on 'monkey-wrenching' tactics that seek to satisfy immediate, short-term goals. A good example of this is the Animal Liberation Front (ALF), involved in sporadic (often violent) actions against the 'abuse' of animals.

Hostility to the Mainstream Media

Grassroots protesters are often highly disillusioned with the mainstream media and openly hostile. The UK organisation Small World provides us with a useful illustration. Set up in the early 1990s by a small number of campaigners with film-making backgrounds, the organisation provides media support to activists working on environment and social justice issues. According to Small World, the rationale for this was, 'If we can't get programmes on important issues onto television we don't give up, nor do we go "down market". Instead we make them and distribute them ourselves.' Director and co-founder, Thomas Harding, observes:

> The major shift came in the late 1980s, with the introduction of the format 8 mm and VHS camcorders. These were very easy to use, high quality and relatively low cost and widely available. . . . Three factors converged at the same time: an emergence of a vibrant form of activism; the availability of new camcorders; and the failure of mainstream TV to adequately cover the boom in grassroots politics. (Harding 1998: 83)

What is interesting is that while in some ways they tend to be critical of technology, they have been at the forefront of developing new forms of political action often through harnessing new media technologies to their own ends. However, as the above quote suggests, their relationship with the mainstream news media is ambivalent.

Alternative Channels of Communication

One response to coverage that is considered unreasonable is to create alternative news sources. Grassroots networks often advocate the use of their own underground alternative channels of communication or, in some cases, actual physical interference through sabotaging transmitters and disrupting broadcasts (Atton 2002; Holloway 1998). Holloway (1998) describes a commonplace scene whereby environmentalists, journalists and even security personnel all record their own versions of the 'news':

> In a copse somewhere in rural Britain, security guards in luminous jackets and hard hats attempt to surround a tree due for felling. A protester takes his opportunity, neatly body swerves a guard and begins to scale a condemned tree. Nearby, an impenetrable human security fence surrounds a tree allowing trained guards, lifted by a hydraulic platform, to grab or 'cherry pick' protesters from their home in the top branches. Elsewhere, contractors remove six-inch spikes from a tree before the chain saw can fell it. In a muddy field somewhere else in rural Britain, a large mechanical digger attempts to inch forward while around it security guards drag and pull protesters out of its path. The machine stops and an activist manages to slide under. Producing a bike lock she secures herself to the digger. Amongst the assembled onlookers in both copse and muddy field are the media: reporters from television and radio, cameramen and women, and sound technicians are all there covering the day's events. Yet these 'mainstream' journalists are also joined by various individuals recording the proceedings with hand-held camcorders, cameras, tape recorders, notebooks, pens. Some are possibly private detectives hired by the Treasury solicitors recording the episode for possible future legal proceedings. Others are there to record the proceedings as part of the production of 'alternative news'. (Holloway 1998: 1197)

Yet there are major tensions among environmentalists about the benefits of alternative channels of communication. Some activists claim that the main focus should be on direct action, not on representing the issues to a wider audience. Also, some view the video-recording of protest events as a threat, as they claim that this makes it easier for undercover individuals to pose as activists and pass on tapes to the police (Paterson 2000). These tensions were very much apparent in the 1990s anti-roads protests in the UK. Here we focus upon perhaps the best-known recent protest in the Spring of 1997 over extending part of the A30 at Fairmile, Honiton, in South West England.

Swampy and the Eco-warriors

Unlike many previous UK anti-roads protests, this gained high profile, often sympathetic, coverage in the national news media. The story had strong appeal in terms of mainstream news values. Indeed, there is some evidence to suggest that it reflected a perception among news editors that the British public's attitude towards direct action environmental protest was changing (Manning 2001). The Fairmile protest came to be personified through one particular protester, 'Swampy' (Daniel Hooper), who temporarily became a media 'star' almost overnight after barricading himself in a tunnel for a week. As Swampy gained notoriety, he had his own column in the *Sunday Mirror*, and appeared on *Have I Got News for You*, the satirical TV news quiz. A rumour circulated about a planned film based on him and there was an attempt to get him to record 'I am a mole and I live in a hole' (Paterson 2000). Swampy even appeared in a *Daily Express* photo-shoot posing in Armani and Paul Smith designer suits and was invited to take part in a fashion shoot for *The Times*. A year later the British soap opera *Coronation Street* decided to model one of their characters on him.

The word 'Swampy' appeared in many newspaper article headlines (which did not feature Swampy) as a byword for direct action and young people's alienation from mainstream politics. Among the tabloid newspapers the *Daily Express* and the *Daily Mirror* gave the A30 protest the most coverage. This appears likely to reflect the perception that their relatively young readerships were interested in following this story. Interestingly the *Sun* only gave one (negative) mention to the Fairmile protest and this was in the Norman Tebbit column (Paterson 2000).

Yet despite gaining much news media attention, it largely became a story about youth lifestyles, side-stepping the real issues at stake. Maggie Wykes's (1999) study of the Fairmile protest suggests that the activists achieved only very limited success in terms of media representation. Coverage of the protest was dispersed among a whole variety of media formats, often being placed within the lifestyle pages, or sections targeting female readers and concentrating on the youth culture element (sex, drugs, violence, student politics). Particular individuals such as 'Swampy' and 'Animal' were treated as celebrities by the media, which proceeded to give detailed accounts of their biographies, lifestyles and so on. Accordingly, while the road protesters managed to attract a lot of media interest in their campaigns, they cannot be seen to have succeeded in terms of effectively setting the political agenda.

One of the disadvantages of the approach taken by grassroots protests is that there are no clearly identifiable leaders, or allocated spokespersons, to speak to the media. This can leave grassroots activists more open to manipulation by the media and take some control away from how they seek to frame the issues. In the case of the Fairmile protest, Swampy became the key individual to whom the media turned. As Derek Wall observes:

> The media celebrated roads protest and crystallised the actions of thousands of grassroots campaigners into the form of a single personality. Swampy became an icon, better known, at least briefly, than many TV presenters and cabinet ministers. Such celebration was a double-edged sword. Daniel Hooper was not asked to be a media star, and, while he attempted to exploit his fame for the benefit of the protest movement, he was clearly embarrassed by his role . . . Media fame brought the theme of protest to millions of individuals, but in doing so raised its exponents to the status of the unique. In short, direct action was transformed from the 'real' to a media spectacle, something for heroes rather than adults and children in local communities. *(Wall 1999: 91–2)*

Grassroots approaches towards the media, then, can be characterised as somewhat ambivalent. While it is recognised that media publicity can be very beneficial in highlighting activities, there are major tensions in terms of conflicting cultures and values. Also, compared to political 'insiders', they are often severely disadvantaged in terms of resources.

Cyber-activism and the Future of Environmental Protest

As discussed above, there are a number of tensions within the environmental movement concerning strategic action and the use of mainstream and alternative media. Increasingly, computer mediated communication (CMC) is coming to play a central part in environmental activism. Many environmental organisations are regularly supplying VNRs to TV news stations and make extensive use of web sites and email networks (Chesters 1999; Manning 2001; Pickerill 2000, 2001). What changes is this likely to bring about in the relationship between environmentalists and the news media? From what we know about the impact of previously introduced new media technologies, it is unlikely that it will replace the importance of direct personal contact via telephone or face-to-face meetings (Golding 2000; Manning 2001). CMC co-exists alongside traditional media rather than replaces them. There is little evidence to suggest that new media technologies have fundamentally changed the nature of environmental activism. As Doherty observes, 'It seems that it may be adding a new weapon in the protester's armoury, rather than simply replacing existing methods' (1999a: xviii). In the case of the 1999 Reclaim the Streets protest in the UK, traditional fly posters accompanied the material on the web. Similarly Pickerill observes, 'despite the potential use of CMC to develop new forms of protest tactics, its use is often restricted to that of an additional communication tool. Relatively few instances of online activism or electronic civil disobedience are practised by British environmentalists, though CMC is still used in many innovative ways' (2001: 143).

Clearly CMC, alongside other campaigning techniques, provides an effective publicity tool for many environmental groups and individual activists. It is

cheaper than having to pay costs of printing and mailing, it has more immedi-
acy, and editorial control enables greater freedom to communicate material on
their terms (Pickerill 2000, 2001; Pipes 1996). As Doherty observes,

> it reduces the reliance upon sympathetic journalists to get the message across in the media.
> For many groups this is the biggest change brought about by the new technology because it
> reduces the imbalance between them and their opponents, often large multinational
> corporations . . . Online magazines such as Squall and Schnews help protesters preserve
> their own solidarity and influence the mainstream media. *(Doherty 1999a: xviii–xix)*

Perhaps one of the best-known examples of the increasing significance of CMCs
in environmental activism is the McSpotlight campaign. McSpotlight was the
name given to the campaign that was established by two members of London
Greenpeace who were accused of making libellous claims against the fast food
chain McDonald's, in the mid-1990s. The McSpotlight web site (launched in
February 1996) had received over 70 million hits by February 1999. It won
several awards and achieved huge mainstream media coverage across the globe.
The web site enabled the case to gain widespread publicity and public access to
the allegedly libellous documents. It also provided an effective means whereby
regular updates could be provided and the issues could be debated on an online
discussion forum.

More recently, the use of the Internet as a mobilising tool was central to the
Reclaim the Streets demonstration, a 'Carnival against Capitalism', in June 1999.
This protest, organised by the anti-roads group, was estimated to involve
around 6,000 individuals and caused over £2 million of damage (Wall 2000).
Live web casts from London and Sydney, together with reports from over 40
countries, linked protesters and interested spectators around the world. A
number of different web sites provided information on the campaign and details
of how to get to the demonstration (Doherty 1999). Global networking through
the Internet also played a crucial role in protests against the World Trade
Organisation (WTO) in Seattle, November 1999 (Chesters 1999).

The Internet, then, is potentially a very powerful tool in widening public
awareness of environmental actions. However, there still remain huge inequalities in Internet access on a global scale (Dordoy and Mellor 2001; Golding 2000;
Hacker and van Dijk 2000). Also the growing quantity of information in cyber-
space means that the ability to find sites often reflects the effectiveness of search
engines; just because information is available on the web does not guarantee that
people will access it (Dordoy and Mellor 2001). Finally, CMC complements
rather than replaces traditional media and therefore the news strategies of
environmentalists are unlikely to be fundamentally altered. CMC is often used
alongside a range of other methods such as telephone trees, word of mouth,
press releases and alternative literature.

As discussed earlier on in this chapter, following the Brent Spar campaign,
journalists exhibited considerable concerns about heavy reliance upon VNRs.
Unless there are major cutbacks in broadcasting that place more pressure upon
journalists to use VNRs, this appears likely to remain the case for the foreseeable
future.

Conclusion

Within this chapter a number of key questions have been raised concerning the analysis of source–media relations with reference to environmental news coverage. It has been suggested that orthodox approaches have underestimated some of the complexities involved in the processes, whereby particular issues become defined as 'problems' before they even arise on media agendas. In order to enable non-official sources to become more heavily accessed, we need to have a greater understanding of these processes. Recent studies have made some headway in furthering what we know about this central aspect of the news production process (see, for example, Anderson 1997; Hansen 2000).

Hall et al.'s theory of 'primary definers' glosses over some of the complexities of news access and the various forms this may take depending upon the specific medium. The environmental lobby encompasses a diverse range of groups with varying strategies and approaches, ranging from international environmental pressure groups through to more locally based grassroots protesters. There are therefore dangers with lumping non-official sources into one category (see Anderson 2000). Also, Hall et al.'s model implies that news sources do not need strategies, since they automatically gain access to the media. As we have seen, the degree to which communicators' and sources' goals become assimilated in covering an environmental issue constitutes a key factor. Despite sometimes competing against powerful institutional sources, environmental groups can sometimes gain considerable media access, as in the cases of the Brent Spar and the anti-roads protest discussed above. The resulting coverage is not necessarily on their terms and sources are constrained in several respects concerning how the issues are 'packaged' (Hansen 2000). In other words, the sheer amount of media coverage gained is, in itself, an inadequate indicator of success since this depends upon how the issues are framed and the degree to which wider political objectives are realised.

CHAPTER SUMMARY

- The mass media (particularly new information and communication technologies) play a central role in the politics of environmentalism.

- Environmental pressure groups have become increasingly sophisticated in their approaches towards the media.

- The environmental lobby encompasses a diverse range of groups which have very different strategies and approaches.

- The relative prominence of an environmental issue is not in any simple way a reflection of public concern but, among other factors, the activities of issue sponsors.

- We cannot judge the success of an environmental group simply by the sheer amount of media attention it enjoys.

- There are often major tensions within environmental groups about focusing upon communication strategies at the expense of engaging in direct action.

- Non-official sources experience differing levels of access to the news media.

- To some extent, success in defining an environmental issue/problem is a reflection of the level of resources an organisation commands.

- There is little evidence to suggest that new media technologies have fundamentally transformed the communication strategies of environmental groups.

PART V

MEDIATING REPRESENTATION AND PARTICIPATION

CHAPTER 8

Tabloid Television and News Culture: Access and Representation

John Langer

What's in a Title?

Tabloid

My dictionary defines this word as a 'newspaper that gives its news in concentrated and easily assimilable form', a derivation from 'tablette' an old French word for 'small slab . . . with or for inscription'. In its earlier connection to journalism, the term 'tabloid' referred to the physical dimensions of a newspaper – half the 'broadsheet' size, hence allowing for more portability and for more 'portable' news, the reading of which could be done by commuters and others on their way to work or during a lunch break. Today, almost invariably, the word 'tabloid' is used in a derogatory way to refer to a type of news which is characterised as 'extravagant', 'sensationalistic', 'over-dramatised' and focused almost entirely on a human interest angle and the 'personality'; in short, a type of news perceived as having almost nothing to do with 'real journalism' (see Bird 1992; Sparks and Tulloch 2000).

Culture

This word is a little more difficult to specify as its usage has been so diverse. Sometimes it refers to the arts and higher learning; sometimes it means 'a whole way of life' in an anthropological sense. For us, the term 'culture' will refer to the making of meaning and, more broadly, to the institutions and institutional routines and practices that allow meaning to be made. In this sense we have to think of news as not just about providing information but as a *cultural* institution which produces meaning; and frequently this meaning in its 'news-message' form is shaped by presentational features very much akin to those of story-telling.

When we combine the first and second terms, we begin to map our direction in this chapter. Despite the many objections lodged against them, the tabloid aspects of news do not seem to want to go away. Indeed, if news on television is examined as a 'case study', as will be done here, it becomes evident that stories which might be described as having tabloid qualities are routinely part of everyday news broadcasts. Hence, as students of mass communication, it seems crucial for us to look more closely at this feature of 'news culture'. But how? Now we can turn to some other title terminology.

Access

The question of who gets into the news or who makes it into a news item has been a longstanding one (see Galtung and Ruge 1981). One view suggests that those who have access to news discourse can shape public opinion and set agendas for action. If we are to examine the tabloidesque features of news culture, it will be useful to specify who makes regular appearances as the subjects of this 'unworthy' journalism.

Representation

To engage fully in an investigation of tabloid news culture, it is important to refer not just to who gets into the news, but how these newsworthy individuals and the occurrences in which they are involved are depicted and *re-presented* to us. Here we have to turn our attention to the institutional practices which allow meanings to be made. How does meaning come about in a news story that might be considered part of this tabloid news culture? What strategies, conventions, devices and stylistics are pressed into service in the news story which permit it to make sense? And perhaps most importantly, are there certain groups who might benefit or be disadvantaged by such sense-making?

The Lament for Television News

During the 1970s when television was consolidating itself as the premier medium of broadcast communication, Diamond (1975: xi) recounted this little slice of journalist lore, apparently professional advice given by a seasoned veteran to a fledgling reporter.

> I'm going to tell you a story and after I tell it, you will know all there is to know about television news . . . The executives of this station [in New York] were watching all three news shows one night. There had been a fire in a Roman Catholic orphanage on Staten Island. One executive complained that a rival station had better film coverage. 'Their flames are higher than ours', he said. But another executive countered: 'Yes, but our nun is crying harder than theirs . . .'

Diamond, and many commentators following him over the years, have been deeply troubled by such tales and what they indicate. Presented less anecdotally, a series of propositions unravel not just about what television news is, but by implication, what it ought to be:

- Television news is primarily a commodity enterprise run by market-oriented managers who place outflanking the 'competition' above journalistic responsibility and integrity.

- Television news is in the business of entertainment, like any other television product, attempting to pull audience for commercial not journalistic reasons.

- Television news has set aside the values of professional journalism in order to indulge in the presentation of gratuitous spectacles.

- Television news is overly dependent on images that create superficiality and lack information content.

- Television news traffics in trivialities and deals in dubious emotionalism.

The list could go on, but essentially the assumptions embedded in such an anecdote lead to what might be designated as the 'lament' for television news (see also Conrad 1982; Esslin 1982; Postman 1985; Bennett 1988; Altheide and Snow 1991; Postman and Powers 1992).

The Path of Irrelevant Coverage

The various manifestations of the 'lament' spring from what is held to be a fundamental relationship which must exist between journalism and the successful workings of liberal democracy. The argument goes this way. A liberal democracy needs an informed citizenry who can make rational decisions on the basis of the kinds of information available, especially in the realm of politics. That information is often complex, untidy or even held back. The task of the journalist is to overcome these obstacles, to shed light in dark corners, to act as the nation's watchdog, to present information on the events of the day with impartiality and objectivity.

It is this contention which provides the foundation for much of the lament. Television news has systematically undermined the crucial arrangement which is meant to operate between a working democracy and its citizens. At its most reprehensible, television news actively turns away from the 'most important stories' completely and is 'content to take the easier path of irrelevant coverage: sports, weather, traffic accidents and smoky fires. Too often "access to facts" has been translated to mean higher flames and more tearful nuns' (Diamond 1975: xiv).

Moreover, it is argued that the orientation and strategies used to produce 'irrelevant' news begin to interfere with, to shape and finally overwhelm the 'consequential' news. For Conrad (1982: 132–3) the restless search for images which accompanies the reporting of what he terms 'non-events' ultimately compromises coverage so that 'significance' is determined by the extraction of 'visual highlights'. Bennett (1988) detects a further wayward trend in contemporary journalism arising out of an unwarranted 'preoccupation with drama', the regrettable spillover from news values most prominent in the production of irrelevant coverage, resulting in the distinctions between news and entertainment becoming blurred. Whichever manifestation is encountered, there seems to be a tendency to link the lament for broadcast journalism to particular *types* of news stories.

> If you are expecting . . . the most important news . . . on any given day, you will often be disappointed. Never forget that the producer of the program is trying to grab you before you zap away . . . Therefore, chances are you will hear a story such as Zsa Zsa's run in with the law, Rob Lowe's home videos, Royal Family happenings, or news of Michael Jackson on tour. Those stories have glitter and glamour in today's journalism. (*Postman and Powers 1992: 38*)

To make matters worse, 'those stories' appear to have propagated more elaborated versions of themselves, growing into what broadcasters like to call 'reality programming' and critics prefer to label 'tabloid tv'. *Rescue 911, Emergency 000, Cops, Hard Copy, Lifestyles of the Rich and Famous, Police, Camera, Action, What Went Wrong?, When Animals Attack* are just a few of the many available examples where smoky fires, accidents, celebrity home videos, royal family happenings, pop music tours and tearful nuns have all become key ingredients for an entire television genre. Perhaps these are developments Altheide and Snow (1991: 51) had in mind when announcing that, as it pertains to television, 'organized journalism is dead'.

Taking the Non-serious News Seriously

Although the lament offers a sustained commentary on broadcast journalism, the basis of its arguments seems to rest on the notion that, given the right conditions and circumstances, news on television has the capacity to act as a transparent and neutral vehicle for relaying information, a 'broadly shared window on reality' (Bennett 1988: xiii). This argument, however, fails to recognise that television news

> is a sequence of socially manufactured messages which carry many of the culturally dominant assumptions of our society. From the accents of the newscasters to the vocabulary of camera angles; from who gets on and what questions they are asked, via selection of stories to presentation of bulletins, the news is a highly mediated product. (*Glasgow University Media Group 1976: 1*)

Another difficulty with the lament's position comes from its desire to define news and the institutional workings of journalism as primarily about the transmission of information which can be used by a citizenry to accumulate knowledge and to engage in responsible judgements and actions. Yet, relying on an 'informational model' to explain television news and its unworthy tendencies may fail to recognise that in the daily recurrence and recognisable features of such programming, viewer linkages to the news and the larger world it represents may be more ritualistic, symbolic and possibly mythic than informational, and in this sense television news might better be conceptualised as a 'form of cultural discourse' (Dahlgren 1988: 289).

The intransigence of broadcast journalists to remove such insignificant reportage from their bulletins could be motivated by news values based on commercial considerations which promote drama, sensation and visual impact. However, if Dahlgren is correct in posing television news as a cultural discourse, a different and perhaps more broadly based explanation still needs to be found for why such news remains 'popular'. This chapter argues that the purportedly insignificant news has to be approached and understood precisely for the reasons the lament would wish it to go. Its longevity, its influential presence, its use of a logic based less on models of information transfer than on structures of sentiment and sensation, its commitment to storytelling, its formulaic qualities as well as its search for visual impact are all key features which provide the grounds for assessing this 'unworthy news' from a *culturalist* perspective.

The significance of the insignificant news also resides in the way it can be thought about in terms of what the Glasgow University Media Group (1976: 13–14) describe as broadcast journalism's 'communicative power'. Whereas the lament leads to a focus on journalistic practice as a 'problem' requiring prescriptive interventions, the culturalist paradigm conceptualises this same practice as a site from which certain 'ideological work' (Hall 1973: 340) can be accomplished by television news.

> Ideology can be used to refer to the ways in which meaning serves, in particular circumstances, to establish and sustain relations of power which are systematically asymmetrical – what I shall call 'relations of domination'. Ideology, broadly speaking, is *meaning in the service of power*. Hence the study of ideology requires us to investigate the ways in which meaning is constructed and conveyed in symbolic forms . . . [and] to ask whether, and if so how, the meaning mobilized by symbolic forms serves, in specific contexts, to establish and sustain relations of domination. (*Thompson 1990: 7; original emphasis*)

Rather than seeing irrelevant coverage as merely tangential to questions of news values due to its ostensible non-serious inflection, it is precisely these characteristics which give such *symbolic forms* their 'communicative power', investing them with a particular, even unique, capacity to do ideological work.

Story-types in the 'Unworthy News'

In a discussion of the 'perennial' quality of the human interest story, Helen Hughes (1968) observes: 'topics that made "good ones" are just the topics that have made "good ones" in the past and have become traditional'. To appreciate this process requires that news stories be acknowledged as 'represent[ing] types and that, while every day's news is fresh, there are essential likenesses and repetitions' (Hughes 1968: 209). The operation of the type can be accorded a similar kind of status to that identified in discussions of film genre. In relation to popular cinema, for example, Alloway explains:

> It is always the schematic parts, the symmetrical plots, the characters known beforehand and their geometrical relationships that characterize the movies . . . A convention is always dominant, the extent to which movies as mass art accords with the accepted manner, model or tradition is the extent to which it will reach its audience. (*Alloway 1971: 60*)

Like a film genre, news story *types* characteristically utilise patterns/forms/styles/structures that transcend individual reports and supervise both their construction and their 'reading' by the audience (Ryall 1975). Knowledge of the generic elements of perennial stories enables television journalists to produce accounts of occurrences as news for various audiences – editors, viewers, sources – as well as to produce copy and images rapidly within accepted codes of presentation. Conversely, organising journalistic production along generic lines ensures that audience expectations are met and the means by which to 'read' a story are provided routinely and systematically.

How then can we uncover and examine these 'schematic parts' that give story-types their shape and meaning? Stuart Hall (1975b: 17) advises that when examining the media's 'messages' we should treat them as 'texts: literary and visual constructs employing symbolic means shaped by rules, conventions and traditions'. With this formulation in mind, news stories might be approached as *cultural artefacts* from which can be 'read' a complex series of interdependent organisational, technical, professional and stylising practices. This would involve examining broadcast news for its *tele-visual and tele-audio* properties – use of camera, pictorial composition, editing, lighting, settings, scripted 'news talk' in newsreader and reporter commentary and strategies for storytelling.

The News World of 'the Especially Remarkable'

In his account of the social and historical conditions that gave rise to the 'phenomena of stars', Francesco Alberoni (1972: 75) observed that in 'every society are to be found persons who, in the eyes of other members of the collectivity, are especially remarkable and who attract universal attention'. At one time this applied to those 'who held power (political, economic, religious)', but now there are others 'whose institutional power is very limited or non-existent, but whose doings and way of life arouse considerable and sometimes even a maximum degree of interest'. This latter group constitutes what Alberoni calls a 'powerless elite' which includes not just stars of cinema but 'idols', 'champions' and 'divi'.

News Values and Structures of Access

Here, the lament is correct. Television news *is* filled with what it would characterise as trivial reportage of this 'powerless elite' and their seemingly insignificant 'doings and way of life' – the television personality playing golf, the theatrical performer discussing a new role, the pop stars on a minor drugs offence. More distressing still, when institutional power-brokers and decision-makers are given coverage in this context, it is overwhelmingly in terms of their informal activities, publicly ritualised displays of attention and 'private lives' (see Lowenthal 1961).

Another way to think about the inclusion of such items might be to locate them as part of what Monaco (1978: 10) has described as a 'calculus of celebrityhood', television journalism, as it were, factoring in its own particular equation in terms of specific news values. According to Galtung and Ruge (1973: 66), there is a structure of access to news which is elite-centred and 'the more the event concerns elite people, the more probable that it becomes a news item'. Because the focus on elites is such a standard news-gathering practice, they become 'naturally newsworthy' simply for their 'very-being-as-they-are' (Hall 1973: 183). An important variation on this news value is found in the extensive coverage given to seemingly very ordinary people whose especially remarkable identities are constituted not by way of their 'being' – because in news terms they are essentially 'nobodies' – but in relation to what might be described as their 'very-acting-as-they-do'. Unlike elites, powerful or powerless, whose actions regardless of how ordinary (marriage plans, a pregnancy, a dieting regime, gift giving, a holiday trip, and so on) are deemed newsworthy (remarkable) by virtue of an already overdetermined presence in journalism's discourse – 'the actions of elites usually, and in the short term perspective [are] more consequential than the activities of others' (Galtung and Ruge 1973: 66) – ordinary people must *become* especially remarkable. Typically, this involves the operation of news values that emphasise the idiosyncratic or fracturing of normal expectancies (Galtung and Ruge 1973: 65):

- a man wins a race in a boat 'made from two thousand beer cans';

- a barber sets a 'world non-stop shaving record';

- a 'cabinet maker' stays in a cage with 'two dozen deadly snakes [for] more than 36 days';

- a woman 'confined to an iron lung' gives birth to 'a baby daughter';

- a truck driver who stops to 'fill out his log book and answer the call of nature' finds a satchel with 'ten million dollars worth of cheques inside'.

All the stories above were part of a sample taken in Australia of early evening news (see Langer 1998).

Representing the Especially Remarkable

News does not merely take note of the especially remarkable, it actively participates in their construction: it makes them 'remarkable' and *especially* so.

Once these individuals are accessed by journalistic discourse as the subject for stories, it becomes relevant to ask: how are they represented? Which 'remarks, attributes, actions and possessions' (Hall 1973: 183) are the focus of interest? How are individuals given meaning as especially remarkable?

Who's in Charge Here?

In an illuminating study of gossip column content and writing style, Smith (1975) found a pervasive admiration for the ability of the column's inhabitants to be in 'control of their own time and environment on a large scale, and to move around effortlessly'. According to Smith (1975: 208), the column's 'latent function is to assert, and celebrate, the persistence of such power in the form of a daily serial'. Contemporary television news stories about showbusiness celebrities, one significant segment of Alberoni's powerless elite, tend to maintain this kind of focus. So, although the basis of much of the coverage could be nothing other than an exercise in promotion and public relations – e.g. the American film director is in Australia to drum up audiences for his newest release; the English comedian gives interviews to ensure interest in his stage appearances – the context of these occasions is never observed as part of a pattern of work and effort. In this case, celebrities are made especially remarkable as they seem to dwell in what Brunsdon and Morley (1978: 24) have described as a 'private leisure-world', glimpsed as a 'free floating sphere from which the productive base has been excised'.

Ordinary people are not so fortunate. Control for them is rarely a given state of affairs, as it can be for elites. To be rendered especially remarkable, ordinary people need to be seen to 'make the effort': their very-acting-as-they-do never 'comes easy'. In order to 'set a new world record [for] domino toppling' a challenger 'spent fifteen days and ten hours setting up the intricate formations'. In order to build his hovercraft, a school boy has to be 'tucked away in the garage [while] most of his class mates were out on the town at weekends'. Ordinary people can also be subject to degrees of variability with regard to control. In the midst of applied effort something can intervene to make completion of the task an elusive affair. Here's one example. A story about 'London's fastest barber' explains that: 'as [he] set off at terrifying speed all seemed to be going well. But then came the problem. Some [volunteers] had backed out at the last minute and [the barber] was running out of willing victims.' As it turns out, he does succeed in breaking his 'own non-stop shaving world record', but 'only by a whisker', as the dialectic of ill-fortune and effort is played out. The badly timed withdrawal of accomplices, which might have proven a lesser person's downfall, becomes the moment in which to demonstrate an *especially remarkable* tenacity of purpose and quick thinking. Instead of floundering in the face of these desertions, the barber resourcefully shaves the same people again ('one hapless [volunteer] was shaved ten times'). Bad luck is turned into good. The reversal is reversed, so that even in all its apparent banality, the reporting of this 'record setting' event produces a forceful statement about the individual will to succeed.

A Different Kind of Language

A short placing phrase, the inclusion or omission of a definite or indefinite article, the first few words of a report, the replacement of common usage with something having a grander ring, all help the gossip column to create an aura around its 'theatrical show' (Smith 1975: 214). Again, gossip column 'stylistics' make the transition to the disreputable news. Whereas you and I might go to a carnival sideshow and toss balls at old chipped plates, when Prince Philip on television news does the same thing, he is 'trying his hand at smashing some crockery'. The use of such 'superlatives', according to Smith (1975: 214), gives the impression that 'these people are not simply degrees above us in the hierarchy, they are different in kind [and] . . . a different kind of language . . . is necessary to apprehend them.'

In stories about celebrities, news talk is more in keeping with a language mobilised from billboards, entertainment magazines and advertising as we hear about 'the star [of] outrageous box office hits', 'the master of the one man show', 'the top American pop group', 'the man who . . . scooped the Academy Awards'. Placement of definite articles before the celebrity's name or in relation to another noun in a descriptive position with regard to the name features regularly: *the* English comedian, *the* rock band, *the* man who made the *Godfather* movie. Definite rather than indefinite articles produce a sense of superiority, uniqueness and recognisability ('*a* man who produced a *Godfather* movie' would hardly be 'remarkable').

The Narrative of Triumph

When it is applied to ordinary people, the 'superlative' is frequently established through a narrative of personal triumph, formed around a sequence of codified storytelling 'moves'. So a report about a 'stunt boy' setting the world motorcycle jump record 'beating Evil Knievel' begins to assemble the superlative with reference to background hardships as news talk explains that '[during] his last attempt at the world record . . . he made it over twenty of the twenty-five cars but hit the last few . . . end[ing] up with the motor bike on top of him and a couple of broken bones'. Then motivation and psychological cueing are inserted: 'for a successful jump [he] knew that he would have to top 160 km an hour by the time he left the ramp'. And finally we *see* and hear about the ultimate success – news film produces visual evidence of the 'amazing leap', once at normal speed, then again in slow motion as news talk describes how 'twelve thousand fans looked on as [the stunt boy] set off on the ride of his life'.

Victim Stories

Another story-type regularly encountered in 'unworthy news' reveals an insistent focus on individuals who, in the process of going about their daily affairs, encounter an unanticipated turn of events which ensnares them in a crisis of great magnitude. If these individuals can be situated as 'characters' in an unfolding drama, their principal role is constituted as victim. This story-type is one of the key structures of access by which 'ordinary people' get placed onto the journalistic agenda of television news. Here we find a world where:

- a 'pre-dawn fire claim[s] the lives of a mother and four of her children';
- a boy is 'mauled and killed by a lion at . . . [a] lion park';
- a 'light plane crash claim[s] the life of an experienced aviator';
- a truck driver has a 'close brush with death' (see Langer, 1998).

The Reflex of Tears

In his discussion of publically observed 'dramatic encounters', sociologist Orrin Klapp (1964) gives details of the conditions that can produce 'symbolic leaders' as 'good victims'. Several features pertaining to social actors in such encounters have resonance in victim stories: infirmity, a sense of helplessness, vulnerability, the incapacity to fight back, the unexpectedness of the circumstances, and the 'magnitude' of the misfortune all make a difference. Crucially for Klapp (1964: 92), 'the trouble [may] be suffered but not chosen', leaving the way open for the introduction of a 'dramatic partner' who can assume the role of 'rescuer'.

The notion of the good victim has links with what literary theorist Northrop Frye (1957) describes as 'low mimetic tragedy'. European fiction, he suggests, can be divided into epochs or periods characterised by 'the different elevations' of the protagonist: 'the hero's power of action . . . may be greater than ours, less or roughly the same'. Through the progressive evolution of the fictional form, the action of the hero moved from a position of superiority (the mythic mode) toward a position of inferiority (the ironic mode). Low mimetic tragedy sits somewhere in the middle: a hero is posited as one of us and we are asked to 'respond to a sense of his [sic] common humanity' (Frye 1957: 34). Typified especially by the realist fiction of the new English middle class, extending from Defoe to the end of the nineteenth century, Frye contends that: 'The best word for low mimetic or domestic tragedy is perhaps pathos, and pathos has a close relationship to the sensational reflex of tears.' Requiring protagonists to be 'isolated by a weakness . . . [which] is on our own level of experience', pathos, Frye insists, frequently taps into some kind of 'queer, ghoulish emotion' (1957: 34–8).

This last comment is not dissimilar to the way the lament characterises 'unworthy news'. But more important perhaps is the underlying issue of identification: news items in this story-type must offer the viewer a position, not of pure spectatorship, but of involvement or affiliation. It might be argued that these stories function differently from the serious news, where reportage is primarily concerned with the worlds of politics, the economy, international affairs and so on. Serious news is often not about those 'on our own level of experience', but concerns the power-brokers and the decision-makers, whereas the majority of victim stories begin with ordinary people and everyday life, with which it is assumed we are all completely familiar. This is not to suggest that the powerful and the influential cannot become victims. A point worth noting is that it is at that moment when these individuals do become victims – think of all those stories about the British royal family – that they can be most personalised, made most like us, brought down to 'our own level of experience'.

Journalism and the Victim Tale

The issue of identification, however, may require more than an experiential moment of recognition on the part of the viewer. Klapp (1964: 92) notes that good victims have always been part of the storytelling tradition of the folk tale. In the light of Hughes's observations (1968), it might be suggested that the perennial quality of victim stories, the reason why they keep cropping up in news despite regular criticism, is not necessarily because television journalists and audiences are indulging in some unsavoury preoccupation with suffering but because, like the folk tale, these stories offer the possibility for telling and hearing such 'good ones'.

The Norm and the Agent

Victim stories attempt to establish an everyday world where it is possible to carry on the normal routines governing our waking, eating and sleeping lives. (These particular routines are worth a special mention here because victim stories are known to begin with a logic like this: the family was eating their evening meal, in bed asleep, etc., when . . . the truck hit the house, the wall caved in, the fire started.) Mundane routines are established, only to be disrupted. Through the use of certain phrases in news talk, the impression is given that some greater design is at work in the creation of misfortune. Inanimate objects seem to manifest a life of their own: 'a light plane crash *has claimed* the life of . . . the plane *hit* a tree and *ploughed* into the ground'; 'his [truck] *kept going, went over* the drop only *to be halted* by the channeling on the tray'.

Accounts and Witnesses

The victim tale also provides an account of the protagonist's plight. This is offered from a number of differing yet overlapping points of view so that the viewer is able to take up a number of positions from which to relate to victims and their circumstances. In this sense an account is constructed out of a number of renditions, something like musical 'variations on a theme'. The first begins with the detached commentary given by the newsreader who frames and focuses the event in general terms (Brunsdon and Morley 1978: 58–61). The story moves on to the reporter, who provides another rendition, reiterating, embellishing and submitting additional detail so that the chain of events begins to take on depth and circumstances become more palpable. The 'aeroplane' first introduced by the newsreader becomes a 'Piper Pawnee', the 'pilot' is given a name, the 'crash' is elaborated as 'the right wing . . . clipped a tree at the edge of the airfield'.

In order to encourage the reflex of tears, the news story can load at least one of the renditions of the event with a certain emotional charge. Inclusion of observations and reactions from witnesses on the scene commonly serve this function. Victims become more authentically sympathetic when an ordinary person located in the real world rather than someone from the potentially manipulative world of professional journalism can guarantee the details of the misfortune: a neighbour, a friend, a care-giver, a coach, a parent. In this sense, newsmakers suspend themselves as narrators. The story provided by witnesses becomes a tale within a tale, a first-hand account which positions the viewer in a more direct relationship with the events and those involved. This sense of engagement can be heightened further if a witness can assume the role of 'dramatic partner' engaged in rescue attempts.

Impact

Stories about victims are structured by 'looking backwards' – the occurrence that becomes news has happened already somewhere in the recent past so that the process of story presentation relies on reconstructing the event on the basis of remaining evidence. The status of 'good victim' is, in part, secured by a strategy that offers an exposition of the aftermath of the occurrence. News film is extremely important in this context. Images selected for such stories serve as condensation symbols (Graber 1976) and can be compelling in the activation of sympathetic responses since they often depict personal realities from 'our own level of experience': a car with its headlights shattered, a charred school note-book, a collapsed house roof. Such images assembled in sequences are submitted as evidence that misfortune has disturbed our 'common humanity'.

Communicative Power

Let us return now to the lament and raise again one of the questions with which we started: despite the very public castigation of news stories like the ones discussed above, why do they persist? What's the 'appeal'? To provide answers we have to get beyond the specifics of good victims, humanised celebrities, and compelling narratives and look to another level of analysis. Instead of thinking about them as separate categories for organising meaning in news, it might be argued that story-types can be examined as a 'structured whole', which can be located as a mutually referential associative field of meaning. And it is in this context that we can address an issue raised earlier in our discussion, namely the ideological work of 'irrelevant coverage'.

On the one hand, we have been examining a domain of reportage centred on instant celebrities and 'elite persons' who, by virtue of either doing-as-they-do in the way of unanticipated achievements or simply being-as-they-are, come to dwell in the realm of the especially remarkable. This domain is constituted and signified by stories that focus on 'ordinary people' who breach expectations (the cabinet maker takes up residence in a cage full of deadly snakes), and on extraordinary people doing ordinary things (the prince plays a sideshow game).

What is *symbolically* represented throughout the variations in surface content is not so much the 'personalities' and their actions but that individuals, through their own special efforts and actions or already established credentials, ought to be and indeed can be the principal instruments for making their own fate, for creating their own destiny. The preferred reading of these stories is governed by a structure of meaning which situates mastery and control as an identifiable and valued 'lived reality'. Here is a world that endows both 'ordinary' and 'elite' persons with all the confidence, authority of conviction, command of resources, will to succeed, and self-motivating optimism to conduct their lives with a 'sense of potency': individuals in these stories are refracted through their own 'subjecthood' (Gouldner 1976: 67), a pantheon of contemporary cultural heroes, both great and small, celebrated for performing masterful deeds which, in turn, transport them into realms of the noteworthy and the exceptional.

At the same time, the imagery of mastery and control is being undermined by another kind of 'lived reality'. This is constituted by the results – physical, psychological, personal, social, economic – of occurrences that have intervened in and transformed ongoing normal activities, unpredictably and often inexplicably. This is the domain of reported events where families get destroyed in house fires, children contract incurable diseases, truck drivers face death on the job. Rather than being makers of their fate, in these news items individuals are made *subject to* fate, becoming the unsuspecting and unprepared victims of capricious happenings. The resources, knowledge and confidence needed to act with a 'sense of potency' disappear, replaced by malevolent external forces that strike indiscriminately, causing changes of fortune and radical disruptions to everyday life (Gouldner 1976: 70).

Emerging from within these two story 'constellations' we begin to detect an underlying generative structure which works symbolically to locate events as news in terms of a paradigmatic system and to postulate the fluctuating conditions of mastery and control. This, in turn, provides for the unfolding of a complex chain of connective meanings:

predictability/capriciousness
action/reaction
strength/vulnerability
safety/risk
knowledge/ignorance
heroes/victims
optimism/pessimism
secure/insecure
subject/object

The conceptual order that shapes the meaning of occurrences as they are represented in the two story-types discussed brings them into the sphere of ideology. By situating the locus of conduct and control in terms of either the personal attributes and deeds of individual actors or the impersonal unaccountable interventions made by forces operating externally on individuals, unworthy news offers modes of explanation and sense-making that displace and mask the social, political and historical context in which events occur and can be made to mean. The personal and the impersonal become 'naturalised' forms of expression and intelligibility within a news discourse which deflects attention from what is perhaps a more crucial factor in explaining the conditions of empowerment and its nemesis – the *structures* of domination and subordination.

Down-to-Earth Philosophising

If 'unworthy news' constructs an ideological system that is specific to its types of stories, this system also has to be seen in the way it draws on and can be read in relation to already existing sets of social representations (Brunsdon and Morley 1978: 88). And this is where the 'popularity' of these types of news stories and their persistence, even in the face of vigorous and sustained criticism, might be further explained. In producing their 'sense' of the world, the story-types that recur in 'irrelevant coverage' appear to have appropriated and synthesised certain aspects of *popular wisdom*: 'orally transmitted tags enshrining generalisations, prejudices and half truths, elevated by epigrammatic phrasing to the status of maxims' (Hoggart 1957: 103).

On the one hand these news stories reproduce the sense that 'there is always someone worse off than yourself', and 'there but for the grace of the gods or fortune go you or I'. If the world is such a dangerous and capricious place, it is best not to risk oneself in it. The rational response is to 'be satisfied with your lot', to 'make the best of what we've got', to cultivate a kind of retreatism ('don't stick your neck out'; 'you can't win so there's no use trying'). On the other hand, paradoxically, it is only 'right and just' that those few individuals who do take risks and are seemingly not afraid of coming in contact with this unpredictable world should be rewarded and celebrated for their mastery and subjecthood; after all, 'nothing ventured nothing gained', 'who dares wins'. These individuals are doubly remarkable: for the deeds they perform and the fact that these performances take place in spite of the hostile, unpredictable world. And if, as it turns out, a handful of people are already 'degrees above us in the hierarchy', they can be handled by other fragments of popular wisdom. In some cases, they are brought down to our level: 'after all is said and done', 'when it comes down to it', 'in the end . . . we're all just human, aren't we?' (he may be the most powerful media mogul in the world, but when it comes to women, he's just as silly as the next guy). In other cases they are made vulnerable: 'the bigger they are, the harder they fall' (sure, she's a famous, sexy in-your-face female pop star, but is she up to caring for her new baby?).

Such 'down-to-earth' everyday philosophising, what the social theorist Antonio Gramsci would call 'folk lore' (in Bennett et al. 1981: 231), can be propitiously conservative in its 'world-view' and implications. This kind of news plays out a commonsense drama of fatalism. It substitutes any expressed potential to act in the world, or to act on that world in order to change it, with a vision of fateful resignation which holds that, however miserable or unrewarding one's life or circumstances might be, people should be satisfied and not complain, because 'things could get worse'. It follows then, that the world is better left untouched, or at least left to only those remarkable few who are capable of dealing with it masterfully, but who still seem bound to us by their 'ordinary' sensibilities. In this way, through the generation of a conceptual structure, unworthy news stories become 'symbolic forms' (Thompson 1990: 7) whereby meaning is mobilised to do ideological work. Existing arrangements and relations of power and privilege retain a resonant measure of legitimacy and the 'thinkability' of alternatives is much harder to accomplish. This might be called the 'politics' of the non-political news.

Irreverent Coverage

The study of broadcast journalism and the issue of pleasure have rarely met on the same investigative agenda (see Stam 1983). Ironically perhaps, those lamenting the decline and fall of television news have been aware of this connection for some considerable time:

> The biggest heist of the 1970's never made it on the five o'clock news. The biggest heist of the 1970's *was* the five o'clock news. The salesmen took it . . . By [then], an extravagant proportion of television news answered less to the description of 'journalism' than to that of 'show business'. *(Powers, cited in Graber 1980: 57)*

This particular reproach is foremost a reaction to the commodification of information; but it is also partially linked to the desire for an idealised 'information model' of news which, in order to exist in a 'pure' form, requires overlooking news as *cultural* discourse. Unresolved tensions like these can open the way for some potentially interesting questions about TV news–audience relations. Show business is, after all, always more than just business, and to account for the 'show' inevitably means addressing issues connected to 'appeal' and 'pleasure'.

Making a Mess

In her essay on the 'imagination of disaster', cultural film critic Susan Sontag (1974) explains her fascination with the 1950s American science fiction film in terms of three generic features:

- the 'ingenuity' applied to the creation disorder;
- the 'artfulness' of the destruction which ensues; and

- the opportunity these films afford to let go of 'normal obligations' in order to gratify certain less-than-wholesome, even sadistic, propensities residing within the spectator in relation to the discomfort and suffering of others.

According to Sontag (1974: 425), this type of cinema deals 'with the aesthetics of destruction, with the peculiar beauties to be found in wreaking havoc, making a mess'. It might be posited that it is just such an aesthetic – the pleasure derived from making a mess – which informs so much of what takes place in victim stories: the physical mess made when the materiality of our world is tampered with, and the social and psychological mess when the orderly arrangements of everyday life collapse.

Victim stories are a litany of 'peculiar beauties'. Each day is filled with unsuspected and ingenious ways in which disruption can occur. Nothing, it seems, is spared or out of range. Although victim stories can produce a sense of fatalism and retreat (which proclaims that we ought to stay put, and make the best of what is ours because things could get worse), there is another possibility offered that contradicts this perspective (which proclaims instead: the worse it gets, the better I like it). In victim stories the world we know is played with, tossed around, stretched and pulled out of shape, and in the end gleefully destroyed; but only momentarily, because it always seems to spring back into shape (like the characters in an animated cartoon, or as in the classic cinema trick, the fallen chimney reassembled in reverse motion) in time for the next day when further misfortunes unfold.

Savouring the Story

There is also 'the pleasure of the text', the grip of the narrative – indeed, a story's status as news, as 'the real', may actually enhance pleasure. Social scientist George Herbert Mead (1926) distinguished between two modes of reportage in journalism, both of which, he argued, needed to be recognised. One is oriented to convey factual material such as election results or financial news, the emphasis on 'the truth value of news'. As distinct from this 'information model', the second is based on 'enjoyability' and the provision of satisfying 'aesthetic' experiences which, for Mead, might help people interpret their own lives. With this model of journalism, 'the reporter is generally sent out to get a story not the facts'. For Stam (1983: 31) the relationship between narrative and broadcast journalism has always been there and 'in this sense all [television] news is good news . . . because [it] entail[s] the pleasurability of fiction itself'.

If Stam is correct and all television news is implicated in the story model of journalism, tabloid news culture seems to produce reportage that might allow for this model to be more forthrightly detected. Whereas the serious news on television uses this approach, it pretends that it does not – it asserts a concern for the important information of the day. 'Irrelevant' news may have a slightly different focus as its news values, in part, are built around a desire to illicit from the viewer a mutually confirming declaration: what a story! By drawing attention to its story-ness, the tabloidesque could be 'blowing the cover' of all the news, revealing that the world of fact and the world of fiction are bound more closely together than those lamenting the demise of television journalism are prepared to have us believe.

CHAPTER SUMMARY

Having completed this chapter you will have been made aware of the cultural (as opposed to the informational) importance of 'irrelevant coverage'. In this chapter we explored the following issues:

- The cultural significance and continuing viewer appeal of tabloid-oriented news on television.

- How newsworthy events are shaped by storytelling techniques which get recycled through every news bulletin.

- How television news reports have significant links with other familiar forms of popular culture.

- The manner in which the seemingly least politically focused news can be implicated in the way meaning-making and the relations of power can be connected.

- The pleasure-giving as opposed to the informational function of news.

CHAPTER 9

TV Journalism and Deliberative Democracy: Mediating Communicative Action

Simon Cottle

Today we live in a world in which conflict and contestation are endemic and in which communicative power is routinely mobilised by strategic interests via the media. This chapter sets out to explore how this communicative action is 'mediated' in and through the principal informational and deliberative genres of television journalism – news and current affairs – and how these variously enable or disable the public elaboration and, importantly, discursive engagement of contending perspectives and interests.[1] This chapter examines a dimension of media access and promotion that all too often is overlooked in empirical sociological studies of hierarchies of access and source media strategies, as well as by culturalist readings of media texts and the discursive positioning of social actors in archetypal story-types, myths and narratives. While these different approaches are necessary for improved understanding of questions of news access and public promotion – as demonstrated admirably by many of the contributors to this book – we must also attend to the *communicative forms* of journalism and examine how these deepen or diminish the possibilities for public deliberation and understanding.

This chapter argues, and against the grain of much current work in the media and communications field, that 'talking heads' remain one of the most efficient and meaningful ways of finding out about and evaluating contending views and arguments, and the interests at stake, within conflicts. People talking in public, embodying differing interests and advancing contending discourses, are fundamental to processes of democracy as well as its deepening through processes of wider deliberation. When we witness the dialogic encounters of others, we are able to consider the reasons and rhetoric, the claims and counter-claims, and the arguments and performances enacted by opposing interests and to evaluate these as they unfold in interaction. It is in this mediated play of difference, where ideas, identities and interests rub up against each other and are communicatively obliged to elaborate, justify and defend their claims and aims, that we, the overseeing, overhearing audience find invaluable resources for deliberation and improved understanding. Ontologically speaking, democracy is all about talking heads.

This chapter aims to explore the communicative architecture of television news and current affairs programmes and the extent to which this provides mediated public spaces of dialogic interaction, spaces that can thereby be seen as constitutive of a televisual public sphere. The communicative forms of television journalism demand close scrutiny if we want to understand how the medium currently discharges its democratic responsibilities and if we want to deepen its contribution to wider processes of public understanding and deliberation in the future.

At the outset of this book we heard how current social theory identifies fundamental processes of social change as the impetus behind the profusion of contending interests, identities and discourses that clash and clamour for recognition, legitimacy and public support via forms of communicative action on the media stage. This backdrop also gives rise to current political theories of 'deliberative democracy' and the need for processes of 'democratic deepening', given the observed deficits of representative systems of government. These ideas provide a rationale and framework of use in our discussion of the communicative forms of television journalism and so we will need to outline these first. There are many strands to ideas of deliberative democracy, however, so we also need to define our terms and argue against overly rationalistic and constitutionally led views in favour of more performative and politically encompassing understandings of deliberation. Armed with these basic ideas, the discussion will then move to examine the range of communicative forms of television journalism and how these currently live up to, or depart from, deliberative ideals. Examples used to illustrate these points include the mediation of 'risk', anti-world trade demonstrations and the events of 'September 11' – three profound, not to say historically momentous issues of our time. Each gives rise to deep-seated social, political and cultural differences of outlook and prescription, and each is emblematic of the kinds of local–global issues that today confront governments and citizens in liberal democracies and that demand widespread deliberation.

The Turn to Deliberative Democracy

The backdrop of social transformation and change, outlined at the outset of this book, has influenced the rise of recent ideas about 'deliberative democracy'; ideas that have sought to address the politically moribund nature of liberal democracies and deepen democratising forms of public engagement (Dryzek 1990, 2000; Benhabib 1996; Habermas 1996; Bohman and Rehg 1997; Warren 2002). Election turn-outs in liberal democracies regularly suggest that voting is in decline and in any case is a poor measure of political engagement. Mark Warren observes,

> So ideally, democratic institutions serve not only to distribute power in the form of votes, but also to secure the connection between the power to make decisions and equal participation

in collective judgement. Thus, communication – argument, challenge, demonstration, symbolisation and bargaining – is as central to democracy as voting. Through communicative processes opinions are cultivated, reasons developed and justifications proffered. *(Warren 2002: 173)*

In large-scale, complex and socially diverse societies, mechanisms for deliberative involvement are necessary for the 'democratising of democracy' (Giddens 1994). Theories of deliberative democracy, then, are based on both normative (what should be), as well as empirical (what already exists) grounds. Seyla Benhabib (1996) defines 'democracy' as inherently and necessarily deliberative:

Democracy, in my view, is best understood as a model for organizing the collective and public exercise of power in the major institutions of a society on the basis of the principle that decisions affecting the well-being of a collectivity can be viewed as the outcome of a procedure of free and reasoned deliberation among individuals considered as moral and political equals. *(Benhabib 1996: 68)*

This definition prompts further reflection in terms of its commitments to an institutional and consensualist model of democracy, a proceduralist view of rationality, and its understanding of the forms of reasoned deliberation.

The cacophony of discourses and radical pluralism of civil society described in Chapter 1, suggests that definitions of, and prescriptions towards, 'the well-being of a collectivity' are unlikely to find uniform consent given the contending interests and agendas, identities and values that exist. The idea of deliberative democracy therefore cannot presume a universal acceptance and identification of matters of mutual concern, nor confine its public deliberations to only those matters where universal concern is presumed – society is too conflicted and differentiated for that (Frazer 1992; Mouffe 1996; Young 1997). This suggests that a definition of deliberative democracy that is too closely tied to a central co-ordinating view of parliamentary processes, perhaps serviced through the 'sluice gates' of a public sphere conveying discourses of civil society upwards to government and state institutions for action (Habermas 1996), is too institutionally restricted. Deliberative processes can take place in diverse arenas and associations, inform inwards as well as extend outwards, move horizontally and culturally as well as vertically and politically.

A proceduralist view of rationality can also be questioned. This view, most forcefully elaborated by Jürgen Habermas, seeks to identify the grounds on which consensus can be reached and by which legitimate decision-making can be enacted. This, according to Habermas, can be arrived at on the basis of 'communicative reason'. Here the validity of statements and arguments is interrogated in relation to their claims to propositional truth, personal sincerity and normative rightness and in this way 'the important function of social integration devolves on the illocutionary binding energies of a use of language oriented to reaching understanding' (Habermas 1996: 8). This is an idealised and context-transcending view of communication – an 'ideal speech situation' – that lends support to Habermas's wider social theory and its pursuit of a normative basis for social reconstruction, but its view of consensus-seeking 'communicative action' is a far cry from the reality of motivated interests and strategic action that informs most public discourse. Arguably we need to develop a sharper sense of how processes of deliberation and the play of power enacted in communicative action are infused in practice (and are destined to remain so). Even so, we can acknowledge with Habermas the unique capacity of engaged forms of public talk, or discursive encounters, for drawing out and prompting reasoned justifications and 'generalising' claims about the 'public good'.

> Most democrats consider deliberation, as one of the many kinds of communication, to be the ideal way of making collective judgements. Deliberation induces individuals to give due consideration to their judgements, so that they know what they want, understand what others want, and can justify their judgements to others as well as to themselves. (Warren 2002: 173)

This surely is the principal defence of the substantive benefits of engaged forms of deliberative encounter. Ideas of deliberation need not always be modelled on, or confined to, legalistic and parliamentary fora and forms of reasoned speech however. Such a rationalist understanding conceals the exclusive (and socially excluding) nature of many 'democratic' arenas.

Iris Young makes the case, based on feminist accounts of dialogical reason as well as African-American and Latino accounts of cultural biases, that theorists of deliberative democracy must have a broader idea of the forms and styles of speaking than usually envisioned by ideas of reason and rationality, and extends deliberative forms of communicative interactions to include greetings, rhetoric and storytelling (Young 1996). 'Greetings' refers to the various ways in which parties establish and maintain trust, respect and mutual understanding through these and other performative aspects of communication, including body language and the care of others' bodies. Rhetoric refers to the styling of speech for its listeners and often plays a powerful role in enhancing argumentative force through figures of speech and the 'pulling on desires'. Storytelling can also serve mutual understanding by revealing (a) particular experiences, (b) distinct values, culture and meanings, and (c) particularised views of the social totality, including those on other social perspectives – all helpful for establishing mutual understanding and grounds for improved communication. These various performative features can therefore also be regarded as important ingredients in engaged encounters, and provide further resources for the formation of deliberative judgements by an overseeing, overhearing audience.

Ideas of deliberative democracy, then, need not be narrowly confined to extant political institutions, presume a proceduralist view of rationality, or work with a delimited understanding of reason – the radical pluralism of civil society and underlying forces of social change militate against such consensualist thinking. Theorists of deliberative democracy can nonetheless agree that deliberative democracy requires a strong concept of the public sphere. Benhabib defines this as 'mutually interlocking and overlapping networks and associations of deliberation, contestation and argumentation' (1996: 73–4). It is remarkable, therefore, that theorists of deliberative democracy, with the exception of Habermas (1989, 1996), have generally failed to integrate analysis of media performance and potential into their own deliberations on deliberative democratic processes. While media theorists, for their part, have pursued the mass media as constitutive of the public sphere, few have focused specifically on the architecture of television's programmes approached as 'discursive designs' (Dryzek 1990) or as deliberative communicative forms.

What follows, then, is an attempt to underline the importance of dialogic forms of news and current affairs programmes and how these communicative forms already provide invaluable resources for wider public deliberation, but also how these need to be 'democratically deepened' in the future.[2]

Risk Society and the Voices of the Side Effects

In a rare moment in British news broadcasting, Frances Hall, the mother of Paul Hall, one of the first victims to die from Creutzfeldt-Jakob Disease (CJD), the human equivalent of Bovine Spongiform Encephalopathy (BSE), was ceded a degree of editorial control by BBC2's *Newsnight* programme and narrated her own film report before participating in a live studio debate. This preliminary film report puts in place a powerful agenda of concerns and provides deliberative resources for dialogic discussion in the studio. Consider Frances Hall's opening narration and the basis of her reasoned challenge to the Government Health Secretary of the day.

> Our son Peter was ill for more than a year. During that time I wrote to request that someone from the government would come and sit with me at his bedside and see what this devastating illness was doing to our strong, handsome young man. No one came. . . .
>
> Given the mounting evidence of a possible link between BSE and CJD can anyone offer me a logical explanation of how my son contracted this disease other than by eating BSE infected meat? Since Peter died I've taken a job in a local café; I see people confused about what's safe to eat. We've been told consistently that British beef is safe and that the most infected parts have been removed, but even if the red meat carries no infection, we still see evidence of incorrectly butchered cattle with possibly infected parts still attached entering the human food chain, and offal being recycled into animal feed. Surely as Health Secretary, Stephen Dorrell, your only duty is to the nation's health? Can you assure me that no one else will be exposed to the dangers of BSE? Are precautions being enforced and will this really protect the public?
>
> Mr Dorrell, I want you to watch the pictures of my son growing up, do they look much different to the pictures you have of your children? Does Peter show any signs of the tragically short span that he would have? I hold the government responsible for his death and their total incompetence and mismanagement of a manmade disease. . . . Will the government now accept that the scientific advice it chose to follow, namely, that there was no conceivable risk from eating British beef, was wrong? Are the experts still the same? Is the government still being selective on the advice that it takes on behalf of the nation or is it now willing to err on the side of caution? These past months have been, and continue to be, a living nightmare for my family. We have been unable to come to terms with Peter's death

because we know that if BSE had been treated with sufficient caution, he and many others would not have suffered this terrible illness. (*BBC2* Newsnight, *20 June 1996*)

The words spoken present an anguished plea and articulate challenge to the Government Health Secretary of the day, Stephen Dorrell MP, requesting information about and an acceptance of responsibility for the (mis)management of the BSE crisis in the UK, and her son's death. Here an ordinary person has won a rare opportunity to convey her feelings, tell her family's story in her own words, develop her reasoned argument through persuasive rhetoric, and directly confront the 'responsible' Secretary of State, sitting (uncomfortably) in the *Newsnight* studio. The opportunity, I think, was not wasted and provides a powerful example of communicative action and mediated deliberative democracy. Her intervention into the world of public discourse, a world generally framed in the impersonal terms and analytical rhetoric of officials, professionals and experts, is arguably all the more forceful for being grounded, in part at least, in the private realm of lived experience, familial relationships and emotions, and everyday concerns. This example of communicative power, prompting deliberative response by the invited speakers in the *Newsnight* studio and by the witnessing audience at home, at a key moment in the unfolding BSE crisis in Britain, has been brought into being by a particular communicative form of news. To what extent this communicative form has been deployed across all mainstream UK TV news providers will be addressed below.

World Trade and the Cacophony of Protest

The power of mediated communicative action is intimately dependent upon the communicative forms in which it takes place. Often news reports are restricted to a delivery of the barest information presented by the news presenter in the studio and with no reference, visual or verbal, to either the sources of such news 'reports' or to the views of those who may well be the subject of news interest. This communicative form serves to ground objectivist claims of news reporting and in fact routinely features across most TV news programmes. Following one of the major anti-capitalist demonstrations in London, Channel Four News reported on the aftermath of these events in the following way.

Channel Four News, 1 Dec. 1999
News Presenter: Jon Snow

Here in London five people have been arrested after an anti-World Trade Organization protest outside Euston station. Three appeared in court today.

As we can see, the report provides the barest of information and remains entirely within the editorial and discursive control of the news presenters. No matter the selection of information, nor its possible dependence upon certain sources and not others, the news presentation serves by default and through its prioritisation of 'arrests' and 'court appearances' to define the demonstration and its aftermath in terms of a 'law and (dis)order' frame. The communicative form is monologic and non-deliberative in nature. As we shall see below, the 'restricted' news format is a standard feature of most TV news programmes, but so too is the ENG ('electronic news gathering' or video/film) report which begins to move towards a more encompassing communicative form – one not so entirely dependent on the voice (and viewpoints) of the news programme.

On 30 November 1999, ITN led its main evening news programme with the 'major' story of the anti-World Trade demonstrations in London and Seattle. The full transcript of the ITN news report as broadcast, including the words spoken by accessed voices, is reproduced below.

ITN 30 Nov. 1999
News presenter: Dermot Murnagham

DM: Good evening. Demonstrators have been fighting riot police in central London tonight in the second protest against capitalism this year. It started peacefully but then degenerated into violence at Euston mainline railway station which was closed for public safety reasons. A police van was set on fire, several people were hurt and several people were arrested by police snatch squads. ITN's Terry Lloyd reports:

TL: For two hours the atmosphere was carnival-like as hundreds of anti-capitalist demonstrators gathered at Euston station for their last rally of the day. Some though had threatened violence and vowed to close down the railway station. At seven o'clock they charged police lines, terrifying the lightly armed officers.

[Police shouting: 'Right come on, get out the way . . .']

Railings were ripped apart and thrown and explosions were heard. Fully kitted-out riot police were eventually sent in to push the rioters back inside the station and surround them. Several arrests were made and the injured taken to nearby ambulances for treatment. But the demonstrators continued to taunt the police, one of them climbed onto an overturned van wearing a policeman's helmet and bib. Then, with the police and fire services helpless, they set the vehicle ablaze ignoring all risks of another explosion. This is exactly what the demonstrators threatened and the police feared, anarchy on the streets of London, albeit for a few hours. Anti-capitalist demonstrators caused £2 million worth of damage in the city of London in June. Tonight they rioted and blocked the main Euston Road, bringing road and rail traffic to a standstill.

Assistant Chief Constable: I can only say that for a group of about 150 people, who were obviously hell-bent on creating a situation of violence and mayhem and damage, there can certainly be no excuse. It was not lawful protest.

TL: Police snatch squads were deployed to pick out and arrest troublemakers who had earlier been identified by undercover officers and photographers. Within the last 90 minutes violence flared again close to Euston station; police baton-charged a group of demonstrators who refused to leave the area. Officers will be kept out in force throughout the night in case protesters congregate elsewhere. Terry Lloyd, ITN Central London.

This is instantly recognisable as a standard communicative form of TV news. The news presenter first introduces the news item from the setting of the TV news studio where the story is 'framed' in terms that will be elaborated in the following ENG report. Following the studio presenter's introduction, the news item then moves to a filmed report by a news reporter whose voice-over commentary narrates the story over visually 'authenticating' scenes – scenes that serve to anchor the reporter's narration firmly within the law and disorder frame. Next the news report includes edited clips from an ENG interview which has been packaged into the final film report. Clearly, this conventionalised TV news format only permits limited forms of access and opportunities for discursive contestation. At no point are the voices of the protesters or those in sympathy with the protest against the World Trade Organization granted direct access to the news report. The film report is thus effectively 'framed' and discursively 'sealed' by the news producers.

When outside voices are granted access in this particular communicative form, they have little opportunity to challenge, much less dislodge, the inform- ing frame of the news producers – assuming, of course, that they would want to. It is apparent that the accessed voice of the Assistant Chief Constable in the ENG report above, for example, serves only to endorse the overall frame and narrative of the news producers. The 'restricted' news report and the 'limited' ENG communicative forms of news presentation, as we shall see, are prevalent across the TV news landscape.

Occasionally, however, deliberatively more 'expansive' communicative forms are deployed, providing enhanced opportunities for discursive engagement and live challenges to the informing 'frames' of the news producers. Channel Four News programme (1 December 1999), for example, devoted a large proportion (22.30 minutes) of its one-hour news programme to the events in Seattle. Consider one extract from this package, a live studio-based discussion.

Channel Four News (1 Dec. 1999)
News presenter; Jon Snow

Tony Benn: I'll tell you the problem. You never interview any of these people. You just show them shouting, fighting and in funny hats, making out they're a lot of nutters.

JS: Well we did have a chap at the top of the programme actually.

TB: Well I didn't see that, but in general 'protest' is the wrong word, it's the beginning of a political campaign. That's how apartheid ended, that's how men got the vote, that's how women got the vote, it was by putting pressure on parliament.

JS: Right, do you find yourself identifying with Tony Benn, or is he of a different era and not something you find a resonance with?

Paul Mobbs, Cyber-activist: I think we're all going in the same direction. Campaigning is all about managing change and different views of how we manage that change. People today are using the Internet, much like in the Civil War people used pamphlets – we've just moved on and it's got a lot more technical.

JS: There's no real identifiable ideology behind what's going on here in Seattle, I mean.

TB: It's anti-capitalist, it's anti-capitalist.

JS: Well, wow hang on a minute, look you were a purist, you wouldn't have bought some piece of equipment from some company that you were protesting against, but there are people there who have got shoes on that were made by people inside the World Trade Organization.

TB: Look this isn't really globalisation is it? The free movement of capital, you can close a factory in London and open it in Malaysia where the wages are lower but if people from Malaysia want to come to London where the wages are higher the Immigration laws keep them out. What you are witnessing now Jon is the globalisation of ideas through the Internet. The Internet is only the street corner meeting on a big scale. And even in the street corner someone was wearing a pair of shoes and stood on a soapbox and so this is really part of a continuing process. My experience of change is that to begin with it's ignored, then you're mad, then you're dangerous, then there's a pause, and then you can't find anyone who didn't claim to have thought of it in the first place and that's what you are witnessing in Seattle.

JS: You're talking about 'one' problem, but there are people there with problems as disparate as the environment, exploitation, child labour.

TB: They're all the same issue Jon, they're all about profit. Genetically modified food is all about profit, the IMF trade is about profit, privatisation is about profit.

In the relatively expansive communicative form of a live studio interview, then, accessed voices are able to challenge and occasionally agenda-shift informing news agendas and frames. Here they can also begin to elaborate alternative interpretative frameworks that help to make sense of newsworthy events and even, as we began to see above, set these within necessary historical, structural and political contexts. Such communicative forms provide relatively generous opportunities for communicative action, but how often do they feature within and across the TV news broadcast landscape? Table 9.1, based on a two-week survey of eight mainstream UK TV news outlets comprising 80 news programmes and a sample of 1,056 separate news items, provides the answer.

As we can see, TV news makes use of different communicative forms, each providing differing opportunities for communicative action and deliberative engagement. For the purpose of this analysis, these have been arranged in a communicative hierarchy of 'restricted' to 'expansive' forms (listed 1–10) with each successive form making use of further presentational elements. These, as we have already begun to see, incrementally enhance the discursive opportunities for accessed voices to put their point of view, contest the ideas of others, and potentially challenge the news presentation agenda and its possible informing frameworks of interpretation. While each communicative form could be discussed in some detail, the key finding here is that formats 1–5 all provide severely restricted opportunities in respect of our concern with dialogic encounter as a key form of deliberative engagement. With 507 news items delivered routinely in these formats, these together represent 48.01 per cent of all news formats deployed across British television news. Nearly half of all TV news items, in other words, provide few if any opportunities for direct access and discursive engagement by non-news voices.

The ENG form, form 6, as previously described, provides limited opportunities of access and with 445 news items within the sample, it represents the single most commonly used of all forms across British TV news at 42.14 per cent. Interestingly, rarely is ENG deployed to interview groups (form 7, 0.09 per cent) where accessed voices could then at least potentially contest and engage directly opposing viewpoints and, in so doing, partially escape the news presentation's 'pseudo-engagement' manufactured from clipped voices juxtaposed later in the editing process.

Discursively, as we have seen, forms 8 (live individual interview) and 9 (live group interview) considerably improve upon the restricted and limited opportunities presented by forms 1–7. Live interviews afford interviewees an 'extended' opportunity to respond to the interviewer's questions, in their own terms, in chronological time, and in the ways that they feel are appropriate. They may even, on occasion, seek to challenge the interviewer's agenda and informing assumptions and agenda-shift to different issues and interpretative frameworks and in so doing fracture the imposition of a particular news frame. Live group

Table 9.1 British TV news and communicative forms

TV news forms	No.	%
Restricted:		
1 Newscaster (NC) only	11	1.04
2 Newscaster + still	104	9.85
3 NC/reporter (Rpt) film/voice over	354	33.52
4 Rpt direct to camera	5	0.47
5 NC + Rpt dialogue	33	3.13
Subtotal	507	48.01
Limited:		
6 ENG interview	445	42.14
7 ENG group interview	1	0.09
Subtotal	446	43.13
Extended:		
8 Studio live interview	61	5.78
9 Studio live group interview	26	2.46
Subtotal	87	8.24
Expansive:		
10 Ceded editorial control	16	1.52
Totals	1056	100.00

interviews also afford interviewees an opportunity not only to question informing news frames, but also to directly engage the ideas and interpretative frameworks of contending interests represented by other accessed voices. While news interviewers will invariably seek to 'hold the ring' on such occasions, the fact that interviewees are inside the ring potentially enables them to engage the ideas and arguments, the claims and counter-claims of their interlocutors. These, then, are deliberatively valuable communicative forms when deployed in relation to social conflicts, where contending interpretative and prescriptive frameworks are at play – and in how many news stories are these not present? Together these communicative forms, however, are only deployed within 8.24 per cent of news stories on British television news.

Finally, we come to ceded editorial control, where news programmes afford, as we have seen, an opportunity for social actors to represent themselves, their experiences and viewpoints in their own words and in ways that may involve accessing voices and views not normally granted a prominent role on the news stage. According to our systematic review, this particular communicative form is rarely deployed and was found in our sample to figure in only 1.52 per cent of all cases – notwithstanding its distinct capability for deepening deliberative processes, as illustrated in our opening example.

September 11 and Intercultural Understanding

Current affairs programmes, like news, are often named in statutory obligations placed upon broadcasters to enhance processes of democratic representation. Because of their longer production gestation they can also often provide a temporally longer view and deeper contextualisation of the events in question, as well as a more expansive forum for engaged public debate. The communicative forms of current affairs programmes, therefore, are no less relevant for a concern with deliberative democracy than news. The forms that current affairs programmes can assume are diverse, however, and are undergoing rapid adaptation and change in response to the changing commercial pressures of the marketplace. In the UK as elsewhere, the genre has recently been subject to enormous pressures to change – more populist magazine formats and 'infotainment' series, schedules offering relatively marginal schedule slots outside of weekdays and prime-time, and new forms of competing 'reality TV' (Cottle 1993a; Bromley 2001). Even so, the genre enjoys flagship status, especially within the public service sector of broadcasting.

This last discussion briefly examines this programme genre and how, in respect of the events and aftermath of September 11, it provided distinctive communicative forms facilitating wider public deliberation of these terrible events. To begin, we can first note how broadcasters produced and transmitted a number of current affairs and documentary programmes dealing with September 11 and its aftermath. Predictably, most confined their sights on the threats posed by Osama Bin Laden and other terrorist organisations to western governments and civilian populations (for example, BBC1 *Panorama*, 'The World's Most

Wanted', 16 Sept. 2001; C4 *Dispatches*, 'Bin Laden's Plan of Terror', 1 Nov. 2001) as well as western government responses to these (BBC1 *Panorama*, 'Britain on the Brink', 30 Sept. 2001; 'Circumstances Unknown', 2 Dec. 2001); the (scant) biographical details known about Osama Bin Laden himself (for example, C5 *Most Evil Men in History* series, 'The World's Most Wanted Man', 29 Nov. 2001); or other human interest dimensions (for example, C4 *Islam and America through the Eyes of Imran Khan*, 2 Nov. 2001; C4 *Heroes of Ground Zero*, 30 Nov. 2001). These programmes provided no doubt interesting and informative ingredients for public understanding and did so via the producers' orchestration of film narrative, juxtaposed and edited interviews, and informing presuppositions about what the audience needed to know or would be interested in. But what they could not do, because this was outside of their communicative forms, was to provide sustained and engaged discussion between involved protagonists and perspectives involving both performative dimensions and live communicative contingencies produced through face-to-face encounters.

This democratic responsibility fell to three programmes only. Each deliberately (deliberatively) sought to provide a wider public forum for contending arguments and perspectives on the events and aftermath of September 11, and it is these 'deliberative' programmes that form the basis of this discussion. Two were produced, as 'specials' within existing BBC programme series – *Panorama* ('Clash of Cultures', BBC1, 21 Oct. 2001) and *Question Time* (*Question Time Special*, BBC1, 13 Sept. 2001) – reflecting the ability of TV institutions to accommodate important developments within extant scheduling and established programme formats. *Panorama* is the BBC's flagship current affairs programme. Broadcast for nearly 50 years, it has become the longest-running public affairs TV programme in the world. *Question Time* was first broadcast in 1979 and has also become something of a national institution in the UK. According to its own publicity, it offers 'British voters a unique opportunity to quiz top decision-makers on the events of the day'. The third programme was especially commissioned by Channel 4 ('War on Trial', 27 Oct. 2001) in a rapidly convened series of programmes under its *War without End* season.

Each provided different public spaces, or 'agora', variously facilitating and containing the engaged display of contending perspectives and political prescriptions. The first, BBC1's *Question Time Special* (BBC1, 13 Sept. 2001) broadcast two days after September 11, provides a programme agora that is closely modelled on the ideas and institutional practices of representative parliamentary democracy. The programme chair (parliamentary 'speaker') officiates from his commanding position centre stage and delegates who is permitted to speak from the studio audience ('represented public') and who is permitted to pose (mainly pre-selected) questions to a panel of 'representatives' (MPs from the main political parties and public opinionated figures) who are assembled either side of the programme chair. These assembled 'senior figures' then hold forth on the various topics put to them.

A different forum or programme agora was enacted by the *Panorama* Special broadcast under the title of 'Clash of Cultures' (BBC1, 21 Oct. 2001). Importantly, this deliberately set out to incorporate a wider range of international opinions and cultural viewpoints than the predominantly national-based opinion of

Question Time, and then forward some of these to senior politicians in studio interviews. To facilitate this, the programme deployed satellite technology to bring into being a simultaneous 'electronic agora' with participants based in London, New York and Islamabad – three parts of the world directly affected by the events and aftermath of September 11. Again hosted by the BBC's ubiquitous David Dimbleby, the programme sought to incorporate differing views and frame these in terms of a deep cultural opposition – a clash of cultures.

The third programme treatment of September 11 provides a further form of programme agora replete with differing discursive opportunities and forms of containment. C4 *War on Trial* (27 Oct. 2001) mirrors the format of a legally conducted trial or debate. Here, though the presenter remains in overall programme control, the actual conduct of the debate is delegated for the most part to the 'prosecution' and 'defence' counsel. Once begun, the trial/debate moves relentlessly towards closure: in this instance a final vote by the studio audience in response to the programme's opening contention. The audience, we are told, are 'representative of the nation as a whole', but unlike the studio audience in *Question Time* bear witness only to the preceding debate and are not allowed to cross the impermeable boundary excluding them from active participation. The structure of this legalistic (debate) agora serves, then, to polarise arguments, heighten combative styles of public engagement, and throw into sharp relief the differences of perspective at play and the issues at stake (as well as differences of personality and public performance).

As this description of these three different programme agorae has illustrated, each is characterised by internal complexities of form that have a direct bearing for wider processes of public deliberation. Each provides qualitatively different opportunities for the public elaboration and dialogic engagement of differing political and cultural perspectives on, and arguments about, the events and aftermath of September 11. Taken together they represented a minority only of TV's September 11 coverage; however, their value in providing spaces for meaningful encounters supportive of wider deliberation should not be underestimated or overlooked. It is useful to consider just a few of the unique forms of deliberative engagement facilitated by these communicative forms – features that could not have been entertained by other programmes. The first extract represents a fairly typical exchange between programme guest and audience member in the *Question Time Special* discussion, chaired by David Dimbleby.

BBC1 Question Time Special (13 Sept. 2001)

David Dimbleby: All right, I'll take a point from the woman in the third row from the back and then I'm going to move on.

Woman in the third row: What scares me about the use of the word 'war' at the moment is the grim task of counting the dead. It's still not finished in America. How can we as a democratic nation justify killing other mothers, fathers, children of another nation?

David Dimbleby: Let me ask quite simply, if anybody in the audience disagrees with that point of view and believes that America should act and act swiftly? You Sir, on the left here [*pointing*].

Man on the left: The Americans that have been innocently killed, Tam Dalyell, you always come in on the side of the terrorists and have done for years.

Tam Dalyell: That I refute. I simply point out that when President Bush says that this is the first war of the twenty-first century, it is not so. A war has been going on for ten years of the daily bombing of Iraq. [*Applause*] Maybe it's the brothers and sisters of these people who are killed that evil men like Bin Laden like to exploit. These are very unpalatable facts; they had better be addressed.

Even within the hierarchical structure and limited opportunities for audience engagement permitted by the *Question Time* agora, opposing arguments, claims and counterclaims as well as reference to the credentials of the speakers involved can all become publicly expressed in a debate requiring the listener/viewer to deliberate on the contending perspectives and performances in play. Lest this exercise in deliberative democracy should be assumed to be pretty much a consensual affair, one need only witness how this can also lead to robust accusations and even attempted defamations of character. This is not genteel democracy or democracy for the faint-hearted but it is part of deliberative democracy nonetheless. Consider, for example, part of an emotionally charged and rhetorically informed exchange between David Aaronovitch, defending the military intervention in Afghanistan, and George Galloway MP, opposed to the war in C4's *War on Trial*.

David Aaronovitch: In the *Guardian*, in April 2001, you said of the things that you had done during the first Labour party administration, 'I am proudest to have stood firmly against a new imperialism, an Anglo-American aggression around the world.' Why aren't you proud to stand up against other aggression?

George Galloway: Your friends are elsewhere for you of course, you were a hard line communist before you shaved your beard off for tickling Tories' backsides.

David Aaronovitch: I am not going to bother to refute that, largely because I have never been 'hard line' in my entire life . . .

George Galloway: You were a hard line communist last . . .

David Aaronovitch: No, no.

George Galloway: You were a communist party member for years.

David Aaronovitch: Well, let's talk about what you are, George Galloway.

George Galloway: You were a communist party member for years.

David Aaronovitch: The Associated Press, and I read from November 1999, Azis, the Deputy Foreign Minister, Prime Minister Tariq Aziz with whom you spent Christmas 1999 said, 'our senior Iraqi leaders give a hero's welcome to British Labour Party member George Galloway who arrived in Baghdad to highlight the plight to the Iraqis of UN sanctions. Young girls sang the praises of Saddam as they showered Aziz and Galloway with roses and offered dates and yoghurt and symbols of war.' How must the Kurds have been choking on the yoghurt and roses that you were showered with!

George Galloway: Hear me out, hear me out. They may have sung hymns of praise to the leaders – I don't but you do.

David Aaronovitch: No, you most certainly do. I have never spent Christmas with a mass murderer and somebody who could have . . .

George Galloway: But you're in bed with, you're in bed with George W. Bush.

Mediated electronic agora facilitated by satellite link, can today serve to bring together normally distant audiences as well as different cultural and political outlooks. One last example taken from BBC1's *Panorama* Special 'Clash of Cultures' illustrates how an invited studio audience in Islamabad both queries the presenter's question premise and elaborates a reasoned response to the events and aftermath of September 11. In so doing the audience provides important insights into a different geo-political outlook to that informing the ideas of the studio audience listening in New York.

Nisha Pillai: Why is it that the people of Pakistan are so hostile towards the US? This is something that has been going on for years, isn't it?

Qazi Zulqader Sidiqui, Internet Consultant: Nisha, I think the issue is not that the people of Pakistan are hostile towards the United States. That is not really the case. I think it's totally misunderstood. The issue really is that just as much as the lives of people in the World Trade Center were valuable, that those people who died here, died wrongly. They should not have died. Nobody had the right to take their lives. Likewise, I don't believe that anybody has a right to take the lives of the innocent people of Afghanistan. It is the civilians of Afghanistan that are being bombed that are being killed, and nobody seems to think that has any value. That's collateral damage, which I think is a horrendous word that has been coined by the government of the United States. It is so bad that it is saying that life has no value whatsoever. How can anybody say that life has no value? If it's a Muslim life, it has no value. If it is somebody else's life that has value?

Nisha Pillai: Well you're nodding your head there Amina. How should a superpower like the US behave under these circumstances? We can't expect them to do nothing when 6000 people were killed?

Amina Sajjad, Teacher: Exactly, exactly. A superpower like America would be expected to show maybe more justice than they are showing. We would expect them to be international benefactors and supporters of international humanitarian causes. But they have proven themselves to be international bullies. They want that terrorism be uprooted. I find it very interesting that they have planted the seeds of terrorism all over the world. Hiroshima, Nagasaki, Cuba, Palestine, Kashmir, you name it. They have supported their interests, and it's really not about the Taliban. It's never been about Iraq invading Kuwait; it's really all about their interests in oil and now their interest in gas.

Nisha Pillai: At this point I'm sorry to say we're going to return to New York to see what their response is to what our Pakistani audience is saying.

Current affairs programme forms such as these are relatively rare in our TV schedules; their capacity to provide meaningful encounters and vital resources for deepened understanding and deliberation should not be overlooked or under-theorised.

Conclusion

This discussion has sought to highlight how extant communicative forms of television journalism, both news and current affairs, can contribute vital resources for processes of deliberative democracy. Though these forms are differentiated in practice and exhibit their own internal complexities of form, at the centre of all of them are dialogical encounters between contending perspectives and interests expressed through 'talking heads'. People talking to each other publicly remains one of the most effective and illuminating ways for an overhearing, overseeing audience to arrive at an improved understanding of the issues, interests and identities at stake within different conflicts and between contending outlooks. Through these communicative forms of television journalism, 'discursive democracy' can variously come into being and provide resources for wider public deliberation and understanding – resources that are both timely and necessary in times of social reflexivity, discursive profusion and democratic deficit. Communicative forms that deliberately (and deliberatively) encompass dialogical encounters between contending perspectives and interests provide unique resources for wider processes of deliberation. They do this in the following ways:

1 Encouraging differing viewpoints to justify and defend their claims and aims publicly through live, close, often combative, sometimes conciliatory engagement with their interlocutors.

2 Enabling, on occasion, programme agendas, presenter presuppositions as well as those of other programme participants to be rendered explicit and open to public challenge.

3 Producing robust, sustained engagement and rhetorical performances enacted and witnessed in chronological (in contrast to edited) time.

4 Providing opportunities for the credentials and legitimacy of speakers to be questioned and challenged, and for these in turn to be defended and challenges rebutted.

5 Facilitating grounds for improved cross-cultural understanding through electronically constituted agora and intercultural exchange of values/stories as well as views/arguments.

6 Presenting both programme participants and audiences with an integral 'live event', displaying communicatively contingent and emergent dynamics – much of which remains unscripted.

In all these ways, extant communicative forms of television journalism can contribute vital resources for wider processes of public deliberation. Their democratic value needs to be more widely acknowledged, however, and we need to understand better how these communicative forms mediate strategic interests and the play of communicative action. In line with recent theories of deliberative democracy, we need to seek out ways of democratically deepening these communicative forms and extending their use in the future. Contrary to popular myth, television's 'talking heads' need not be 'boring'; they contribute to the lifeblood of democracy.

CHAPTER SUMMARY

- In today's conflicted societies an increased plurality of contending interests, identities and discourses vie and contend for public recognition, support and legitimacy. The media are prime sites in which communicative action may be pursued.

- Ideas of 'deliberative democracy', that is of 'democratic deepening' via processes of public deliberation, seek to address both the radical pluralism of civil society and also the moribund nature of representative processes of liberal democracy.

- The media, and forms of news and current affairs programming particularly, can here be seen as meaningful vehicles for wider deliberative processes. It is therefore necessary to investigate extant forms of TV journalism and explore how these enable or disable the politics of engaged debate and discussion and the public elaboration of contending views (and performances) for a wider overhearing, overseeing audience.

- Extant forms of TV journalism provide some opportunities for engaged dialogical encounters and the justification and defence of contending views and values. These 'meaningful' forms currently exist, provide unique features of deliberative communication and value, but are rarely used.

- Deliberative formats of TV journalism are needed in conditions of increased social reflexivity and radical pluralism. Contrary to popular claims, 'talking heads' need not be boring. Deliberative forms of television need to be taken more seriously by media academics and extended and developed in their use in the future.

Notes

1 This study confines its sights to an initial examination of the deliberative forms of news and current affairs programmes. Future work is needed to go behind these forms and examine their historical evolution and possible dependency on, or determination by, changing political economy, technologies, institutional contexts and wider cultural and political settings (see Winston 1993; MacGregor 1997; Cottle 1999). The author is currently undertaking an international comparative, historical and production-based study of TV news and current affairs in Australia, the USA, UK, India and Singapore 'TV News, Current Affairs and Deliberative Democracy'. Ideas of 'communicative action' as well as 'deliberative democracy', the subject of this discussion, have been influenced by the writings of Habermas (1984, 1996), but both here necessarily depart from Habermas's original formulation.

2 The examples used here first appeared in Cottle (2000, 2001, 2002), where further discussion and details of each can be found. Here they help to illustrate for the first time an encompassing argument about TV journalism and deliberative democracy.

References

Abercrombie, N., Hill, S. and Turner, B. (1980) *The Dominant Ideology Thesis*. London: Allen & Unwin.

Alberoni, F. (1972) 'The Powerless Elite: Theory and Sociological Research on the Phenomenon of the Stars', in D. McQuail (ed.) *Sociology of Mass Communications: Selected Readings*. Harmondsworth: Penguin.

Alexander, J.C. (1988) 'Culture and Political Crisis: "Watergate" and Durkheimian Sociology', in J.C. Alexander (ed.) *Durkheimian Sociology: Cultural Studies*. New York: Cambridge University Press, pp. 187–224.

Alexander, J.C. and Jacobs, R.N. (1998) 'Mass Communication, Ritual and Civil Society', in T. Liebes and J. Curran (eds) *Media, Ritual and Identity*. London: Routledge, pp. 23–41.

Alinsky, S.D. (1971) *Rules for Radicals*. New York: Vantage.

Allan, S., Adam, B. and Carter, C. (eds) (2000) *Environmental Risks and the Media*. London: Routledge.

Alloway, L. (1971) *Violent America: the Movies 1946–1964*. New York: Museum of Modern Art.

Altheide, D.L. (1976) *Creating Reality*. Beverly Hills, CA, and London: Sage.

Altheide, D.L. (1995) *An Ecology of Communication: Cultural Formats of Control*. New York: Aldine de Gruyter.

Altheide, D.L and Snow, R.P. (1979) *Media Logic*. Beverly Hills, CA: Sage.

Altheide, D.L. and Snow, R.P. (1991) *Media Worlds in the Postjournalism Era*. Hawthorne, NY: Aldine de Gruyter.

Altschull, J.H. (1997) 'Boundaries of Journalistic Autonomy', in D. Berkowitz (ed.) *Social Meanings of News*. Thousand Oaks, CA, and London: Sage, pp. 259–68.

Anderson, A. (1991) 'Source Strategies and the Communication of Environmental Affairs', *Media, Culture and Society*, 13 (4): 459–76.

Anderson, A. (1993) 'Source–Media Relations: the Production of the Environmental Agenda', in A. Hansen (ed.) *Mass Media and Environmental Issues*. Leicester: Leicester University Press, pp. 51–68.

Anderson, A. (1997) *Media, Culture and the Environment*. London: UCL Press.

Anderson, A. (2000) 'Environmental Pressure Politics and the Risk Society', in S. Allan, B. Adam and C. Carter (eds) *Environmental Risks and the Media*. London: Routledge, pp. 93–104.

Atton, C. (2002) *Alternative Media*. London: Sage.

Badsey, S. (1995) 'Twenty Things You Thought You Knew about the Media', *Despatches*, 5 (Spring).

Ball-Rokeach, S. and De Fleur, M. (1976) 'A Dependency Model of Mass Media Effects', *Communication Research*, 3: 3–21.

Barkin, S.M. and Gurevitch, M. (1987) 'Out of Work and on the Air: Television News and Unemployment', *Critical Studies in Mass Communication*, 4 (4): 1–20.

Barnett, S. and Gaber, I. (2001) *Westminster Tales: the Twenty First Century Crisis in Political Journalism*. London: Continuum.

Beck, U. (1992) *Risk Society*. London: Sage.

Beck, U. (1997) *The Reinvention of Politics*. Cambridge: Polity Press.

Beck, U., Giddens, A. and Lash, S. (eds) (1994) *Reflexive Modernization*. Cambridge: Polity Press.

Becker, H. (1963) *Outsiders Studies in the Sociology of Deviance*. New York: The Free Press of Glencoe.

Becker, H. (1967) 'Whose Side Are We On?' *Social Problems*, 14: 239–47.

Bell, M. (1995) *In Harm's Way: Reflections of a War Zone Thug*. London: Hamish Hamilton.

Benhabib, S. (ed.) (1996) *Democracy and Difference*. Princeton, IL: Princeton University Press.

Bennett, L. and Paletz, D. (eds) (1994) *Taken by Storm: the Media, Public Opinion, and U.S. Foreign Policy in the Gulf War*. Chicago and London: The University of Chicago Press.

Bennett, T., Martin, G., Mercer, C. and Woollacott, J. (eds) (1981) *Culture Ideology and Social Process: A Reader*. London: Batsford Academic and Educational.

Bennett, W.L. (1983) *News: the Politics of Illusion* (2nd edn). New York: Longman.

Bennett, W.L. (1988) *News: The Politics of Illusion*. New York: Longman.

Bennett, W.L. (1990) 'Towards a Theory of Press–State Relations in the United States', *Journal of Communication*, 40 (2): 103–25.

Bennie, L.G. (1998) 'Brent Spar, Atlantic Oil and

Greenpeace', *Parliamentary Affairs*, 51 (3): 397–410.

Berkowitz, D. (1992) 'Non-routine News and Newswork: Exploring What-a-Story', *Journal of Communication*, 43 (4): 80–8.

Berry, J. (1984) *The Interest Group Society*. Boston, MA: Little, Brown & Company.

Bird, E. (1990) 'Storytelling on the Far Side: Journalism and the Weekly Tabloid', *Critical Studies in Mass Communication*, 7: 377–89.

Bird, E. and Dardenne, R.W. (1988) 'Myth, Chronicle and Story: Exploring the Narrative Qualities of News', in J. Carey (ed.) *Media, Myths and Narratives: Television and the Press*. Thousand Oaks, CA, and London: Sage Publications, pp. 67–86.

Bird, S.E. (1992) *For Enquiring Minds: A Cultural Sudy of Supermarket Tabloids*. Knoxville: University of Tennessee Press.

Blau, P.F. (1964) *Exchange and Power in Social Life*. New York: John Wiley & Sons.

Blumer, H. (1969) *Symbolic Interactionism: Perspectives on Method*. Englewood Cliff, NJ: Prentice-Hall.

Blumer, H. (1971) 'Social Problems as Collective Behaviour', *Social Problems*, 18: 298–306.

Blumler, J.G. and Gurevitch, M. (1981) 'Politicians and the Press: An Essay on Role Relationships', in D.D. Nimmo and K.R. Sanders (eds) *Handbook of Political Communication*. London: Sage.

Blumler, J.G. and Gurevitch, M. (1986) 'Journalists' Orientations to Political Institutions: The Case of Parliamentary Broadcasting', in P. Golding, G. Murdock and P. Schlesinger (eds) *Communicating Politics: Mass Communications and the Political Process*. Leicester: Leicester University Press, pp. 67–92.

Blumler, J. and Gurevitch, M. (1996) 'Media Change and Social Change: Linkages and Junctures', in J. Curran and M. Gurevitch (eds) *Mass Media and Society*. London: Edward Arnold.

Bohman, J. and Rehg, W. (eds) (1997) *Deliberative Democracy: Essays on Reason and Politics*. Cambridge, MA: MIT Press.

Boorstein, D.J. (1964) *The Image: A Guide to Pseudo-events in America*. New York: Harper & Row.

Bourdieu, P. (1979) *Distinction*. London: Routledge.

Brindle, D. (1999) 'Media Coverage of Social Policy: a Journalist's Perspective', in B. Franklin (ed.) *Social Policy, the Media and Misrepresentation*. London: Routledge.

Bromley, M. (ed.) (2001) *No News Is Bad News*. Harlow: Longman.

Brunsdon, C. and Morley, D. (1978) *Everyday Television: 'Nationwide'*. London: British Film Institute.

Butler, D. (1995) *The Trouble with Reporting Northern Ireland*. Aldershot: Avebury.

Cabinet Office (1997) *Guidance on the Working of the Government Information Service*. London: HMSO.

Campbell, R. (1987) 'Securing the Middle Ground: Reporter Formulas in 60 Minutes', *Critical Studies in Mass Communication*, 4 (4): 325–50.

Carruthers, S. (2000) *The Media at War: Communication and Conflict in the Twentieth Century*. Basingstoke: Macmillan.

Castells, M. (1996) *The Rise of the Network Society*. Oxford: Blackwell.

Castells, M. (1997) *The Power of Identity*. Oxford: Blackwell.

Challener, A. (ed.) (1970) *The Papers of Dwight David Eisenhower Vol. 4: The War Years*. Baltimore: Johns Hopkins University Press.

Chaney, D. (1986) 'The Symbolic Form of Ritual in Mass Communication', in P. Golding, G. Murdock and P. Schlesinger (eds) *Communicating Politics: Mass Communication and Political Process*. Leicester: Leicester University Press, pp. 115–32.

Chesters, G. (1999) 'Resist to Exist: Radical Environmentalism at the End of the Millennium', *ECOS: A Review of Conservation*, 20 (2): 19–25.

Chibnall, S. (1977) *Law and Order News: An Analysis of Crime Reporting in the British Press*. London: Tavistock.

Clayman, S.E. (2002) 'Tribune of the People: Maintaining the Legitimacy of the People', *Media, Culture and Society*, 24 (2): 197–216.

Cohen, N. (1999a) *Cruel Britannia: Reports on the Sinister and the Preposterous*. London: Verso.

Cohen, N. (1999b) 'An Explosion of Puffery', *New Statesman*, 29 November, pp. 14–15.

Cohen, N. (2001) 'Not Spinning but Drowning', *New Statesman*, 19 February, pp. 16–19.

Cohen, S. (1972) *Folk Devils and Moral Panics*. London: MacGibbon & Kee.

Cohen, S. and Young, J. (eds) (1981) *The Manufacture of News: Social Problems, Deviance and the Mass Media*. London: Constable.

COI (Central Office of Information) (1970–99) *The IPO Directory: Information and Press Officers in Government Departments and Public Corporations*. London: COI.

Conrad, P. (1982) *Television: the Medium and Its Manners*. London: Routledge & Kegan Paul.

Cottle, S. (1993a) *TV News, Urban Conflicts and the Inner City*. Leicester: Leicester University Press.

Cottle, S. (1993b) 'Mediating the Environment: Modalities of TV News', in A. Hansen (ed.) *The*

Mass Media and Environmental Issues. Leicester: Leicester University Press, pp. 107–33.

Cottle, S. (1999) 'From BBC Newsroom to BBC Newscentre: on Changing Technology and Journalist Practices', *Convergence: The Journal of Research into New Media Technologies*, 5 (3): 22–43.

Cottle, S. (2000a) 'TV News, Lay Voices and the Visualisation of Environmental Risks', in S. Allan, B. Adam and C. Carter (eds) *Environmental Risks and the Media.* London: Routledge, pp. 29–44.

Cottle, S. (2000b) 'New(s) Times: towards a "Second Wave" of News Ethnography', *Communications: European Journal of Communication Research*, 25 (1): 19–41.

Cottle, S. (2000c) 'Rethinking News Access', *Journalism Studies*, 1 (3): 427–48.

Cottle, S. (2001) 'Television News and Citizenship: Packaging the Public Sphere', in M. Bromley (ed.) *No News Is Bad News.* Harlow: Pearson Education, pp. 61–79.

Cottle, S. (2002) 'TV Agora and Agoraphobia Post September 11', in B. Zelizer and S. Allan (eds) *Journalism after September 11.* London: Routledge, pp. 178–98.

Cottle, S. (forthcoming a) *Media Performance and Public Transformation: The Racist Murder of Stephen Lawrence.* New York: Praeger Publishers.

Cottle, S. (ed.) (forthcoming b) *Media Organisation and Production.* London: Sage.

Coxall, W. (1986) *Political Realities: Parties and Pressure Groups.* Harlow: Longman.

Cracknell, J. (1993) 'Issue Arenas, Pressure Groups and Agendas', in A. Hansen (ed.) *Mass Media and Environmental Issues.* Leicester: Leicester University Press, pp. 3–21.

Cumberbatch, G., McGregor, R., Brown, J. and Morrison, D. (1986) *Television and the Miners' Strike.* London: Broadcasting Research Unit.

Cumberbatch, G., Brown, J. and McGregor, R. (1988) 'Arresting Knowledge: a Response to the Debate about TV and the Miners' Strike', *Media, Culture and Society*, 10 (2): 112–16.

Curran, J. (1991) 'Rethinking the Media as Public Sphere', in P. Dahlgren and C. Sparks (eds) *Communication and Citizenship.* London: Routledge, pp. 27–57.

Curran, J. (1996) 'Rethinking Mass Communications', in J. Curran, D. Morley and V. Walkerdine (eds) *Cultural Studies and Communications.* London: Arnold, pp. 119–65.

Curran, J. and Seaton, J. (1997) *Power without Responsibility.* London: Routledge.

Cutlip, S., Center, A. and Broom, G. (2000) *Effective Public Relations.* Englewood Cliff, NJ: Prentice-Hall.

Dahlgren, P. (1988) 'What's the Meaning of This? Viewers' Plural Sense: Making of TV News', *Media, Culture and Society*, 10 (3): 285–301.

Dahlgren, P. (1995) *Television and the Public Sphere: Citizenship, Democracy and the Media.* London: Sage.

Danielian, L.H. (1988) 'From "bouncing bosoms" to the ERA: *L.A. Times* coverage of L.A. N.O.W.: Mass media activities from 1980–1983', Paper presented at International Communication Association Convention, New Orleans.

Davis, A. (1998) *Trade Union Communications in the 1990s: A Report for the TUC and its Affiliate Unions.* London: TUC.

Davis, A. (2000a) 'Public Relations, News Production and Changing Patterns of Source Access in British National Media', *Media, Culture and Society*, 22 (1): 39–59.

Davis, A. (2000b) 'Public Relations Campaigning and News Production: the Case of New Unionism in Britain', in J. Curran (ed.) *Media Organisations in Society.* London: Arnold, pp. 173–92.

Davis, A. (2000c) 'Public Relations, Business News and the Reproduction of Corporate Elite Power', *Journalism, Theory, Practice and Criticism*, 1 (3): 282–304.

Davis, A. (2002) *Public Relations Democracy.* Manchester: Manchester University Press.

Davis, A. (forthcoming) 'Whither Mass Media: Evidence for a Critical Elite Theory Alternative', *Media, Culture and Society.*

Dayan, D. and Katz, E. (1992) *Media Events: The Live Broadcasting of History.* Cambridge, MA: Harvard University Press.

Deacon, D. (1996) 'The Voluntary Sector in a Changing Communication Environment: a Case Study of Non-official News Sources', *European Journal of Communication*, 11 (2): 173–99.

Deacon, D. (1999) 'Charitable Images: the Construction of Voluntary Sector News', in B. Franklin (ed.) *Social Policy, the Media and Misrepresentation.* London: Routledge.

Deacon, D. and Golding, P. (1994) *Taxation and Representation: the Media, Political Communication and the Poll Tax.* London: John Libbey.

Deacon, D. and Monk, W. (2000) 'Executive Stressed? News Reporting of Quangos in Britain', *Press/Politics*, 5 (3): 45–63.

Deacon, D. and Monk, W. (2001) 'Quangos and the "Communications Dependent Society": Part of the Process or Exceptions to the Rule?', *European Journal of Communication*, 16 (1): 25–49.

Deacon, D., Fenton, N. and Walker, B. (1995) 'Communicating Philanthropy: the Media and the Voluntary Sector in Britain', *Voluntas*, 6 (1): 119–39.

Diamond, E. (1975) *The Tin Kazoo: Television, Politics and the News*. Cambridge, MA: MIT Press.

Doherty, B. (1999a) 'Change the World via E-Mail', *New Statesman*, 1 November, pp. xviii–xix.

Doherty, B. (1999b) 'Paving the Way: the Rise of Direct Action against Road-Building and the Changing Character of British Environmentalism', *Political Studies*, 47 (2): 275–91.

Dordoy, A. and Mellor, M. (2001) 'Grassroots Environmental Movements: Mobilisation in an Information Age', in F. Webster (ed.) *Culture and Politics in the Information Age*. London: Routledge, pp. 167–82.

Downing, J. (1986) 'Government Secrecy and the Media', in P. Golding, G. Murdock and P. Schlesinger (eds) *Communicating Politics*. Leicester: Leicester University Press, pp. 153–70.

Dryzek, J. (1990) *Discursive Democracy*. Cambridge: Cambridge University Press.

Dryzek, J. (2000) *Deliberative Democracy and Beyond*. Oxford: Oxford University Press.

DTI (1994) Stoy Hayward Management Consultants, *The Public Relations Sector: An Analysis for the Department of Trade and Industry*. London: DTI.

Dunwoody, S. (1978) 'Science Writers at Work', in D. Berkowitz (ed.) *Social Meanings of News*. Thousand Oaks, CA, and London: Sage Publications, pp. 155–67.

Edwards, R. (1988) 'Spirit of Outrage', *New Statesman and Society*, 29 July, pp. 16–18.

Ehrlich, M.C. (1995) 'The Competitive Ethos of Television News', *Critical Studies in Mass Communication*, 12: 196–212.

Ekstein, M. (1989) *Rights of Spring: the Great War and the Birth of the Modern Age*. London: Bantam Press.

Eldridge, J. (ed.) (1993) *Getting the Message: News, Truth and Power*. London: Routledge.

Eldridge, J. (ed.) (1995) *News Content, Language and Visuals*. Glasgow University media reader. London: Routledge.

Eliasoph, E. (1988) 'Routines and the Making of Oppositional News', *Critical Studies in Mass Communication*, 5: 313–34.

Elliott, P. (1980) 'Press Performance as Political Ritual', in H. Christian (ed.) *The Sociology of Journalism and the Press*. University of Keele:

Sociological Review Monograph No. 29, pp. 141–77.

Elliott, P. (1986) 'Intellectuals, "the Information Society" and the Disappearance of the Public Sphere', in R. Collins, J. Curran, N. Garnham, P. Scannell, P. Schlesinger and C. Sparks (eds) *Media, Culture and Society: A Critical Reader*. London: Sage, pp. 247–63.

Emerson, R. (1972) 'Power–Dependence Relations', *American Sociological Review*, 27: 31–41.

Entman, R. (1989) *Democracy without Citizens*. New York: Oxford University Press.

Epstein, E.J. (1973) *News from Nowhere: Television and the News*. New York: Random House.

Ericson, R.V., Baranek, P.M. and Chan, J.B.L. (1987) *Visualizing Deviance: A Study of News Organisation*. Milton Keynes: Open University Press.

Ericson, R.V., Baranek, P.M. and Chan, J.B.L. (1989) *Negotiating Control: A Study of News Sources*. Milton Keynes: Open University Press.

Esslin, M. (1982) *The Age of Television*. San Francisco: W.H. Freeman.

Ettema, J. (1990) 'Press Rites and Race Relations: A Study of Mass-Mediated Ritual', *Critical Studies in Mass Communication*, 7: 309–31.

Evans, H.M. (2001) 'The Combat Correspondent', *Media Studies Journal*, 15 (1): 2–7.

Ewen, S. (1996) *PR! A Social History of Spin*. New York: Basic Books.

Fialka, J.K. (1992) *Hotel Warriors: Covering the Gulf War*. Washington: Woodrow Wilson Press.

Fishman, M. (1980) *Manufacturing News*. Austin: University of Texas Press.

Fishman, M. (1981) 'Crime Waves as Ideology', in S. Cohen and J. Young (eds) *The Manufacture of News*. London: Constable, pp. 98–117.

Fiske, J. (1987) *Television Culture*. London: Methuen.

Franklin, B. (1991) 'Watchdog or Lapdog? Local Press/Politicians Relations in West Yorkshire', *Local Government Studies*, September/October: 15–32.

Franklin, B. (1994) *Packaging Politics: Political Communication in Britain's Media Democracy*. London: Arnold.

Franklin, B. (1997) *Newzak and News Media*. London: Arnold.

Franklin, B. (1998) *Tough on Soundbites, Tough on the Causes of Soundbites: New Labour and News Management*. London: Catalyst Trust.

Franklin, B. (1999) 'Soft-Soaping the Public? The Government and Media Promotion of Social Policy', in B. Franklin (ed.) *Social Policy, the Media and Misrepresentation*. London: Routledge.

Franklin, B. and Murphy, D. (1998) 'Changing

Times: Local Newspapers, Technology and Markets', in B. Franklin and D. Murphy (eds) *Making the Local News: Local Journalism in Context*. London: Routledge, pp. 7–24.

Franklin, B. and Parry, J. (1998) 'Old Habits Die Hard: Journalism's Changing Professional Commitments and Local Newspaper Reporting of the 1997 General Election', in B. Franklin and D. Murphy (eds) *Making the Local News: Local Journalism in Context*. London: Routledge, pp. 209–28.

Franklin, B. and Richardson, J. (2002) 'A Journalist's Duty? Continuity and Change in Local Newspaper Reporting of Recent UK General Elections', *Journalism Studies*, 3 (1): 35–53.

Frazer, N. (1992) 'Rethinking the Public Sphere: A Contribution to the Critique of Actually Existing Democracy', in C. Calhoun (ed.) *Habermas and the Public Sphere*. Cambridge, MA, and London: MIT Press, pp. 109–42.

Frye, N. (1957) *Anatomy of Criticism: Four Essays*. Princeton, NJ: Princeton University Press.

Fussell, P. (1975) *The Great War and Modern Memory*. Oxford: Oxford University Press.

Gaber, I. (1998) 'A World of Dogs and Lamp-posts', *New Statesman*, 19 June, p. 14.

Galtung, J. and Ruge, M. (1981) 'Structuring and Selecting News', in S. Cohen and J. Young (eds) *The Manufacture of News: Deviance, Social Problems and the Mass Media* (2nd edn). London: Constable.

Gamson, W.A. (1988) 'Political Discourse and Collective Action', in B. Klandermans, H. Kriesi, H. Tarrow and S. Tarrow (eds) *From Structure to Action: Social Movement Participation across Cultures*. Greenwich, CT: JAI Press.

Gamson, W.A. (1989) 'News as Framing', *American Behavioral Scientist*, 33: 157–61.

Gamson, W.A. (1992) *Talking Politics*. Cambridge: Cambridge University Press.

Gamson, W.A. and Modigliani, A. (1989) 'Media Discourse and Public Opinion on Nuclear Power: A Constructionist Approach', *American Journal of Sociology*, 95: 1–37.

Gamson, W. and Wolfsfeld, G. (1993) 'Movements and Media as Interacting Systems', *The Annals of the American Academy of Political and Social Science*, 528: 114–25.

Gamson, W.A., Croteau, D., Hoynes, W. and Sasson, T. (1992) 'Media Images and the Social Construction of Reality', *Annual Review of Sociology*, 18: 373–93.

Gandy, O. (1980) 'Information in Health: Subsidised News', *Media Culture and Society*, 2 (2): 103–15.

Gandy, O.H. (1982) *Beyond Agenda Setting: Information Subsidies and Public Policy*. Norwood, NJ: Ablex Publishing.

Gans, H.J. (1979) *Deciding What's News: A Study of CBS Evening News, NBC Nightly News, Newsweek and Time*. New York: Pantheon.

Garnham, N. (1986) 'The Media as Public Sphere', in P. Golding, G. Murdock and P. Schlesinger (eds) *Communicating Politics*. Leicester: Leicester University Press, pp. 37–53.

Garrow, D.J. (1978) *Protest at Selma*. New Haven, CT: Yale University Press.

Gerbner, G. (1992) 'Violence and Terror in and by the Media', in M. Raboy and B. Dagenais (eds) *Media, Crisis and Democracy*. London: Sage, pp. 94–107.

Giddens, A. (1990) *The Consequences of Modernity*. Cambridge: Polity Press.

Giddens, A. (1994) *Beyond Left and Right*. Cambridge: Polity Press.

Gitlin, T. (1980) *The Whole World Is Watching: Mass Media and the Making and Unmaking of the New Left*. Berkeley, CA: University of California Press.

Glasgow University Media Group (GUMG) (1976) *Bad News*. London: Routledge & Kegan Paul.

Glasgow University Media Group (GUMG) (1980) *More Bad News*. London: Routledge & Kegan Paul.

Goffman, E. (1963) *Stigma. Notes on the Management of Spoiled Identity*. London: Penguin Books.

Goldenberg, E. (1975) *Making the Papers: The Access of Resource-Poor Groups to the Metropolitan Press*. Lexington, MA: D.C. Heath.

Golding, P. (2000) 'Forthcoming Features: Information and Communications Technologies and the Sociology of the Future', *Sociology*, 34 (1): 165–84.

Golding, P. and Elliott, P. (1979) *Making the News*. London: Longman.

Golding, P. and Murdock, G. (1979) 'Ideology and the Mass Media: The Question of Determination', in M. Barrett (ed.) *Ideology and Cultural Production*. London: Croom Helm, pp. 198–224.

Goodwin, A. (1990) 'TV News: Striking the Right Balance?' in A. Goodwin and G. Whannel (eds) *Understanding Television*. London: Routledge.

Gouldner, A.W. (1976) *The Dialectic of Ideology and Technology*. London: Macmillan.

Graber, D.A. (1976) *Verbal Behavior and Politics*. Urbana, IL: University of Illinois Press.

Graber, D.A. (1980) *Mass Media and American Politics*. Washington: Professional Quarterly.

Grant, W. (1993) *Business and Politics in Britain.* London: Macmillan.

Grant, W. (2001) 'Pressure Politics: From "Insider" Politics to Direct Action?' *Parliamentary Affairs*, 54: 337–48.

Greatbatch, D. (1986) 'Aspects of Topical Organisation in News Interviews: the Use of Agenda-shifting Procedures by Interviewees', *Media, Culture and Society*, 8 (4): 441–55.

Grossman, M.B. and Rourke, F.E. (1976) 'The Media and the Presidency: an Exchange Analysis', *Political Science Quarterly*, 91: 455–70.

Habermas, J. (1984) *The Theory of Communicative Action.* Vol. 1. Cambridge: Polity Press.

Habermas, J. (1989) *The Structural Transformation of the Public Sphere.* Cambridge: Polity Press.

Habermas, J. (1996) *Between Facts and Norms.* Cambridge: Polity Press.

Hacker, K.L. and van Dijk, J. (eds) (2000) *Digital Democracy: Issues of Theory and Practice.* London: Sage.

Hall, S. (1973) 'The Determinations of News Photographs', in S. Cohen and J. Young (eds) *The Manufacture of News.* London: Constable.

Hall, S. (1974) 'Deviancy, Politics and the Media', in P. Rock and M. McIntosh (eds) *Deviance and Social Control.* London: Tavistock.

Hall, S. (1975a) 'The "Structured" Communication of Events', in UNESCO (ed.) *Getting the Message Across.* Paris: UNESCO, pp. 115–45.

Hall, S. (1975b) 'Introduction', in A.C.H. Smith (ed.) *Paper Voices: the Popular Press and Social Change, 1935–1965.* London: Chatto & Windus.

Hall, S. (1982) 'The Rediscovery of Ideology: Return of the Repressed in Media Studies', in M. Gurevitch, T. Bennett, J. Curran and J. Woollacott (eds) *Culture, Society, Media.* London: Methuen, pp. 56–90.

Hall, S. and Jacques, M. (eds) (1989) *New Times.* London: Lawrence & Wishart.

Hall, S., Critcher, C., Jefferson, T., Clarke, J. and Roberts, B. (1978) *Policing the Crisis: Mugging, the State and Law and Order.* London: Macmillan.

Hallin, D. (1986) *The Uncensored War: The Media and Vietnam.* Oxford: Oxford University Press.

Hallin, D. (1994) *We Keep America on Top of the World: Television Journalism and the Public Sphere.* London: Routledge.

Hansen, A. (ed.) (1993a) *The Mass Media and Environmental Issues.* Leicester: Leicester University Press.

Hansen, A. (1993b) 'Greenpeace and Press Coverage of Environmental Issues', in A. Hansen (ed.) *The Mass Media and Environmental Issues.* Leicester: Leicester University Press, pp. 150–78.

Hansen, A. (2000) 'Claims-making and Framing in the British Newspaper Coverage of the Brent Spar Controversy', in S. Allan, B. Adam and C. Carter (eds) *Environmental Risks and the Media.* London: Routledge, pp. 55–72.

Harding, T. (1998) 'Viva Camcordistas! Video Activism and the Protest Movement', in G. McKay (ed.) *DiY Culture: Party and Protest in Nineties Britain.* London: Verso.

Harrison, M. (1985) *Television News: Whose Bias?* Berkhemstead: Policy Journals Publication.

Haste, C. (1977) *Keep the Home Fires Burning. Propaganda in the First World War.* London: Allen Lane.

Held, D., McGrew, A., Goldblatt, D. and Perraton, J. (1999) *Global Transformations: Politics, Economics, Culture.* Cambridge: Polity Press.

Heritage, J. and Greatbatch, D. (1993) 'On the Institutional Character of Institutional Talk: the Case of News Interviews', in D. Boden and D. Zimmerman (eds) *Talk and Social Structure: Studies in Ethnomethodology and Conversation Analysis.* Cambridge: Polity Press, pp. 93–137.

Herman, E. and Chomsky, N. (1988) *Manufacturing Consent: The Political Economy of the Mass Media.* New York: Pantheon.

Hilgartner, S. and Bosk, C.L. (1988) 'The Rise and Fall of Social Problems: a Public Arenas Model', *American Journal of Sociology*, 94 (1): 53–78.

Hills, J. (ed.) (1996) *New Inequalities: the Changing Distribution of Income and Wealth in the United Kingdom.* Cambridge: Cambridge University Press.

Hoggart, R. (1957) *The Uses of Literacy.* London: Pelican.

Holloway, J. (1998) 'Undercurrent Affairs: Radical Environmentalism and Alternative News', *Environment and Planning A*, 30: 1197–217.

Hughes, H.M. (1968) *News and the Human Interest Story.* New York: Greenwood Press.

Hunt, D. (1999) *O.J. Simpson Facts and Fictions: News Rituals in the Construction of Reality.* Cambridge: Cambridge University Press.

Husband, C. (2000) 'Media and the Public Sphere in Multi-ethnic Societies', in S. Cottle (ed.) *Ethnic Minorities and the Media: Changing Cultural Boundaries.* Buckingham: Open University Press, pp. 119–214.

Hutton, W. (1996) *The State We're In.* London: Vintage.

Ingham, B. (1990) 'Government and Media Co-existence and Tension', Unpublished Lecture delivered at Trinity and All Saints University College, Leeds, 22 November.

Ingham, B. (2001) 'Spin and the 2001 UK General Election', *Journalism Studies*, 2 (4): 585–90.

Institute of Public Relations (1998) *Membership Surveys*. London: IPR.

Jacobs, R.N. (1996) 'Producing the News, Producing the Crisis: Narrativity, Television and News Work', *Media, Culture and Society*, 18 (3): 373–97.

Jones, N. (1986) *Strikes and the Media: Communication and Conflict*. Oxford: Basil Blackwell.

Jones, N. (1995) *Soundbites and Spin Doctors: How Politicians Manipulate the Media and Vice Versa*. London: Cassell.

Jones, N. (1999) *Sultans of Spin: the Media and the New Labour Government*. London: Orion.

Jones, N. (2001) *The Control Freaks: How New Labour Gets its Own Way*. London: Politico's.

Kellner, P. (1983) 'The Lobby, Official Secrets and Good Government', *Parliamentary Affairs*, 36 (3) Summer: 275–82.

Kerr, A. and Sachdev, S. (1992) 'Third among Equals: an Analysis of the 1989 Ambulance Dispute', *British Journal of Industrial Relations*, 30 (1): 127–43.

Kitzinger, J. and Reilly, J. (1997) 'The Rise and Fall of Risk Reporting: Media Coverage of Human Genetics Research, "False Memory Syndrome" and Mad Cow Disease', *European Journal of Communication*, 12 (3): 319–50.

Klapp, O.E. (1964) *Symbolic Leaders, Public Dramas and Public Men*. Chicago: Aldine de Gruyter.

Knightley, P. (1975) *First Casualty: from the Crimea to Vietnam: the War Correspondent as Hero, Propagandist and Myth Maker*. New York: Harcourt Brace Jovanovich.

Langer, J. (1998) *Tabloid Television: Popular Journalism and the 'Other News'*. London: Routledge.

Larson, L. (2002) 'Journalists and Politicians: A Relationship Requiring Manouvering Space', *Journalism Studies*, 3 (1): 21–34.

Lash, S. and Urry, J. (1994) *Economies of Signs and Space*. London: Sage

Lasswell, H.D. (1927) *Propaganda Technique in the World War*. New York: Alfred A. Knopf.

Lasswell, H.D. (1935) *World Politics and Personal Insecurity*. New York: McGraw-Hill.

L'Etang, J. (1998) 'State Propaganda and Bureaucratic Intelligence: the Creation of Public Relations in 20th Century Britain', *Public Relations Review*, 24 (4): 413–41.

Lowe, P. and Morrison, D. (1984) 'Bad News or Good News: Environmental Politics and the Mass Media', *Sociological Review*, 32: 75–90.

Lowenthal, L. (1961) 'The Triumph of Mass Idols', in *Literature, Popular Culture and Society*. Palo Alto, CA: Pacific Books.

Lule, J. (1997) 'The Rape of Mike Tyson', in D. Berkowitz (ed.) *Social Meaning of News*. London: Sage, pp. 376–95.

MacAskill, E. (1997) 'Cabinet Watch', *Red Pepper*, September, p. 34.

MacGregor, B. (1997) *Live, Direct and Biased? Television News in the Satellite Age*. London: Edward Arnold.

McGwire, S. (1997) 'Dance to the Music of Spin', *New Statesman*, 17 October, p. 11.

McKay, G. (ed.) (1998) *DiY Culture: Party and Protest in Nineties Britain*. London: Verso.

McManus, J.H. (1997) 'The First Stage of News Production: Learning What's Happening', in D. Berkowitz (ed.) *Social Meanings of News*. Thousand Oaks, CA, and London: Sage, pp. 286–99.

McNair, B. (1999) *An Introduction to Political Communication*. London: Routledge.

McNair, B. (2000) *Journalism and Democracy*. London: Routledge.

McQuail, D. (1977) *Analysis of Newspaper Content. Report for the Royal Commission on the Press*. London: HMSO.

McRobbie, A. (1994) 'The Moral Panic in the Age of the Postmodern Mass Media', in A. McRobbie (ed.) *Postmodernism and Popular Culture*. London: Routledge, pp. 198–219.

Mancini, P. (1993) 'Between Trust and Suspicion: How Political Journalists Solve the Dilemma', *European Journal of Communication*, 8 (1): 33–53.

Manning, P. (1998) *Spinning for Labour: Trade Unions and the New Media Environment*. Aldershot: Avebury.

Manning, P. (1999) 'Categories of Knowledge and Information Flows: Reasons for the Decline of the British Labour and Industrial Correspondents Group', *Media, Culture and Society*, 21 (3): 313–36.

Manning, P. (2001) *News and News Sources: A Critical Introduction*. London: Sage.

Marsh, D. (1992) *The New Politics of British Trade Unionism*. Basingstoke: Macmillan.

Martin, R., Sunley, P. and Wills, J. (1996) *Union Retreat and the Regions: the Shrinking Landscape of Organised Labour*. London: Jessica Kingsley.

Mazzolena, G. and Schulz, W. (1999)

'"Mediatization" of Politics: A Challenge for Democracy?', *Political Communication*, 16: 247–61.

Mead, G.H. (1926) 'The Nature of Aesthetic Experience', *International Journal of Ethics*, 36 (4): 382–93.

Meyer, D.S. and Tarrow, S. (1998) *The Social Movement Society*. Maryland: Rowman & Littlefield.

Mill, J. (1997) 'Liberty of the Press', in M. Bromley and T. O'Malley (eds) *A Journalism Reader*. London: Routledge, pp. 16–21. (Essay first published in 1811.)

Mill, J.S. (1997) 'Of the Liberty of Thought and Discussion', in M. Bromley and T. O'Malley (eds) *A Journalism Reader*. London: Routledge, pp. 22–7. (Essay first published in 1859.)

Miller, D. (1993) 'Official Sources and "Primary Definition": The Case of Northern Ireland', *Media, Culture and Society*, 15 (3): 385–406.

Miller, D. (1994) *Don't Mention the War: Northern Ireland, Propaganda and the Media*. London: Pluto Press.

Miller, D. (1999) 'Risk, Science and Policy: Declinational Struggles, Information Management, the Media and BSE', *Social Science and Medicine*, 49: 1239–55.

Miller, D. and Dinan, W. (2000) 'The Rise of the PR Industry in Britain, 1979–98', *European Journal of Communication*, 15 (1): 5–35.

Miller, D. and Williams, K. (1993) 'Negotiating HIV/AIDS Information: Agendas, Media Strategies and the News', in J. Eldridge (ed.) *Getting the Message: News, Truth and Power*. London: Routledge, pp. 126–42.

Miller, D. and Williams, K. (1998) 'Sourcing AIDS News', in D. Miller, J. Kitzenger, K. Williams and P. Beharrell (eds) *The Circuits of Mass Communication*. London: Sage, pp. 123–46.

Miller, D., Kitzenger, J., Williams, K. and Beharrell, P. (1998) *The Circuits of Mass Communication*. London: Sage.

Mitchell, N. (1997) *The Conspicuous Corporation: Business, Publicity, and Representative Democracy*. Ann Arbor: University of Michigan Press.

Moeller, S. (1999) *Compassion Fatigue: How the Media Sell Disease, Famine, War and Death*. New York: Routledge.

Molotch, H. and Lester, M. (1981) 'News as Purposive Behavior: On the Strategic Use of Routine Events, Accidents and Scandals', *American Political Science Review*, 39: 101–12.

Molotch, H., Protess, D.L. and Gordon, M.T. (1987) 'The Media–Policy Connection: Ecologies of News', in D.L. Paletz (ed.) *Political Communication Research: Approaches, Studies, Assessments*. Norwood, NJ: Ablex Publishing.

Monaco, J. (1978) *Celebrity: the Media as Image Makers*. New York: Delta.

Morrison, D. (1992) *Television and the Gulf War*. London: Libbey.

Morrison, D. (1994) 'Journalists and the Social Construction of War', *Contemporary Record*, 8 (2): 305–20.

Morrison, D. and Tumber, H. (1988) *Journalists at War: the Dynamics of News Reporting during the Falklands War*. London: Sage.

Mouffe, C. (1996) 'Democracy, Power and the "Political"', in S. Benhabib (ed.) *Democracy and Difference*. Princeton, NJ: Princeton University Press, pp. 245–56.

Mountfield, L. (1997) *Report of the Working Group on the Government Information Service*. London: HMSO.

Murdock, G. (1999) 'Rights and Representations: Public Discourse and Cultural Citizenship', in J. Gripsrud (ed.) *Television and Common Knowledge*. London: Routledge, pp. 7–17.

Negrine, R. (1996) *The Communication of Politics*. London: Sage.

Neill, L. (1998) *Neill Report: 5th Report of the Committee on Standards in Public Life: The Funding of Political Parties in the United Kingdom*. London: HMSO Cm 4057-1.

Oborne, P. (1999) *Alastair Campbell, New Labour and the Rise of the Media Class*. London: Aurum Press.

Paletz, D.L. and Entman, R.M. (1981) *Media, Power, Politics*. New York: Free Press.

Palmer, J. (2000) *Spinning into Control: News Values and Source Strategies*. London: Leicester University Press.

Paterson, M. (2000) 'Swampy Fever: Media Constructions and Direct Action Politics', in B. Seel, M. Paterson and B. Doherty (eds) *Direct Action in British Environmentalism*. London: Routledge, pp. 151–66.

Pedelty, M. (1995) *War Stories*. London: Routledge.

Pharoah, C. and Welchman, R. (1997) *Keeping Posted: Current Approaches to Communication in the Voluntary Sector*. London: CAF Research Programme.

Philo, G. (ed.) (1995) *Glasgow Media Group Reader, Vol. 2: Industry, Economy, War and Politics*. London: Routledge.

Pick, D. (1993) *War Machine: the Rationalisation of Slaughter in the Modern Age*. New Haven, CT: Yale University Press.

Pickerill, J. (2000) 'Environmentalism and the Net', in R. Gibson and S. Ward (eds) *Reinvigorating Government*. Aldershot: Ashgate.

Pickerill, J. (2001) 'Weaving a Green Web: Environmental Protest and Computer-Mediated Communication in Britain', in F. Webster (ed.) *Culture and Politics in the Information Age*. London: Routledge, pp. 142–66.

Pipes, S. (1996) 'Environmental Information on the Internet', *ECOS: A Review of Conservation*, 17 (2): 63–66.

Pollard, S. (1992) *The Development of the British Economy 1914–90* (4th edn). London: Edward Arnold.

Postman, N. (1985) *Amusing Ourselves to Death: Public Discourse in the Age of Show Business*. London: Methuen.

Postman, N. and Powers, S. (1992) *How to Watch TV News*. New York: Penguin Books.

PRCA (1986) *The Public Relations Year Book*. London: PRCA.

PRCA (2001) *The Public Relations Year Book*. London: PRCA.

Preston, P. (2001) 'What That Email Said', *Guardian*, 15 October, p. 17.

Reese, S. (1991) 'Setting the Media's Agenda: A Power Balance Perspective', in J. Anderson (ed.) *Communication Yearbook*, 14: 309–40.

Reese, S., Grant, A. and Danielian, L. (1994) 'The Structure of News Sources on Television: A Network Analysis of *CBS News*, *Nightline*, *MacNeil/Lehrer*, and *This Week with David Brinkley*', *Journal of Communication*, 44: 84–107.

Rock, P. (1981) 'News as Eternal Recurrence', in S. Cohen and J. Young (eds) *The Manufacture of News: Deviance, Social Problems and the Mass Media*. London: Constable, pp. 64–70.

Roeder, G.H. (1993) *The Censored War: American Visual Experience during World War Two*. New Haven, CT: Yale University Press.

Rootes, C. (2000) 'Environmental Protest in Britain 1988–1997', in B. Seel, M. Paterson and B. Doherty (eds) *Direct Action in British Environmentalism*. London: Routledge, pp. 25–61.

Rose, C. (1998) *The Turning of the Spar*. London: Greenpeace.

Rose, R. (1989) *Politics in England: Change and Perspective*. Basingstoke: Macmillan.

Rosenbaum, M. (1997) *From Soapbox to Soundbite: Party Political Campaigning in Britain since 1945*. London: Macmillan.

Rosenblum, M. (1993) *Who Stole the News?* New York: John Wiley & Son.

Routledge, P. (2001) 'It May Pay But Journalism It Ain't', *British Journalism Review*, 12 (4): 31–6.

Royle, T. (1987) *War Report: the War Correspondent's View of Battle from Crimea to the Falklands*. London: Grafton Books.

Ryall, T. (1975) 'Teaching through Genre', *Screen Education*, 17: 27.

Ryan, C. (1991) *Prime Time Activism*. Boston, MA: South End Press.

Sanders, M.L. and Taylor, P.M. (1982) *British Propaganda during the First World War*. Basingstoke: Macmillan.

Scammell, M. (1995) *Designer Politics: How Elections Are Won*. London: Macmillan.

Scannell, P. (1992) 'Public Service Broadcasting and Modern Public Life', in P. Scannell, P. Schlesinger and C. Sparks (eds) *Culture and Power*. London: Sage, pp. 317–48.

Scannell, P. (1996) *Radio, Television and Modern Life*. Oxford: Blackwell.

Scannell, P. (forthcoming) 'The Brains Trust: a Historical Study of the Management of Liveness on Radio', in S. Cottle (ed.) *Media Organisation and Production*. London: Sage.

Schattschneider, E.E. (1960) *The Semi-sovereign People*. New York: Holt, Rinehart & Winston.

Schatz, H. (1992) 'Televising the Bundestag', in B. Franklin (ed.) *Televising Democracies*. London: Routledge, pp. 234–54.

Scheufele, D.A. (1999) 'Framing as a Theory of Media Effects', *Journal of Communication*, 49: 103–22.

Schlesinger, P. (1978) *Putting 'Reality' Together*. London: Methuen.

Schlesinger, P. (1990) 'Rethinking the Sociology of Journalism: Source Strategies and the Limits of Media-Centrism', in M. Ferguson (ed.) *Public Communication: the New Imperative*. London: Sage, pp. 61–83.

Schlesinger, P. and Tumber, H. (1994) *Reporting Crime: The Media Politics of Criminal Justice*. Oxford: Clarendon Press.

Schlesinger, P., Miller, D. and Dinan, W. (2001) *Open Scotland? Journalists, Spin Doctors and Lobbyists*. Edinburgh: Polygon.

Schudson, M. (1991) 'The Sociology of News Production Revisited', in J. Curran and M. Gurevitch (eds) *Mass Media and Society*. London: Arnold, pp. 141–59.

Seel, B., Paterson, M. and Doherty, B. (2000) *Direct Action in British Environmentalism*. London: Routledge.

Select Committee on Public Administration (1998) *The Government Information and Communications Service: Report and Proceedings of the Select*

Committee together with Minutes of Evidence and Appendices. London: HSMO, HC770.

Seymour-Ure, C. (1968) *The Press, Politics and the Public.* London: Methuen.

Shoemaker, P. (1989) 'Public Relations versus Journalism: Comments on Turrow', *American Behavioral Scientist*, 33 (2): 213–15.

Shoemaker, P.J. and Reese, S.D. (1991) *Mediating the Message: Theories of Influences on Mass Media Content.* New York: Longman.

Shorenstein, J. (1993) *Turmoil at Tiananmen: A Study of U.S. Press Coverage of the Beijing Spring of 1989.* Barone Center on the Press, Politics, and Public Policy. Cambridge, MA: John F. Kennedy School of Government, Harvard University.

Sigal, L.V. (1973) *Reporters and Officials: The Organisation and Politics of Newsmaking.* Lexington, MA: Lexington Books.

Simpson, J. (1995) *From the House of War.* London: Arrow Books.

Smith, A.C.H. (1975) *Paper Voices: the Popular Press and Social Change, 1935–1968.* London: Chatto & Windus.

Smith, R.R. (1979) 'Mythic Elements in Television News', *Journal of Communication*, 29: 75–82.

Soloski, J. (1989) 'News Reporting and Professionalism: Some Constraints on the Reporting of News', *Media, Culture and Society*, 11: 207–28.

Sontag, S. (1974) 'The Imagination of Disaster', in G. Mast and M. Cohen (eds) *Film Theory and Criticism: Introductory Readings.* New York: Oxford University Press.

Sparks, C. (1987) 'Striking Results?', *Media Culture and Society*, 9 (3): 369–77.

Sparks, C. and Tulloch, J. (eds) (2000) *Tabloid Tales: Global Debates over Media Standards.* Boulder, CO: Rowman & Littlefield.

Staggenborg, S. (1993) 'Critical Events and the Mobilization of the Pro-choice Movement', *Political Sociology*, 6: 319–45.

Stam, R. (1983) 'Television News and Its Spectator', in E.A. Kaplan (ed.) *Regarding Television.* Los Angeles: University Publications of America.

Stevenson, N. (1995) *Understanding Media Cultures.* London: Sage.

Strodthoff, G.G., Hawkins, R.P. and Schoenfeld, A.C. (1985) 'Media Roles in a Social Movement: A Model of Ideology Diffusion', *Journal of Communication*, 35: 135–53.

Taylor, P.M. (1987) 'Censorship in Britain in World War Two: An Overview', in A.C. Duke and G. Tanse (eds) *Too Mighty to be Free: Censorship and the Press in Britain and Netherlands.* Zutphen: de Walburg Pers.

Taylor, P.M. (1995) *Munitions of the Mind: a History of Propaganda from the Ancient World to the Present Day.* Manchester: Manchester University Press.

Taylor, P.M. (1998) *War and the Media: Propaganda and Persuasion in the Gulf War.* Manchester: Manchester University Press.

Thompson, J.B. (1990) *Ideology and Modern Culture: Critical Social Theory in the Era of Mass Communication.* Stanford: Stanford University Press.

Thompson, J. (1995) *The Media and Modernity: A Social Theory of the Media.* Cambridge: Polity Press.

Thompson, J. (2000) *Political Scandal: Power and Visibility in the Media Age.* Cambridge: Polity Press.

Thomson, S., Stancich, L. and Dickson, L. (1998) 'Gun Control and Snowdrop', *Parliamentary Affairs*, 51 (3): 329–44.

Tiffen, R. (1989) *News and Power.* Sydney: Allen & Unwin.

Tilly, C. (1978) *From Mobilization to Revolution.* Reading, MA: Addison-Wesley.

Timmins, N. (1997) 'Blair Aide Calls on Whitehall to Raise its PR Game', *Financial Times*, 9 October, p. 2.

Toolis, K. (1998) 'The Enforcer', *Guardian Weekend*, 4 April, pp. 29–36.

Tuchman, G. (1972) 'Objectivity as Strategic Ritual: an Examination of Newsmen's Notions of Objectivity', *American Journal of Sociology*, 77: 660–79.

Tuchman, G. (1973) 'Making News by Doing Work: Routinizing the Unexpected', *American Journal of Sociology*, 79 (1): 110–31.

Tuchman, G. (1978) *Making News: A Study in the Social Construction of Reality.* New York: Free Press.

Tulloch, J. (1993) 'Policing the Public Sphere: the British Machinery of News Management', *Media, Culture and Society*, 15 (3): 363–84.

Tumber, H. (1993) 'Selling Scandal: Business and the Media', *Media, Culture and Society*, 15 (3): 345–61.

Tunstall, J. (1970) *The Westminster Lobby Correspondents: A Sociological Study of National Political Journalism.* London: Routledge & Kegan Paul.

Tunstall, J. (1971) *Journalists at Work.* London: Constable.

Tunstall, J. (1996) *Newspaper Power: The National Press in Britain.* Oxford: Oxford University Press.

Turner, V. (1969) *The Ritual Process.* Ithaca, NY: Cornell University Press.

Turner, V. (1974) *Dramas, Fields, and Metaphors: Symbolic Action in Human Society*. Ithaca, NY: Cornell University Press.

Van Dijk, T. (1991) *Racism and the Press*. London: Routledge.

Voss, F. (1989) *Reporting the War: the Journalistic Coverage of World War II*. New York: Greenwood Press.

Wagner-Pacifici, R. (1986) *The Moro Morality Play*. Chicago: University of Chicago Press.

Wall, D. (1999) *Earth First! and the Anti-Roads Protest: Radical Environmentalism and Comparative Social Movements*. London: Routledge.

Wall, D. (2000) 'Genealogies of Environmental Direct Action', in B. Seel, M. Paterson and B. Doherty (eds) *Direct Action in British Environmentalism*. London: Routledge, pp. 79–92.

Walsh, E.J. (1988) *Democracy in the Shadows: Citizen Mobilization in the Wake of the Accident at Three Mile Island*. Westport, CT: Greenwood Press.

Warren, G. (2002) 'Deliberative Democracy', in A. Carter and G. Stokes (eds) *Democratic Theory Today*. Cambridge: Polity Press, pp. 173–202.

Watts, R. (2001) 'Blair in Row as Whitehall Adverts Soar by 157%', *Guardian*, 26 April, p. 13.

Weir, S. and Hall, W. (1996) *The Untouchables*. London: Democratic Audit/Scarman Trust.

Wernick, A. (1991) *Promotional Culture: Advertising, Ideology and Symbolic Expression*. London: Sage.

Williams, M. (2000) 'The Impact of Mountfield: A Detailed Analysis in the Department for Education and Employment', Department of Public Media, Trinity and All Saints University College, unpublished MA thesis.

Wilson, D. (1984) *Pressure: The A to Z of Campaigning in Britain*. London: Heinemann.

Winston, B. (1993) 'The CBS Evening News, 7 April 1949: Creating an Ineffable Television Form', in J. Eldridge (ed.) *Getting the Message: News, Truth and Power*. London: Routledge, pp. 181–209.

Wolfsfeld, G. (1984a) 'Collective Political Action and Media Strategy: the Case of Yamit', *Journal of Conflict Resolution*, 28: 1–36.

Wolfsfeld, G. (1984b) 'The Symbiosis of Press and Protest: an Exchange Analysis', *Journalism Quarterly*, 61: 550–6.

Wolfsfeld, G. (1991) 'Media, Protest and Political Violence: a Transactional Analysis', *Journalism Monographs*, 127.

Wolfsfeld, G. (1993) 'Introduction: Framing Political Conflict', in A. Cohen and G. Wolfsfeld (eds) *Framing the Intifada: People and Media*. Norwood, NJ: Ablex Publishing.

Wolfsfeld, G. (1997) *Media and Political Conflict*. Cambridge: Cambridge University Press.

Wykes, M. (2000) 'The Burrowers: News about Bodies, Tunnels and Green Guerillas', in S. Allan, B. Adam and C. Carter (eds) *Environmental Risks and the Media*. London: Routledge, pp. 29–44.

Young, I. (1996) 'Communication and the Other: Beyond Deliberative Democracy', in S. Benhabib (ed.) *Democracy and Difference*. Princeton, NJ: Princeton University Press, pp. 120–36.

Young, I. (1997) 'Difference as a Resource for Democratic Communication', in J. Bohman and W. Rehg (eds) *Deliberative Democracy: Essays on Reason and Politics*. Cambridge, MA: MIT Press, pp. 383–406.

Young, P. and Jesser, P. (1995) *The Media and the Military from the Crimea to Desert Strike*. Basingstoke: Macmillan.

Zelizer, B. and Allan, S. (eds) (2002) *Journalism after September 11*. London: Routledge.

Index